246

KANSAS SCHOOL OF RELIGION
University of Kansas
1300 Oread Avenue
LAWRENCE, KANSAS 66044

KANSAS SCHOOL OF RELIGION
University of Kansas
1300 Oread Avenue
LAWRENCE, KANSAS 66044

JUDAISM AND CHRISTIANITY: **What We Believe**

BEHRMAN HOUSE, INC. • PUBLISHERS • NEW YORK

JUDAISM AND CHRISTIANITY

WHAT WE BELIEVE

by William B. Silverman

MS: Judaism -- Juvenile literature
Christianity & other religions -- Judaism -- 1945 -
Judaism -- Relations -- Christianity -- 1945 -

Acknowledgments

The author and the publisher wish to express their gratitude to the syna-
gogues and churches, the information offices, the museums, the religious, social
and civic agencies, and the commercial services that have helped in assem-
bling the illustrations for this book and have permitted their reproduction in it.

PICTURE CREDITS

Alinari-Art Reference Bureau and the Sistine Chapel, the Vatican: p. 36.
Allegro, John M.: p. 135.
Art Reference Bureau and the Gemäldegalerie Kunsthistorisches Museum,
    Vienna: p. 98.
Bettmann Archive, Inc.: pp. 126, 145 (top), 192.
Danish Information Office, New York (copyright Royal Danish Ministry for
    Foreign Affairs, Press Department, Copenhagen): p. 103.
Gendreau, Philip, New York: 45, 47, 70, 74, 84, 226.
Israel Consulate, New York: pp. 163, 172, 186, 187.
Israel Government Tourist Office, New York: pp. 79, 159.
Israel Ministry for Foreign Affairs, Department of Information, Jerusalem:
    p. 182.
Jewish Museum (Frank J. Darmstaedter, photographer): 83, 110.
    The Tobe Pascher Workshop, craftsman Ludwig Wolpert ©: p. 195.
Joint Distribution Committee: p. 140.
Louise Wise Services (Margot Kaiser, photographer): p. 211.
Magnum Photos, Inc. (Photo by Capa): p. 143.
Methodist Missions: pp. 154, 179.
Methodist Prints (Photo by Togi Fujihira): p. 87.
The Metropolitan Museum of Art, New York: p. 192.
National Conference of Christians and Jews, Chicago: p. 30.
National Gallery of Art, Mellon Collection: p. 93.
The Pierpont Morgan Library, New York (French psalter, third quarter of
    13th century, M. 72. folio 139v): p. 235.
Rapho-Guilumette Pictures: pp. 39 (Photo by Louis Goldman), 196 (Photo
    by J. Allan Cash, London), 237 (Photo by Bruce Roberts).
Religious News Service Photos: pp. 16, 17, 22, 30, 32, 34, 41, 51, 53, 58, 60,
    64, 93, 101, 115, 119, 128, 145 (bottom), 152, 207, 212, 219, 231.
Scope Associates, Inc. (Photo by Martin J. Dain): p. 209.
Shanks, Ann Zane: p. 133.
The Society of Friends of Touro Synagogue (John T. Hopf, photographer):
    p. 19.
Unations: p. 68.
UNESCO (Photo by Dominique Roger): p. 227.

UNICEF: pp. 70 (Photo by Jean Speiser), 76 (Photo by Almasy), 176 and
    199 (Photos by Jack Ling), 215.
Union of American Hebrew Congregations
    Commission of Social Action of Reform Judaism: p. 203.
    Synagogue Architectural Library: p. 158.
United Press International Newspictures: p. 241.
University of Chicago, Oriental Institute: p. 123.
University of the South (Photo by Don Ormsby): p. 17.
Wide World Photos: pp. 27, 38, 67, 109, 167, 171, 195, 222, 239, 246.
Wolpert, Ludwig: p. 195.

A Word to Teachers

Although the author has made every effort to be just and fair in his evaluation of the basic teachings of Judaism and Christianity, by the nature of his vocation and calling he cannot be completely objective. As a rabbi he has been conditioned to a great and overwhelming love for his own faith. Since he believes so strongly in the teachings and practices of Judaism, some prejudices will undoubtedly be revealed.

It was his intention in writing this volume to use a comparative technique to teach the basic beliefs of Judaism, to afford a glimpse into the Christian tradition, and to stimulate further learning on the part of the student to respect faiths other than his own. The effort to inculcate a love for Judaism, however, must not be made at the expense of belittling Christianity or Christians.

Judaism has given to Christianity an exalted moral heritage. There are similarities in ethics and differences in theology. There are areas of agreement and disagreement. Judaism and Christianity are not the same, nor should they be equated as equally true. We believe that Judaism is more consistent with truth and reason than is Christianity. Christians undoubtedly believe the same about their faith. Regardless of our differences, however, we are partners in faith— a faith that transcends all sectarian demarcations. Jews and Christians join hands, not as rivals, but as partners in faith, partners of a dream—a dream that may be fulfilled as we join together and work together for the building of a future society of justice, brotherhood and universal peace on earth.

W. B. S.

Have we not all one Father?
Hath not
one God created us?

MALACHI 2:10

CONTENTS

JUDAISM AND CHRISTIANITY: What We Believe

What Do We Believe?

Dear Rabbi:

I'll bet that you're surprised to hear from me—all the way from northern Maine. The camp is wonderful, and I'm having a swell time—except for one thing. That's why I'm writing to you. You always told us that in case we ever had any problems to come to you. Right now I have a whopper of a problem and I need your help.

I'll try to explain it the best I can. My three bunk-mates are Christians. They are wonderful boys and swell pals. They all said they are glad that they could bunk with a Jewish boy because they have so many questions to ask about Judaism. That's my problem. They have the questions but I don't have the answers.

They seem to know a lot about their religion, and when they ask me questions about what Jews believe, I feel like a real dummy. Of course, I can tell them about our Holy Days and festivals, and some of the things I learned in Religious School. They are interested, but that isn't what they really want to know. They want me to tell them what Judaism believes about God, the Bible, prayer, and what happens in the next world. They want to know how Judaism is different from

Christianity in these things. They have so many questions that I made a list of them on another page. I need some help on how to answer these questions. It sure is embarrassing to be so ignorant about my own religion.

Thanks for everything.

Your friend and pupil,

Joseph

JOSEPH'S LIST

What do we believe about God? (I know the *Shema Yisrael,* but that isn't enough.) Is our God cruel, vengeful and without mercy?

What do we believe about prayer? (Does God answer all our prayers?)

Do we believe in miracles?

What don't Jews believe about Jesus?

What do Jews believe about Jesus?

Do we believe in the New Testament as well as the Old?

Do we believe in Heaven and Hell? What happens in the next life?

Is mankind good or evil? (What do Christians mean by *original sin?*)

How are we punished for our sins, and rewarded for our goodness?

The Torah scrolls, containing the Law, the word of God, are the core of Jewish belief. Bar Mitzvah, when a boy first reads from the Torah in the synagogue, marks his acceptance as a responsible member of the congregation.

Do we believe in baptism? If not, why not?

Do we believe that we are the Chosen People?

What do we believe about the Messiah?

HOW ABOUT YOU?

Are you able to answer the questions on Joseph's list? You may have some ideas and opinions, but do you *really know* what Judaism teaches and what Jews believe? Do you know what Christianity teaches and what Christians believe?

Most of us are like Joseph. We know our Holy Days and festivals. We know about the Sabbath candles and the Ḥanukkah Menorah, and other symbols and ceremonies of Judaism, but we are not sure what Judaism teaches about many of the *beliefs* and problems that puzzle us.

We want to know more about the beliefs of Judaism. We want to know what Judaism teaches us about God, Torah, prayer, miracles, and the mystery of the "next life." We must search for answers to the questions: Are we the Chosen People? When will the Messiah come? Are we rewarded for being good? Are we punished when we are bad?

Then, too, there are the things we want to know about the religion of our Christian friends, and how their beliefs compare with ours—where we differ, and where we agree.

There are many reasons why we should know "What We Believe." Joseph wanted to know about Jewish beliefs because he was embarrassed to be so ignorant before his Christian friends. Is that a good reason? What are some other reasons why we should know "What We Believe"?

IS BELIEVING IMPORTANT?

There are some people who say that what we believe isn't very important, our actions are the only things that count. Actions are important, but does that mean that what we believe isn't important? Suppose we think about these questions before we decide:

1. David says that he tries to do kind and thoughtful deeds to make his parents happy. Do you think David would do these deeds if he didn't believe that his parents loved him, and he loved them?

2. Marsha says that she always wants to act like a good American. Do you think Marsha would say that if she didn't believe in the greatness and the goodness of the American way of life?

3. Billy says that he must do his "good deed" every day because he is a Boy Scout. Would he do this if he didn't believe in the ideas and principles of scouting?

4. Judith lights the Sabbath candles every Friday night, and always says her prayers before going to sleep. What do you think she believes? Why are her beliefs so important?

THE CHRISTIAN CREED

Joel was invited by his friend Paul to attend the Episcopal church service on a Sunday morning. At first, Joel didn't want to accept, but he decided that since his friend was kind enough to invite him, he shouldn't hurt his feelings by refusing.

The service was beautiful and Joel was impressed with the pageantry of the ministers in their robes, the choir, the flags and the procession in general. When the others knelt down, Joel also kneeled.

Then came the time during the service for the reading of the Nicene Creed. This is what Joel saw in the Episcopalian *Book of Common Prayer:*

I believe in one God the Father Almighty, Maker of heaven and earth. And of all things visible and invisible:

The central symbol of Christianity is the cross. It is here seen centered in the chancel of All Souls' Chapel, University of the South.

And in one Lord Jesus Christ, the only-begotten Son of God; Begotten of his Father before all worlds, God of God, Light of Light; Very God of very God; Begotten, not made; Being of one substance with the Father; By whom all things were made; Who for us men and for our salvation came down from heaven, And was incarnate by the Holy Ghost of the Virgin Mary, and was made man: And was crucified also for us under Pontius Pilate; He suffered and was buried: And the third day he rose again according to the Scriptures: And ascended into heaven, And sitteth on the right hand of the Father: And he shall come again, with glory, to judge both the quick and the dead; Whose kingdom shall have no end.

And I believe in the Holy Ghost, the Lord, and Giver of Life, Who proceedeth from the Father and the Son: Who with the Father and the Son together is worshipped and glorified; Who spake by the Prophets: And I believe one Catholic and and Apostolic Church: I acknowledge one Baptism for the remission of sins: And I look for the Resurrection of the dead: And the Life of the world to come. Amen.

The service continued, and after the concluding benediction, the boys walked home together. On the way Paul asked Joel, "Is the Episcopal service very different from your Jewish service? I've always been curious to know."

"Oh, yes, our Jewish service is quite different—although we, too, have responsive reading, psalms, scripture, hymns, a sermon and the benediction. Why don't you come to temple with us this Friday night, Paul, and see for yourself?"

"But is it all right for me to come? I mean not being Jewish?" asked Paul.

Joel said, "Didn't I just attend your church service, and I'm not a Christian? Just as I

was welcome in your church, so you will be welcome in the temple."

Paul agreed to accompany Joel to services that Friday night, and the two boys finally reached home after the long walk. Joel thanked his friend for inviting him to his church, but before saying, "Good-bye," he asked, "Paul, before I go in the house, tell me, what is the long creed that was said during the service? Just what is a creed?"

"Why, that's the Nicene Creed," Paul replied. "It's what we believe—about God, Jesus and the Church. Don't you have a creed in your religion, Joel?"

Joel kicked at a stone. He seemed uncertain. "Well, to tell you the truth, Paul, I'm not sure. I know that we believe in one God, but honestly, I can't tell you whether we have a creed or not. That's something I'll have to find out. See you tomorrow at school. Thanks for everything."

WHAT DO YOU THINK?

1. Was Joel right in accepting the invitation of his friend to attend a Christian church service? Would you accept an invitation to worship in a Christian church? What are your reasons?

2. Do you think that Joel should have joined in repeating the prayers from the Episcopal prayer book? What would you have done?

3. Do you think that Joel did the proper thing when he invited Paul to attend the Sabbath services in his temple? Do you think that Paul will stand for the *Shema* when he attends a temple service with Joel and repeat the prayers from the Jewish prayer book?

4. Reread the Nicene Creed. With which statements of belief do you agree? With which do you disagree?

5. Paul asked Joel whether the Jewish religion has a creed. What would you answer if someone asked you this question?

DOES JUDAISM HAVE A CREED?

There are some who say, "Christianity is a religion of creed, and Judaism is a religion of deed." That statement isn't exactly fair to Christianity or to Judaism. It is true that Christianity puts more emphasis upon a creed than does Judaism, but Christianity is also concerned with deeds, acts of goodness and kindness.

If you will look up the dictionary meaning of "creed," you will find that it is a statement of essential beliefs, guiding rules or principles. Judaism has essential beliefs, guiding rules and principles, therefore shall we say that Judaism has a creed?

If you were asked to write up the main beliefs and teachings of Judaism, how would you begin? What would you include in your statement? Suppose you write this statement about what you think are the beliefs and teachings of Judaism. Ask your teacher to save the statement and at the end of the year, when you have completed this study of "The Beliefs of Judaism," you will be asked to write another statement so that you can compare the two.

The Shema

We say that the *Shema Yisrael* is the watchword of the Jewish faith. This is the most important belief of Judaism. You have repeated it many times but now think about what it means and what it teaches.

This statement of belief is found in the Bible, in the Book of Deuteronomy, Chapter 6, verse 4. Find the passage in the Bible and read it: "Hear, O Israel, the Lord our God, the Lord is One."

The belief that God is One is the most important teaching of Judaism. In the next chapter we will find out the reasons why this is the motto and the watchword of our faith.

Do you think that the *Shema* is our Jewish creed? Suppose someone born a Jew says that he doesn't believe in one God. Is he still a Jew? Does he have a right to say that he is of the Jewish faith?

The Ten Commandments

In almost every synagogue there may be found above the Holy Ark the two tablets upon which are inscribed the Ten Commandments. Judaism gave these moral laws of right and wrong to all mankind. We say that we

The Ten Commandments enshrined in the Holy Ark section of the Touro Synagogue, Newport, Rhode Island, a National Historic Site.

believe in the Ten Commandments. Turn to Exodus, Chapter 20, or Deuteronomy, Chapter 5, beginning with verse 6, and read these commandments. Here we find essential beliefs, guiding rules and principles of Judaism. These are the sacred rules of conduct, commanded by God.

Do you think that the Ten Commandments are part of a Jewish creed? Suppose someone born a Jew says that he doesn't believe in the Ten Commandments. Is he still a Jew? Does he have a right to say he is of the Jewish faith?

The Thirteen Principles of Faith

The great Jewish physician-philosopher Moses Maimonides, who lived from 1135 to 1204, summed up the teachings of Judaism in Thirteen Principles of Faith. These have been the guiding principles of Judaism for many, many years. So important were these beliefs, that they were included in the prayer book. Even to this day, we may read Maimonides' Thirteen Principles of Faith in Orthodox prayer books, and in some of the prayer books used by Conservative Jews.

Here are the first five of the thirteen beliefs in Maimonides. Study them carefully and decide whether or not you believe in them, too.

1. I believe with complete faith that the Creator, blessed be His name, is the Author and Guide of everything that has been created, and that He alone has made, does make, and will make all things.

2. I believe with complete faith that the Creator, blessed be His name, is a Unity, and that there is no unity in any manner like unto His, and that He alone is our God, who was, is, and will be.

3. I believe with complete faith that the Creator, blessed be His name, is not a body, and that He is free from all the accidents of matter, and that He has not any form whatsoever.

4. I believe with complete faith that the Creator, blessed be His name, is the first and the last.

5. I believe with complete faith that to the Creator, blessed be His name, and to Him alone, it is right to pray, and that it is not right to pray to any being besides Him.

The first five principles

As you have probably discovered, the first five principles of faith are concerned with God.

Maimonides believed that:

> God is the creator.
> God is one—*unity*.
> God is not a body.
> God is the first and the last.
> We pray only to God.

Which of the five principles do you think Christianity would accept? Which would Christianity reject? Give your reasons.

In what way do Judaism and Christianity disagree on the fifth principle?

The other principles

6. I believe with complete faith that all the words of the prophets are true.

7. I believe with complete faith that the prophecy of Moses our teacher, peace be unto him, was true, and that he was the chief of the prophets, both of those that preceded and those that followed him.

Do you agree that all the statements made by Moses are true?

Do you agree that Moses was the greatest of all the prophets? If not, who was a greater prophet than Moses? Give your reasons.

8. I believe with complete faith that the whole Law, now in our possession, is the same that was given to Moses our Teacher, peace be unto him.

9. I believe with complete faith that this Law will not be changed, and that there will never be any other law from the Creator, blessed be His name.

Ask your rabbi to come to class and explain what Orthodox, Conservative and Reform Judaism teach about the eighth and ninth principles of faith.

God, the All-knowing

10. I believe with complete faith that the Creator, blessed be His name, knows every deed of the children of men, and all their thoughts, as it is said: It is He that fashioneth the hearts of them all, that giveth heed to all their deeds.

How should the belief that God knows all our thoughts and all our deeds influence our actions and our thoughts?

If God knows all our deeds and thoughts, does this mean that we don't have the freedom to choose between right and wrong?

If God knows all our deeds and all our thoughts, why should we pray?

First, discuss these questions in class. Then ask your parents for their views. After you have thought about all these answers, then ask your rabbi to give his explanation.

The last three principles

The last three principles of faith will be discussed more fully in the chapters that follow. Read them carefully now, and then answer the questions that are asked. The same questions will be asked again after a more careful study. Then you will have a chance to compare your answers.

Punishment and reward

11. I believe with complete faith that the Creator, blessed be His name, rewards those that keep His commandments, and punishes those that transgress them.

Do you agree with this?

Do you think that you will be rewarded every time you do a kind deed, and punished every time you do an evil deed?

Doesn't it happen that the wrongdoer sometimes gets away with it?

How does God punish and reward?

The Messiah

12. I believe with complete faith in the coming of the Messiah, and though he tarry, I will wait daily for his coming.

What is meant by the Messiah?

What will happen when the Messiah comes?

How do Christianity and Judaism differ in the belief about the Messiah?

How do Orthodox, Conservative and Reform Judaism differ in the belief about the Messiah?

Explain how the House of David and the prophet Elijah are involved with the idea of the Messiah.

The resurrection

13. I believe with complete faith that there will be a resurrection of the dead at the time when it shall please the Creator, blessed be His name, and exalted be the remembrance of Him forever and ever.

Look up the dictionary meaning of *resurrection*.

Do you believe that the resurrection of the dead is possible?

What would science say about this idea of the dead coming back to life?

What does Christianity teach about the resurrection of Jesus?

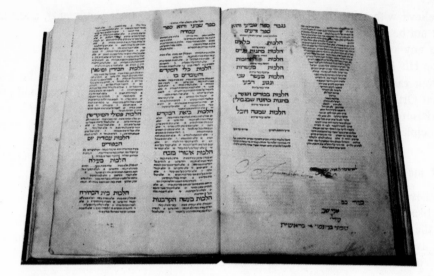

*These pages are from the first edition of the Mishneh Torah,
summarizing the rulings of Talmudic and other rabbinic laws.*

What do Orthodox, Conservative and Reform Judaism teach about this thirteenth principle of faith? Interview the Orthodox, Conservative and Reform rabbis in your community and ask them to explain what this means. Discuss results of the interviews in class.

Does this discussion of resurrection in Judaism sound somewhat strange to you? If it does, remember that this idea was taught a long time ago. Before you make up your mind that it is true or not, wait until you have all the facts and have completed all the interviews. Then you will find out that not all Jews agree on this thirteenth principle of faith.

Read all the Thirteen Principles again, and then write an essay explaining those you can accept and those you do not accept. Be sure and give reasons for your choices.

Do you remember the question that Paul asked Joel? He asked him whether the Jew-

ish religion has a creed. After considering the *Shema,* the Ten Commandments, and the Thirteen Principles of Faith, what would you answer?

QUESTIONS FOR DISCUSSION

1. What should you reply to a Christian friend when he asks you questions about Judaism that you can't answer?

2. If you are unable to answer questions about your own religion, do you think that you drop a little in the estimation of your Christian friends? How about your Jewish friends? Do they expect you to know about your own religion?

3. Do you think that a Christian your age knows more about his religion than you know about your religion? What are your reasons?

4. According to our Jewish tradition, when the Torah was given at Sinai, the children of Israel responded, "We will do and we will

hearken" (Ex. 24:7). Since they said, "We will do" first, doesn't it seem that Judaism places more importance upon doing than believing?

5. Is it necessary "to believe" in order to perform good deeds with the whole heart?

6. Is it easier for a Jew to attend a Christian religious service than it is for a Christian to attend a Jewish religious service? Give your reasons.

7. Christianity requires the belief in a creed. It is an important part of being a Christian. If there is a creed in Judaism, is it an important part of being a Jew?

8. Suppose someone of the Jewish faith says, "I believe in the Ten Commandments," but doesn't obey them. How significant is his belief? Suppose he says, "I don't believe in the Ten Commandments," but obeys them. Is he a good Jew?

9. Maimonides' Thirteen Principles of Faith were compiled in the thirteenth century. Do you think they are modern enough to be included in our prayer book today?

10. Usually when a person says he believes in something, he can give reasons for his belief. Why do you believe in God? What reasons can you give?

11. Is Judaism more a matter of birth or belief? If belief is more important, may we choose not to be Jews?

THINGS TO DO

1. Look up the dictionary definition of *creed*. Then look up the dictionary definition of *theology*. Is there a difference between these two words? What is meant by *Jewish theology?*

2. Find out if the Boy Scouts and Girl Scouts have creeds. If so, write out copies of these creeds.

3. Does America have a creed? If so, what is it? Would you consider the Pledge of Allegiance to be a creed?

4. When a person who is not born in this country becomes an American citizen, does he have to say what he believes? Find out what a candidate for citizenship has to believe in order for him to become a new American.

5. Go over Joseph's list of questions about "The Beliefs of Judaism," and add other questions about Judaism you would like to have answered.

6. Jonathan Jay of Houston, Texas wrote this statement:

I believe in one God. I believe in the Ten Commandments . . . I believe in the dignity of man—to pay respect to each human being no matter what his place in life or society is. I believe in the American Declaration of Independence and the Constitution of the United States . . . two of the finest documents in world history guaranteeing the rights of man. I believe in the United Nations and in its work for peace.
—JONATHAN JAY

This is what Jonathan Jay believes. Write a paragraph on what you believe.

7. Interview a Christian minister and ask him questions about the importance of creed in Christianity. Interview a rabbi and ask him about the importance of creed in Judaism.

8. Write out the Nicene Creed. Then pencil out every belief that Judaism cannot accept and then submit your paper to your teacher.

9. Debate in class the proposition, "Resolved: One can be a good Jew without knowing what Judaism teaches."

10. Edward R. Murrow, the radio and television news analyst said, "After all, the only way of discovering what people believe is to ask them." Make up a list of questions about Jewish beliefs and interview some prominent Jews in your community.

SELECTED QUOTATIONS

Democracy and brotherhood

Democracy rests upon brotherhood. Justice, amity, understanding and cooperation among Protestants, Catholics and Jews throughout our nation are cornerstones of democracy, even as they are the requirements of brotherhood. With them we can maintain our national unity and keep up the teamwork needed in peace as in war.

—DAVID SCHWARTZ

Albert Einstein's credo

The striving after knowledge for its own sake, the love of justice verging on fanaticism, and the quest for personal independence — these are the motivating traditions of the Jewish people which cause me to regard my adherence thereto as a gift of destiny. Those who rage today against the ideals of reason and of individual freedom, and seek to impose an insensate state slavery by means of brutal force, rightly see in us their irreconcilable opponents. History has imposed upon us a severe struggle. But as long as we remain devoted servants of truth, justice and freedom, we shall not only continue to exist as the oldest of all living peoples, but we shall also, as hitherto, create, through productive effort, values which shall contribute to the ennobling of mankind.

The heart of Judaism

The heart of Judaism and its chief contribution to religion is the doctrine of the One, Living God, Who rules the world through law and love. In Him all existence has its creative source and mankind its ideal of conduct. Though transcending time and space, He is the indwelling Pres-ence of the world. We worship Him as the Lord of the universe and as our merciful Father.

—From *Guiding Principles
of Reform Judaism*
Central Conference of
American Rabbis, 1937

I believe

"I believe in the sun even when it is not shining, I believe in love even when feeling it not; I believe in God even when He is silent." (An inscription on the wall of a cellar in Cologne where a number of Jews hid themselves for the entire duration of World War II.)

—Quoted in ZVI KOLITZ,
Tiger Beneath the Skin

Communion with God

Judaism is a way of life which endeavors to transform virtually every human action into a means of communion with God. Through this communion with God, the Jew is enabled to make his contribution to the establishment of the Kingdom of God and the brotherhood of men on earth.

—RABBI LOUIS FINKELSTEIN

The power of faith

The Jewish power of endurance and survival is due to their religious faith.

For the whole civilized world this people has been the source of all the highest conceptions of God, man and nature. Through this people was developed not only the Hebrew religion, but also the Christian religion; for the Christian religion was only an outcome or development of the religion of the Hebrews, the early

expounders of the new religion, afterwards
called Christian, being exclusively Jews....
—PRESIDENT CHARLES W. ELIOT,
of Harvard University, 1905

What Protestants and Catholics believe

The Protestant, the Roman or Western,
the Greek or Eastern — profess the faith
set forth in the general creeds of Christian-
dom, commonly called the Apostles' Creed
and the Nicene Creed. They each claim to
be Catholic, that is universal, and all —
Protestant, Roman and Greek (Orthodox)
—believe:

In God the Father, maker of
  heaven and earth;
In Jesus Christ, His only Son, our Lord;
In the Holy Spirit, the Lord and
  Giver of life;
In the Holy Catholic Church;
In the communion of saints;
In the forgiveness of sins;
In the life ever lasting.
—REV. HUGH THOMPSON KERR

The law of mankind

The Talmud interprets the verse from
Scriptures, "Ye shall therefore keep My
statutes, and Mine ordinances, which if a
man do, he shall live by them" (Lev. 18:5).
Whence is it deduced that even a Gentile who
obeys the Torah is the equal of the high
priest? From the words "which if a man do
he shall live by them." Similarly it is said,
"and this too after the manner of mankind,
Lord God" (II Sam. 7:19). It is not stated,
"This is the law of the priests, or the Levites,
or of Israel," but "the law of mankind."

SELECTED READINGS

FITCH, FLORENCE MARY, *One God*
SILVERMAN, WILLIAM B., *The Still Small Voice
  Today*, Chapter 8

2

The Right to Be Different

THE RIGHT TO BE DIFFERENT

You have heard the story of Ḥanukkah many times, but have you ever thought of what might have happened if the Maccabees hadn't resisted and fought for their religious freedom and the right to follow Judaism and worship God in their own way?

What if the tyrant, Antiochus Epiphanes, had won? If he had, there wouldn't have been any festival of Ḥanukkah and Judaism might well have disappeared as a religion. If this had happened, it is doubtful that Christianity would have come into existence.

The following is an imaginary description of what might have been a true story if the Jews had refused in those times of trial to be loyal to their religion.

THE TREASURE IN THE JARS

An Arab lad had been wandering around the caves of southern Judea for several hours when he came upon a pile of old cracked jars in one of them. He had heard about other boys who had found such piles and had been able to sell the jars to foreign men in Jerusalem. These boys had received much money and many gifts. The Arab lad thought that maybe the jars he had discovered were worth something too, so he gathered them up and started the long trek to the big city. Sure enough, after asking several friends, he was directed to an Englishman who became quite interested when he saw the jars. The Englishman called in some friends who looked at the jars and the old papers which were inside them. Several hours passed this way and the Arab boy began to feel that the men had completely forgotten about him. Suddenly, the first man he had met turned to him and offered him a large sum of money for his jars. This was exactly what the lad had hoped for and he gladly accepted and ran off.

The men were archaeologists interested in the ancient history of Israel. They had recognized that the papers contained in the jars had been written centuries ago and were very important for understanding the ancient history of Israel. They worked for a year in deciphering one scroll. When they had come to understand what it said they published the following fascinating text:

In the last month of the year 167, the Emperor Antiochus IV issued five decrees which were to be enforced throughout Judea. They were:

1. *The Law of Moses is no longer to be observed by the Jews. Punishment for those caught following this Law is death.*

2. *All Jews are required to worship pagan gods and sacrifice to them.*

3. *The Temple in Jerusalem is to be used as a house of worship of Greek gods.*

4. *The Jews will learn Greek ways by attending Greek schools called gymnasia.*

5. *The name of Jerusalem is to be changed to the name of the Greek city Antioch.*

Many prominent Jews in Jerusalem wanted to imitate their Greek-Syrian conquerers and be accepted by them. These Jews did not object to the decrees. In fact, they obeyed them immediately. The Temple was dese-

crated. Jews sacrificed swine to Zeus, went to the gymnasia, changed their Hebrew names to Greek names, and tried in every way to make themselves Greek.

Reports, however, reached Jerusalem that people in the countryside were resisting such changes. Therefore, Antiochus sent his troops from village to village to enforce the decrees. The small village of Modin was rumored to be the center of the resistance. When the Greek troops arrived there, Mattathias, chief of the village and high priest, was summoned to appear before the general. In front of the entire village he was ordered to sacrifice a pig to Zeus. Mattathias mounted the steps of the altar, slew the pig and laid the animal over the coals. Others followed him. No re-

The victory of the Maccabees is commemorated at Ḥanukkah. Here the rabbi lights the first candle for the first day of the festivities.

sistance was offered and soon the entire countryside accepted the ways of the Greeks.

Thus Antiochus unified his empire. Everyone believed the same thing, performed the same religious rites and was obedient to the same imperial authority. The unique beliefs of Israel disappeared. Jews were now Greeks —all but one. I, the author of this document, still remember and cherish the old ways. In secret I still worship the One God. But when I die there will be no one left and all will be forgotten forever.

The history of the world would have been very different indeed if this had actually happened in Judea between 167 and 164 B.C.E. If the story of the finding of the jar and its scroll were really true, Judaism might well have disappeared and the Jews would have been absorbed into the Greek peoples. Many other nations disappeared from history in just that way. The Jews would belong to the long list of peoples who did not have the strength to survive in history. And if this were so, there would be no record of Christianity or Islam altogether. Christianity and Islam emerged out of Judaism, and if Judaism had been lost at this period Christianity and Islam would never have developed.

But, as we know, the story of the scroll is imaginary and history did not actually take this course. Mattathias refused to sacrifice on the altar of Zeus but rather fled to the hills with his sons where they organized an army of resistance. This small army won many victories. After several years the Greek emperor decided to offer peace to the troublesome Jews. In the treaty which the Jews accepted, the king wrote the following:

As for our Jewish subjects we understand that they object to our father's project of bringing them over to Hellenism (Greek ways), preferring their own ways of life and asking permission to follow

their own customs. [He therefore agreed] to give them back their Temple and permit them to live after the manner of their ancestors.

—THE BOOK OF MACCABEES

The Maccabees had won for the Jews the freedom to live in the way which they chose. Rather than conforming to the style of life and the beliefs of their Greek conquerors, they resisted and eventually succeeded in reestablishing their own ways. The Law of Judea was to continue to be the Law of Moses and not the laws of the Greeks. The Jews were granted the right to maintain their own distinct way of life and live in peace.

THE DANGER OF UNIFORMITY

We have discussed the story of the scroll because it indicates a point which is of crucial importance to citizens of the United States and particularly to us as we begin a study of Judaism and Christianity. In the United States many types of people with many different backgrounds live together. Some men have suggested that it would be good for the country if the government sought to eliminate these differences by making all Americans conform to a single pattern. The government would then pass laws of conformity much like the decrees of Antiochus IV. All citizens would have to wear the same kind of clothes, speak with the same accent, vote the same way, and attend the same church. Thus there would be uniformity in American society. This is what Hitler tried to do in Germany and this is also a part of the Communist philosophy. *Uniformity* means thinking the same, believing the same —with no room for difference.

Many years ago the Psalmist said, "How good and how pleasant it is for brethren to dwell in unity" (Ps. 133:1). What if he had said, "How good and how pleasant it is for brethren to dwell together in uniformity"? What a tremendous difference there is between these two words. *Uniformity* means that everything must be the same. It means the elimination of all differences.

Hitler's motto was: "One Fuehrer, One People, One German Reich." Under their dictatorial leaders the Communists insist upon "thought control," and people were and are being punished if they dare to think or speak or act differently. In a democracy, we have the right to be different, to think differently and speak and act differently. That is why we prefer the word "unity," which means the harmonization of differences.

UNITY

Think of a symphony orchestra as an example of unity. Imagine an orchestra made up of all brass instruments, or all strings, or all woodwinds, or all percussion instruments like drums. It would make a kind of music, but it wouldn't be an orchestra. A real symphony orchestra has different instruments united into a beautiful and inspiring harmony. Each section of instruments plays its own part and does not clash with other sections, nor does it blend into another and disappear.

How does this example of a symphony orchestra apply to different peoples and different religions? The United States government has not tried to enforce uniformity, but has encouraged unity. It has not demanded that all citizens of all ages conform to any one pattern. In a democracy we have the right to be different, to think differently and to believe differently. Americans are encouraged to develop themselves in the way they choose. Each has the right to retain the elements of his own background which he chooses. Each is free to make himself according to the image which he selects. America is a pluralistic society in which many

forms and many patterns exist side by side in peace. But pluralism implies that each man must accept the responsibility of making a choice and then developing himself according to it.

In order to understand this difficult idea a little better consider these two questions of the great sage Hillel: "If I am not for myself who will be for me? And if I am only for myself, what am I"? (See *Sayings of the Fathers.*) First, Hillel is saying that it is up to every man to be himself and take care of himself. And Hillel means much more than that each man must earn money and supply himself with material goods. He means that each man must develop his inner self—it is his obligation and no one can do it for him. Of course, parents and teachers help. But in the end, each man should make himself into the kind of person he wants to be.

If a man does not become a self-respecting, mature human being he will not have the respect of others. "If I am not for myself, who will be for me?" In order for others to regard you as a man worthy of admiration you must regard yourself that way. This does not mean that one should be boastful, self-centered, or selfish. For a man is nothing if he cares only for himself. "And if I am only for myself, what am I?" Hillel is saying in this second line that if a man worries only about his own advantage and thinks only about his own interest, he has actually failed in being a human being. A genuine person is one who is involved with and cares about others. Man does not live alone but in relation to other men. The truly developed individual lives not only for himself but in relationship with others.

This is what is taught by the Biblical commandment, "Love thy neighbor as thyself" (Lev. 19:18). Man must love his neighbor, but he cannot do so unless he respects and loves himself. As we saw in Hillel's statement, self-love and love of others go together. The Bible teaches that man must become a

Children of different races make music together in this Protestant church-sponsored instrumental group in the Midwest.

self-respecting and self-loving individual without becoming a purely selfish one. For he must love his neighbors to the same degree and in the same way that he loves himself.

Thus we can understand that all men striving to be themselves and to respect themselves must know who they are and how they got to be that way. As Jews, this means that we must understand Judaism because it is such an important part of our background and has played such an important role in making us what we are today.

It is only after we know something about our own religion that we can really understand another's beliefs and recognize what another's religion means to him. In the following chapters we shall try to learn about Christianity and Judaism — gaining understanding and respect of ourselves and others.

THE BED OF TORTURE

In the Talmud there is a rabbinic legend that tells about a strange bed of torture and an unbelievable custom. The evil judges of the cities of Sodom and Gomorrah instructed the inhabitants to set up beds on their commons. When a stranger arrived, three men seized him by his head, and three by his feet and they forced him to lie upon one of the beds. If he happened to be a short man and didn't fit into the bed exactly, his six attendants pulled and wrenched his limbs, stretching him until he conformed to the exact size of the bed. He would be killed in the process, but what did the people care? They hated strangers. If it happened that he was tall and his legs extended beyond the end of the bed, they would either cut off his legs or try to jam him in with their combined strength until the victim was on the verge of death. His outcries and screams were met with the words, "Thus will be done to any man that comes into our land" (Talmud Sanhedrin 109b).

Other stories are told about the wicked inhabitants of the cities of Sodom and Gomorrah. When a stranger would enter the gates they would give him gold, silver and precious jewels—but no food or water. He was not permitted to leave the town, but died of thirst and starvation with all the gold, silver and jewels in his pockets.

Our rabbis give this as the reason for the destruction of Sodom and Gemorrah. Not only did the people hate strangers, but they never permitted differences of opinion or religious conviction. Everyone had to believe the same and act the same, dress the same way and speak the same language.

1. How would you apply this story to the early history of the United States?

2. How does this legend relate to the idea of democracy?

Accepting differences

The Midrash relates the following: Human beings mint coins bearing the picture of one original (a king or a prince), and all coins are identical. However, the King of Kings, the Holy One, blessed be He, patterned all human beings after the image of Adam, the first man, and yet no two human beings are exactly alike.

The Talmud asks the question: "Why did God begin the creation of man with Adam?" The answer is: "To teach us that all human beings are descended from one ancestor, so that no man may be able to say: 'My family is better than thine. My nation is better and more superior to yours.'"

The Midrash teaches:
The Lord took dust from the four corners of the earth in equal measure. Some of the dust was red, some black, some white and some as yellow as sand. These He mixed with water from all the oceans and seas, to indicate that all races of mankind have the same beginning, and that none can be counted better than the other.

1. What do you think the Talmud and Midrash are trying to teach?

2. How does this Midrash apply to different religions as well as to the differences in people?

THE LAWS OF NOAH

In our Jewish tradition, we are taught that the Laws of Noah, or the Noahide Laws, apply to all peoples, all nations and all faiths. According to the rabbis, Noah and his descendants (the whole human race) were commanded by God to observe the following seven commandments by refraining from (1) idolatry; (2) adultery and incest; (3) bloodshed; (4) blasphemy; (5) robbery; (6) social injustice; (7) eating flesh cut from a living animal.

These laws and commandments apply to non-Jews as well as Jews. This means that the rabbis believed that there were ideals and moral commandments that applied to all peoples, all religions and all races.

WHAT DO YOU THINK?

1. These laws were written in ancient times. Do you think they still apply today?

2. What additional commandments and moral laws do you believe apply to all peoples regardless of their religious faith?

3. Discuss in class how modern people should interpret these Noahide laws to apply to their own times and their own lives.

Tell how would you answer these questions:

a. Do you think there should be one, universal religion, the same for all peoples and all nations? What would be the advantages and disadvantages? How would the nations determine what the universal religion should be? Would it be one of the great religions such as Christianity, Judaism, Islam, or the best that is in all religions, with a new name given to the new religion?

b. Do you think America would be a better nation if all Americans observed and believed in the same religion, which would be the official religion of the United States? If so, what would be a fair way of determining what that religion should be? If so, what religion should the official religion of the United States be?

THE RELIGION OF OUR NEIGHBORS

We, in America, live with Christians. We believe that we should learn more about the religion of our neighbors, and we hope they will learn more about our Jewish re-

ligion. It is only when we know about each other and understand each other, that we may have respect for other religions even though we may disagree with their beliefs and practices.

In the next few weeks we are going to study what happens when a Jewish group visits a Christian church and worships with Christian friends. No one will be forced to attend, although I do hope that every member of the class will want to be present. We are going to invite a Protestant minister and a Catholic priest to visit our classroom and explain their religious beliefs and practices to us. This does not mean that we will be disloyal to our own religion, or that we are going to accept what other religions believe. We will be better Americans and better Jews if we understand the religion of our Christian

Sisters of Mercy, nuns studying or teaching at Salve Regina College summer school, visit the historic Touro Synagogue in Newport.

neighbors, and how their religion differs from and agrees with our own.

Some of us may find this a bit unusual. Perhaps you may think to yourself, "What does this have to do with Judaism?" If we are really to understand the spirit of Judaism, we must learn to respect differences of religion—differences in the way we worship.

QUESTIONS FOR DISCUSSION

1. What are some other examples of the difference between uniformity and unity?

2. Will a study of other religions weaken or strengthen your faith in Judaism?

3. Do you think that Jewish students should learn more about Christianity in a Jewish religious school? Should Christian students study about Judaism in Christian religious schools?

4. Instead of having Jewish religious schools and Christian religious schools, would it be better to have one religious school where Jewish and Christian children study about Judaism and Christianity together? What are the advantages and disadvantages?

5. Instead of studying about Christian beliefs and practices in a Jewish religious school, would it be better for Jewish students to spend the time studying more about their own religion?

THINGS TO DO

1. Look up in the dictionary the meaning of these words: xenophobia, cultural pluralism, unity, uniformity, diversity.

2. Study and discuss the filmstrip: "Our World of Happy Differences" (Cokesbury).

3. Invite Protestant and Catholic students to your religious school to discuss the differences and similarities of Judaism, Protestantism and Catholicism.

4. Look up in the *Universal Jewish En-*

cyclopedia the article on Midrash. Write a page giving a summary of the article.

5. When Moses was about to die, he asked God to appoint a successor to lead the children of Israel. According to Midrash, Moses prayed: "Sovereign of the universe, Thou knowest the minds of all men, and how the mind of one man differs from that of another. Appoint over them a leader, who will be able to bear with the differing minds of every one of Thy Children."

Discuss in class the modern meaning of this Midrash.

6. Show cartoon of "The Rabbit Brothers," and discuss it in class.

7. Present a pageant from *Men Are All Brothers,* by Weil and Kohan. (Order from Anti-Defamation League.)

SELECTED READINGS

God's work

Christianity and Judaism can never blend without the surrender by the one or the other of its fundamental principles. But they could learn to understand and respect each other and recognize that each religion has God's work to do, and cannot do it without the help and presence, yes, even the sympathy of the other. And it would be a great help to this end if it were recognized that the hard things spoken and written of old belong to the old time alone, and have no meaning now—let the dead past bury its dead.

—PROFESSOR TRAVERS HERFORD,
"A Christian Scholar," in
*Jewish Studies in Memory of
Israel Abrahams,* 1927

Hoping for the great day

Judaism, which differed and continues to differ from other religions in significant matters of belief and practice, has sought and seeks opportunities of friendly cooperation with them in all things which contribute to the building of the good society, firm in its own convictions, reverent of theirs, hoping for the great day of universal reconciliation of all peoples, when "they shall not hurt nor destroy in all My holy mountain, and the earth shall be full of the knowledge of God as the waters over the sea.

—RABBI ABBA HILLEL SILVER,
Where Judaism Differed

One great common mission

In our own time, in a world full of pain and confusion and bitterness, the world's religions find themselves faced with one great common mission:

The Mission of Peace.

Regardless of the differences between religion and religion, or creed and creed, to fulfill their promise to their followers, they must all gather under the one banner bearing the inscription:

The Mission of Mankind is Peace.

—JOSEPH GAER,
How the Great Religions Began

The right to be different

Four centuries ago Charles V was emperor of the Holy Roman (German) Empire, which then included most of Europe. Like other monarchs, he found the job of ruling people a troublous occupation. In his old age he retired to a monastery to rest his frazzled nerves. There he amused himself by tinkering with clocks. He had a house full of them. His pet ambition was to regulate them so that they would all strike at precisely the same time. But despite his most persistent painstaking efforts, he could not make them do it.

Finally he gave it up. One day he philosophised as follows: "I was a fool, trying to make my subjects think alike on everything. I can't even make these helpless clocks strike alike!"

Star and cross together form the background for Armistice Day ceremonies in Springfield, Mass. Both faiths seek for peace.

SELECTED READINGS

BOND, GLADYS BAKER, *Little Stories on Big Subjects* (May be ordered from Anti-Defamation League.)

GAER, JOSEPH, *How the Great Religions Began*, pp. 412–415

GUGGENHEIM, HANS, *The World of Wonderful Differences* (May be ordered from Anti-Defamation League.)

KRAUS, ROBERT, *The Rabbit Brothers* (Pamphlet — may be ordered from Anti-Defamation League.)

LEVINE, RAPHAEL H., *Two Paths to One God*, pp. 207ff.

WILSON, BETTYE D., *We are All Americans* (May be ordered from Anti-Defamation League.)

3

The Jewish Concept of God

THE MYSTERY OF GOD

Kaufmann Kohler, one of the great leaders of Reform Judaism in America, tells a story in his book called *Jewish Theology*. It is a story about the teacher who is preparing to lecture to his students on the nature of God. Reviewing his subject he walked along the seashore and saw two boys digging in the sand. They took buckets and filled them with water and poured the contents into the hole in the sand.

"What are you boys trying to do?" asked the teacher. "Can't you see?" answered the boys, "we're emptying the sea into this hole."

"Fools," retorted the professor, "Don't you know that you can't empty the sea into that hole you are digging? Why, it's too. . ." Then he paused, struck by a sudden thought. "I called these boys 'fools,' " said the professor to himself. "But the sea is measurable. It *can* be emptied. Fool? I am the fool, because I am trying to put into the human mind a concept of a God who is immeasurable and infinite. I should learn humility in the presence of the God of the universe before I attempt to teach all about Him to my students." He realized how impossible it was for a human being to know all about God.

This feeling of awe that the professor experienced, was also experienced by the author of the 8th Psalm as he looked at the heavens and said:

*When I behold Thy heavens, the work of
  Thy fingers,
The moon and the stars, which Thou hast
  established;
What is man that Thou art mindful of
  him?
And the son of man, that Thou thinkest of
  him?*

It is this same sense of wonder expressed in another Psalm that extols the wonders of the human body: "I am wonderfully and awesomely made" (Ps. 139:14).

Modern physicists, botanists and astronomers have expressed this same sense of wonder when they considered the breathtaking size of the universe, and the precision and order of God's creation. One scientist said, "When I consider the magnitude of the universe I can only repeat the words of the 139th Psalm:

*Whither shall I go from Thy spirit?
Or whither shall I flee from Thy presence?*

Jewish law forbids depicting God in human form, as in Michelangelo's powerful scene of the creation of Adam, in the Sistine Chapel of the Vatican.

If I ascend up into heaven, Thou art there;
If I make my bed in the netherworld;
  behold, Thou art there.
If I take the wings of the morning,
And dwell in the uttermost parts of the sea;
Even there would Thy hand lead me,
And Thy right hand would hold me!

You may be wondering, "If God doesn't have a body, how can He have fingers and a hand?"

The idea of God as having human limbs and human qualities is called by a big word: *anthropomorphism.* This very long word means thinking of God in physical terms, making God like a man. When we read that God walked, God talked, God touched, the eyes of God, the hand of God—these are all anthropomorphisms. The Bible doesn't really mean that God has fingers, hands, eyes, legs or other human organs. This was the way that our ancestors described God. In the way they knew. It was childish and primitive, but our civilization was very young, and it was difficult to think of an invisible spirit. It is very difficult to think of an invisible spirit and even more difficult to describe it. How else can we talk about God except in human terms? That is why the Talmud explains this by saying that "the Bible speaks in the language of man."

Let us try to illustrate why we sometimes think of God as having some physical form or substance. Suppose you were putting on a play and you wanted to show the presence of God. How would you do it? Perhaps you would show God's presence by a light, or have someone speak with a deep voice.

It's practically impossible to describe God without something physical or something like a substance—such as light, or smokelike fog, or ectoplasm or something visible. Even to think of God having a voice would mean that God has a tongue and a larynx or voice box or whatever produces sound.

Early man used wooden or stone idols to worship as gods. Later on, we will see that Christianity believed that God became incarnate, that is, became flesh as a human being. That human being was called Jesus. But we don't want to get into this subject before we study the views of Catholicism. Right now we want to study the Jewish concept of God and consider how important it is to have humility when we think of God.

WHAT DO YOU THINK?

After his historic journey into space, the Russian cosmonaut, Gherman Titov, said that he saw "Neither God nor angels" during his orbital flight. "I don't believe in God," he added.

1. Give your opinion of the statement made by the Russian cosmonaut.

2. What do you think is the Jewish answer to Titov?

3. How do you think a Christian would answer Titov?

4. What is the belief of modern Judaism about angels? How do Orthodox, Conservative and Reform Jews differ in their belief about angels?

5. Titov suggests that there is no God because he could not see any physical manifestation or appearance of God. Compare what you think is the Jewish and Protestant belief about whether or not God has a body and may be seen in physical form.

6. How do these two statements from the Jewish Bible apply to Titov's statement?

a. "And God said: 'Thou canst not see My face, for man shall not see Me and live." (Ex. 33:20)

b. "And the Lord spoke unto you out of the midst of the fire. Ye heard the voice of words, but ye saw no form." (Deut. 4:12)

7. Reread Maimonides' principles of faith in Chapter 1 and tell how you think Maimonides would have responded to Titov's statement.

I WILL BE WHAT I WILL BE

Some people try to define God, but in the book of Exodus when Moses asked God to tell him how to explain God to the children of Israel, God answered: *"Eheyeh asher eheyeh"*—which means, "I am what I am." The great commentator Rashi interpreted this in the future tense, "I will be what I will be." These puzzling words mean that God is saying that no man can define God or know God completely.

That is why an ancient Jewish psalmist wrote after thinking about God, and hoping to understand God:
Such knowledge is too wonderful for me;
Too high, I cannot attain unto it.
—PSALM 139:6

Years later, Job about whom you will hear more later, said:
Canst thou find out the deep things of God?
Canst thou attain unto the purpose of the Almighty?
It is as high as heaven; what canst thou do?
—JOB 11:7–8

Show me your God

The Talmud relates that the Roman Emperor, Hadrian, once summoned Rabbi Joshua and demanded, "Show me your God!

Let me see your God, or you and your people will be punished." Rabbi Joshua tried to convince the Emperor that no human being can see God, but the Emperor insisted and so the rabbi told him to meet him in the town square at noon.

When the sun was high in the heavens, Rabbi Joshua said to the Emperor, "Look, look at the sun!" He looked up but the sun was so bright he averted his eyes. "Look up at the sun," said Rabbi Joshua more emphatically. Hadrian tried again but cried out, "I cannot look, the sun is too bright."

Rabbi Joshua said, "You can't look at the sun, which is only a tiny servant of God. How then do you expect to look upon the radiance and brilliance of the Supreme Master of the Universe who created the sun?"

This homily, or story, illustrates how impossible it is for man to see God or know God completely. That is why we approach the subject of God with reverence and humility —knowing that we may be able to understand just a little and to see only glimpses of the divine.

But Judaism doesn't say, "We can't know God completely and so that's that," dropping the search for God. We may not know completely but through the thousands of years of searching and questing for a greater understanding of God, Judaism has come to embrace the following beliefs:

GOD IS THE CREATOR OF THE UNIVERSE AND ALL THAT IS THEREIN.

In the Beginning God . . .

The Bible starts with these words:

In the beginning God created the heaven and the earth.

In order to explain the creation of man, anthropologists trace the development of the human species back through millions of years

"Mountains and all hills, fruitful trees, and all cedars: . . . Let them praise the name of the Lord, For His name alone is exalted; His glory is above the earth and heaven."
—Psalms 148:9, 13

to the one cell from which human life eventually evolved, but the question to be answered is, "How did the one cell originate?" The scientists offer theories that it came about through subcellular parts. There are many theories of how life evolved from neutrons, protons and electrons, but the question is still to be asked, "How did these originate?" The answer of Judaism, no matter how far back human life may be traced, is, "In the beginning, God."

God not only started the beginning process by which life evolved, but God's presence is to be found in all of life. The prayer book tells us that "God renews the work of creation daily." God is in everything and yet is more than the sum total of all things. The Supreme Being is the *makom* (the place), imminent, in the universe, and yet transcendent, beyond the universe.

The intelligence of God is revealed in part through the order, wonder and precision of the universe. Sir James Jeans, a great physicist, estimated that a collision between two stars could occur once in 600,000,000,000,-000,000 years. The atmosphere surrounding the earth is about 78 per cent nitrogen and 21 per cent oxygen which permits life to exist on this planet. With too much or too little nitrogen or oxygen it is unlikely that life could continue on earth. The marvelous order of heaven and earth inspires many scientists today to say what the psalmist said thousands of years ago: "the heavens declare the glory of God and the firmament showeth His handiwork" (Ps. 19:1).

According to the Midrash, a certain man, who always looked for proof of everything, once came to Rabbi Akiba and asked him:

"Rabbi, tell me, who created the world?"

"God created the world," answered the rabbi.

"I want you to give me proof positive that it was God who created the world," persisted the man.

"Come back tomorrow," said Rabbi Akiba.

The following day, when the man returned, Rabbi Akiba pointed to the man's coat and asked:

"What is this you are wearing?"

"It's my coat," said the man.

"Who made the cloth?" asked the rabbi.

"The weaver, of course," answered the man.

"I don't believe you. Prove it," said the rabbi.

"But everyone knows that the weaver weaves the cloth," exclaimed the man.

"You are so readily convinced that the weaver weaves the cloth," said Rabbi Akiba. "You will readily admit that the carpenter makes a wooden door, and that a house is proof that there is a builder! Yet you are so blind to the clear fact that the very existence of the world and everything in it gives proof that there is a Creator, the Almighty God!"

Without the belief in God as the Creator, we would have to conclude that the earth came about through chance, and that our world is a cosmic accident, and that life is without meaning and purpose.

GOD IS ONE

The declaration of the unity of God is the watchword and the foundation of the Jewish faith. When we declare, "Hear, O Israel, the Lord our God, the Lord is One" (Deut. 6:4), we indicate our belief that there are no other gods, and that God is indivisible and unique. The Hebrew word *ehad* not only means *oneness,* but it also means *"uniqueness."* There is nothing that can compare with God. The faith of Israel declares with stubborn conviction: not "Hear, O Israel, the Lord our God, the Lord is two." Not

"Hear, O Israel, the Lord our God, the Lord is three." Not "Hear, O Israel, the Lord our God, the Lord is many," but "Hear, O Israel, the Lord our God, the Lord is One."

If God is the Creator of all, and if God is One, then God is the Father of all mankind. Therefore, since God is our heavenly Father, we are all His children, Jew, Protestant, Catholic, Moslem, Buddhist, white, black, brown, yellow and red, American, Chinese, German, Russian and Congolese. The belief that God is one also leads us to the belief that mankind is one. That is why our prayer book expresses the hope: "One God over all. One brotherhood of all."

GOD IS OMNIPRESENT

This means that God is everywhere, in heaven, on earth, and in the heart and soul of man. God is in every leaf, in every molecule, in everything that was, is and shall yet be.

That is why the story is told of the time when Rabbi Yitzhak Meir was a little boy and his mother once took him to see the *maggid* (traveling preacher) of a town called Koznitz. There someone said to him, "Yitzhak Meir, I'll give you a gulden [a coin] if you'll tell me where God lives."

The boy replied, "And I'll give you two gulden if you tell me where He doesn't live!"

Perhaps you are wondering: if God doesn't have a body, then God doesn't have a sex. Why, then, is God called He, Him, Father, Lord, King?

This may be the result of male pride. A patriarchal society, which means a civilization dominated by men, thinks of God as a man. A matriarchal society, dominated by women, would probably think of God as a Goddess and refer to the deity as Her, She, Mother, Lady, Queen. Again, it is what the Talmud calls "speaking in the language of man."

The "I-thou" relationship between father and child typifies the guidance and trusting obedience relationship between God and mankind living by God's law.

Judaism believes that God is *omnipresent* and cannot be confined to one place or one nation. That is why Rabbi Joshua of Siknin gave the example of a cave near the seashore that filled up with water, and yet just as much water remained in the sea. The presence of God filled the sanctuary, but the world was no less filled with God's glory. Just as the sun seems to be shining in one place, yet we know that the light of the sun is cast for great distances, so the infinite God casts the glow of divinity throughout not only the world, but the whole universe.

Recently, in an article by a religious teacher who is not Jewish, the author worried about what would happen if astronauts discovered human beings on other planets. How would such a discovery affect a theology that thinks of God ruling over *this earth* alone?

This would be no problem to Jewish theology because every blessing we use tells us that God is more than the God of the earth: *Barukh attah Adonai Eloheinu Melekh ha-Olam,* Blessed art Thou, O Lord, our God, King of the Universe. . . .

Notice that when we praise God, we praise Him not as King of the *Jews,* or King of the *Earth,* but as *King of the Universe.* God is omnipresent. He is everywhere. No matter where we are, in the words of the psalmist: "The Lord is near unto all who call upon Him, to all who call upon Him in truth." That, too, is why the prayer book speaks of God, Who is "farther than the farthermost star, and yet is as close to us as breathing."

GOD IS OMNISCIENT

Perhaps you see the word for *science* in the latter part of the word, *omniscient.* Science is derived from the word *scientia* which means "to know." "God is omniscient" means that God is all-knowing.

The Jewish philosophers debated this

quality or attribute of God. Some of them said that if God knows everything that is going to happen, then everything is decided on before it happens.

This means that man does not have freedom of will, for every actoin is really determined. If this is true, then man really doesn't have a choice between right and wrong.

Other philosophers believed that God could know everything, but God purposely does not know because He wants to let man make his own moral choices.

Still others taught that God knows everything but gives man freedom of will to choose right or wrong, good or evil.

Oh, how the Jewish scholars argued this question! Some said, "If God knows everything that is going to happen, then He should stop evil from happening." Others said: "No. God knows what is going to happen, but He still gives man the freedom of will to choose, otherwise man would be like a puppet or a marionette, without will of his own."

One thing is certain about Jewish belief. Judaism believes that God has given man freedom of will. Man must make his choice between good and evil, and abide by the consequences. The Bible states clearly that God said: "I have set before thee life and death, the blessing and the curse; therefore choose life, that thou mayest live" (Deut. 30:19).

GOD IS OMNIPOTENT

This means that God is all-powerful. The Bible asks: "Is anything too difficult for the Lord?" (Gen. 18:14) Should we not believe that the God who created the heaven and the earth, the wonders of the human body, and the miracles of nature that are all around us, should be able to do anything and everything?

Some Jewish thinkers have said that God is omnipotent, but there are some things that

God will not do. God will not break His own laws of nature. That is why Judaism doesn't place very much emphasis on what people call "miracles." If we mean that something is wondrous, yes, Judaism believes in this. If we mean that God will suspend the law of gravity to save a good person from danger— no, Judaism doesn't believe in this kind of miracle.

The sages considered the problem of how to account for the plagues in Egypt and the miracle of the Sea of Reeds splitting and permitting the children of Israel to cross over on dry land, and they explained all the so-called miracles in very natural and realistic ways. One rabbi said that the greatest miracle was not the splitting of the sea, but the real miracle was that a slave rabble, a mob, made its way from slavery to freedom, and then to the moral laws given at Sinai.

There is another problem that still bothers people to this day. It bothered the Biblical Job. If God is all-powerful, why is there so much suffering, misery and evil in the world? That was the problem of Job, who wanted to know why the wicked were rewarded and why the righteous people suffered so much. Scholars call this problem *theodicy*. It raises the question, "How do we reconcile, or harmonize, God's goodness and mercy, with all the evil and suffering in this world?"

Should we blame God?

During the terrible years when Jews suffered and died in concentration camps because of the cruelty of the Nazis under Hitler, a sorrowing Jew cried out, "How can there be a God and yet permit all these innocent people to suffer so?" He shook his fist at the sky and shouted, "God, You are cruel. I don't love You. I hate You because You could have stopped all this, and You didn't."

When there is unhappiness and misery in the world, it is only natural that people who suffer should cry out in their misery asking why God doesn't help. But we blame God too much for the faults of man. It wasn't God Who created a Hitler and allowed him to come to power. It was because man strayed far from the ways of God that this happened. Some people blame God for wars, but it is man who creates and causes wars. Most of the misery in our world is not caused by God, but by man's disobedience to God's commandments. Man forgets God and the ways of God, and then when there is trouble, he blames God.

Unfortunately, sometimes innocent people suffer for what seems to us to be no just reason. We cannot understand, and so we wonder why God doesn't perform a miracle and take away the sickness, or bring the dead back to life, or stop wars, or prevent epidemics, hunger and misery. This would mean that God would have to perform miracles and break His own laws.

This is a very difficult problem. We can't solve it or even begin to understand it in one morning. We will have to think about it again and again but now we should think about some things that may appear evil, and yet not be evil.

DISCUSS IN CLASS

A. A person is ill and the doctor takes his temperature. It is above normal. The doctor says: "Hmm, this temperature is bad." How could the temperature be good and not evil? Has fever a purpose?

B. A child drowns in a river. The grieving parents curse the river and call it evil. Is it evil? Is it good, or neither good nor evil?

C. A man holds a sharp knife in his hand. He says, "That's a wicked looking thing, isn't it?" Is the knife wicked or evil? What if that knife is used by a skilled surgeon to save a child's life? Is it still wicked-looking to the eyes of the child's parents?

D. A busy executive had a slight heart attack. How can that affliction be bad? How can it be good?

E. Most people say that death is bad. We know that we all have to die sometime. Is death really bad? How can it be merciful and good?

F. An atheist, one who does not believe in God, sneers, "If God is so all-powerful and good, why doesn't he stop atomic bombs from killing innocent people?" What would you answer?

GOD IS HOLY

Some people say that *monotheism,* the belief in one God, is the greatest contribution of the Jewish religion. There is a greater contribution that Judaism has made: not only that God is one, but that God is a moral God, a God of Justice, Mercy, Truth and Holiness, who demands the practice of justice, mercy, truth and holiness from those who worship Him. This is called *ethical monotheism,* which means a belief in a moral God of holiness Who demands holiness and justice from those who worship Him. Just to say, "I believe in God," isn't enough in the Jewish faith. If our belief in God does not encourage us to follow God's ways and keep His commandments, what good is the belief in God? We might as well believe in a piece of wood, or a carved pagan idol.

It is because we believe that God is good, that we must be good—not just for the sake of a reward or pie in the sky by and by. The Book of Leviticus, Chapter 19, commands: "Ye shall be holy, for I the Lord your God am holy." It is because God is holy that we must be holy. It is because God is just that we must be just. It is because God is merciful that we must be merciful in all that we do. We must be just because we are made in the divine image. There is a portion of God within each of us. We must be just because it is God's way and God's way is the right way and good for us.

The prophets of Israel believed in this moral God, and they taught that man must worship God with his deeds and actions as well as with his words and his ritual.

What did the prophets teach us about ethical monotheism?

Micah proclaimed: "It hath been told thee, O man, what is good, and what the Lord doth require of thee: but to do justly and love mercy and walk humbly with thy God." (Mic. 6:8)

Amos said in the name of God: "I hate and I despise your feasts, and I will take no delight in your solemn assemblies. Yea, though ye offer me burnt-offerings and your meal offerings, I will not accept them. Neither will I regard the peace offerings of your fat beasts." And he continued:

*Take thou away from Me the noise of thy
  songs;*
*And let Me not hear the melody of thy
  psalteries;*
But let justice well up as waters,
And righteousness as a mighty stream."
                              —AMOS 5:21–24

Isaiah said in the name of God:

*I cannot endure iniquity along with
  the solemn assembly,*
*Your new moons and your appointed
  seasons,*
My soul hateth;
They are a burden unto Me;
I am weary to bear them.
*And when ye spread forth your hands
  [in prayer]*
I will hide Mine eyes from you;
Yea, when ye make many prayers,
I will not hear;

Your hands are full of blood.
Wash you, make you clean,
Put away, the evil of your doings
From before Mine eyes,
Cease to do evil;
Learn to do well;
Seek justice, relieve the oppressed,
*Judge the fatherless, plead for the
  widow.*
                              —ISAIAH 1:13–17

Malachi said: "Have we not all one Father? Hath not one God created us? Why then do ye deal treacherously every man against his neighbor?" (Mal. 2:10)

Habakkuk said: "The righteous shall live by his faith." (Hab. 2:4)

If we are to understand the Jewish concept of God, then it must be very clear to us that we show our love of God by service to our fellow men, God's children. Every act of kindness is a prayer. Every deed of holiness is worship in action.

QUESTIONS FOR DISCUSSION

1. Jewish tradition tells us that Rabbi Simeon ben Shetach asked his disciples to buy him a camel from an Arab. As they brought him the animal, they gleefully announced that they had found a precious stone in its collar. "Did the seller know of this gem?" asked their teacher. On being answered in the negative, he called out angrily, "Do you think me a barbarian that I should take advantage of the letter of the law by which the gem is mine together with the camel? Return the gem to the Arab immediately." When the heathen received it back he exclaimed, "Blessed be the God of Simeon ben Shetach!"

   a. Why did the Arab bless the rabbi's God instead of the rabbi?

   b. Do you think the rabbi was right in

returning the gem even though it was legally his?

c. If you bought a used car and found a diamond worth $2,000 in the glove compartment, would you keep it, or return it to the man from who you purchased the car? How would your decision relate to your belief in God?

2. Rabbi Solomon B. Freehof in his book, *Preface to Scripture,* wrote: It is evident that many of the phrases which are used about God in Scripture, such as God "speaking" with human words, "walking" or "stretching out his hand," are not to be explained as mere primitive ideas of God. It is the natural genius of Scripture to speak of . . . God in language that is vivid to human beings. It is not that they were naive enough to think of God as having feet or hands; it was simply that God's presence was so real to them that they could not talk of Him in abstract terms. . . .

a. Explain why you agree or disagree with Rabbi Freehof.

b. How is it possible for man to refer to God without using physical terms, or designating a sex?

3. Rabbi Akiba once said "Everything is foreseen, yet free will is given." Doesn't this seem to be contradictory? How would you explain it?

4. Dr. Charles W. Eliot once wrote this to an atheist, "If you say: 'There is no God,' I can only ask how a speck of a mortal, living for a moment on an atom of an earth in plain sight of an infinite universe full of beauty, wonder and design, can confidently hold so improbable a view."

a. What did Dr. Eliot mean by this statement?

b. If God did not create the world, or

The "beauty, wonder, and design" of creation are seen even in the shimmering web of a spider.

that from which the world evolved, how did the world come into being?

c. Do you think that without the belief in God, mankind could still strive for morality, truth and goodness for goodness' sake?

5. Would your belief in God be strengthened or weakened if God performed miracles upon request and changed the laws of nature? Would your respect and reverence for God be increased if God broke His own natural laws?

6. The Supreme Court reviewed a decision that a person who does not believe in God is "incompetent to hold public office, to give testimony, or serve as a juror" under Maryland's constitution.

What would your decision be if you were a Justice of the Supreme Court? Why?

7. How can the belief in ethical monotheism be good for you and bring greater happiness to you and to others?

THINGS TO DO

1. Write an essay on the religious meaning of this question raised by Bachya ibn Pakuda, a medieval Jewish philosopher:

If one should bring an ordered manuscript and claim that the writing was produced by the accidental spilling of ink upon the paper, would he be believed?

2. Look up the following passages in the Bible to find out if God is described as spiritual or physical: Deuteronomy 4:12–15; Exodus 3:17–23.

3. Read through the Book of Jonah carefully, and discuss in class the real meaning of the story of the reluctant prophet. What does the Book of Jonah teach us about the Jewish concept of God?

4. Write a paragraph on the Jewish idea of holiness after reading Leviticus, Chapter 19. How would you apply holiness to the life of someone your age in modern times?

5. The teacher should tell the story of the Book of Job after reading the prologue in class. Discuss in class, "What the Book of Job tells us about the question 'why do the righteous suffer?' "

6. Consider the following anecdote:

A minister noticed a little boy holding securely the end of a long string. The attached kite was indistinguishable in the evening twilight. When he inquired of the lad why he was acting so, the boy said he was flying a kite. "I can't see it; but I know it's there, for I feel the pull."

—BERNARD L. DUNHAM

Write an essay telling how you feel God's presence pulling us upward and tugging at you in your daily life.

SELECTED QUOTATIONS

How to recognize God's work

God saw the light—that it was good. He said, Let dry land appear, and trees and herbs and flowers, fish, and birds and creeping things and the luminaries of heaven. He beheld everything that He had made and saw that it was good. So God recognized His work; its goodness proclaimed it His.

God clothed the naked Eve and Adam and threadbare Israel in their wandering; sick Abraham He visited and buried Moses when he died; fed hungry Elijah and Israel in the wilderness.

What can men ever know of God?— what they see of goodness in His world. Where find the greatest goodness? In God's best effort: man himself.

We give evidence of His in-breathed image when we imitate God—feeding the hungry, clothing the naked, tending the sick, relieving the burdened. We are His instruments, helping men to recognize God's work by this: that it is good.

—RABBI ALBERT S. GOLDSTEIN

The idea of God

There is an old legend that when Abraham began to reflect upon the nature of God he at first took the stars for deities, because of their luster and beauty. But when he realized that they were outshone by the moon, he thought of the moon as divine. The moon's light, however, faded before the light of the sun and made him think of the latter as divine. Yet at night the light of the sun also disappeared. There

The patterned flight of migrating waterfowl, following the path of the seasons, shows forth the orderliness of a planned and purposeful creation.

must be something in the world greater than all these constellations, mused Abraham. Thus, gradually he rose from the deification of nature to the God of nature.

—RABBI H. G. ENELOW

God as the All

Belief in God must begin with the postulate that God is All. If this be true, how can the mature mind reconcile its thinking with the fragmentized beliefs taught by the various religions? It cannot accept the division of Ultimate Reality into a Jewish God, a Christian God, a Mohammedan God, and the like. A fundamental question arises: Do Jews believe in God or in a Jewish God? Do Christians believe in God or in a Christian God?

Do Mohammedans believe in God or in a Mohammedan God? This perplexing dilemma confronts every searcher whose belief in God is predicated upon the premise that God is All. His Allness must be indivisible. Since each religion espouses its particular God concept as the sole agent of Supreme Truth, there can be but one logical conclusion: each captures fragments of Supreme Truth, but cannot claim to represent the Ultimate which becomes Allness only when completely stripped of labels.

—RABBI ALEXANDER ALAN STEINBACH

The orderliness of the universe

To an astronomer the most remarkable thing about the universe is not its immense size, its great age, or even the violence of the forces operating within its borders. The thing which strikes an astronomer with awe is the element of perfect orderliness. From the tiny satellites of our solar system to the vast galaxies far beyond our own there is no trace of confusion. There is nothing haphazard, nothing capricious. The orderliness of the universe is the supreme discovery of science.

—F. R. MOULTON,
The Nature of the World and of Men

The burning bush

"And the angel of the Lord appeared unto him in a flame of fire out of the midst of a bush." (Ex. 3:2)

A heathen asked Rabbi Joshua ben Karḥah:

"Why did the Holy One, blessed be He, choose to speak to Moses out of the midst of a thornbush?"

The rabbi answered him:

Had it been out of the midst of a carob tree or out of the midst of a sycamore, you would have asked the same question.

Still, I cannot send you away empty-handed.

Well then: Why out of the midst of a thornbush?

To teach you that there is no place void of the Presence of God, not even a thornbush!"

—Midrash, from NAHUM M. GLATZER'S
In Time and Eternity

What is God?

When in the west at evening I behold
Lit one by one upon the dusky sky
Torches, like sparks of silver and of gold,
Gazing in wonder, to those lights I cry:
"Tell me, ye stars, ah, tell me, what is
God?"

"Order," the stars reply.

When in her festive garb the earth is
decked,
Green valley, hill and field, and river bank,
With many-colored flowery garlands
flecked,
Gazing, I ask: "Tell me, ye fragrant
bowers,
Ye blazing colors, tell me, what is God?"
"Beauty," reply the flowers.

When the caressing eyes upon me turn
Their softly sparkling ray,
I ask of those pure fires that in them burn:
"Where were ye kindled? Ah, can ye not
say,
Bright stars, can ye not tell me what is
God?"
They answer: "God is love."

—ALEARDO ALEARDI,
from *Anthology of*
Italian Lyrics, R. Rendel

The awareness of God

Solomon ibn Gabirol, enumerating the "three things which stand together to bring the awareness of Thee ever before me," lists first the "heavens and second the earth in its expanse, but as a climactic third "the stirring of my heart when I look inward."

—MILTON STEINBERG,
Basic Judaism,
Harcourt, Brace & World, Inc.

SELECTED READINGS

FACKENHEIM, EMIL L., *Paths to Jewish Belief,*
Chapters 1–5
GITTELSOHN, ROLAND B., *The Jewish Concept of*
God, BBYO Pamphlet Series
———*Little Lower Than the Angels,* Chapters
2–8

KRIPKE, DOROTHY, AND LEVIN, MEYER, *God and the Story of Judaism*, Unit Two

SILVERMAN, WILLIAM B., *The Still Small Voice*, Chapter 2

UNIVERSAL JEWISH ENCYCLOPEDIA, Vol. 5, God, pp. 1–8

GLOSSARY

Anthropomorphism: Thinking of God in humans terms, as having a body, eyes, hands, ears, voice, etc.

Atheist: One who denies the existence of God.

Attribute: A characteristic or quality.

Cosmic: Relating to an orderly, harmonious, systematic universe.

Deification: Making into a God or gods.

Deity: Supreme being.

Ethical monotheism: Belief in moral God of holiness, Who demands holiness and justice from those who worship Him.

Imminent: Ready to take place; at hand; near; within.

Infinite: Subject to no limitation; immeasurably or inconceivably great or extensive.

Maggid: Traveling preacher.

Midrash: Explanation of Bible, stories and interpretations, written between fourth century B.C.E. and eleventh century C.E.

Monotheism: Belief that there is but one God.

Omnipotent: Almighty; all-powerful.

Omnipresent: Present in all places at all times. (God is everywhere.)

Omniscient: All-knowing. (God is All-knowing.)

Talmud: Decisions of rabbis, known as Oral Law, explaining Written Law of Bible.

Theodicy: Defense of God's goodness and power in view of existence of evils and suffering.

Theology: Study of God and religious beliefs.

Transcendent: Exceeding all limits—being beyond limits of all possible experience and knowledge; beyond the universe.

4

The Christian Concept of God

Just as there are differences of belief in Judaism, so there are differences of belief in Christianity. There are Orthodox, Conservative and Reform Jews. So there are Catholics, Greek Orthodox and Protestants who all call themselves Christians and follow the Christian religion.

Even the titles of Christian religious leaders are different. The Catholics call their religious leader, father, and refer to him as a priest. Those who belong to the Greek Orthodox Church also call their religious leader father and priest. Most Protestants call their religious leader Mr., Dr., Pastor or Reverend, and refer to him as a minister.

Because Protestantism grew out of Catholicism we are going to continue our comparison of Judaism and Christianity by studying first about Catholicism. There are many false and twisted ideas about Catholics and Catholicism, just as there are untrue and strange ideas about Jews and Judaism. We, as Jews, disagree with many of the beliefs and practices of our Catholic friends, but we respect each other's differences.

The term *catholic* was first used by Ignatius of Antioch, an early church leader who lived during the second century C.E. By *catholic* he meant "universal" or "worldwide." Peter, the chief disciple of Jesus, is believed to be the founder of the church of Rome and to have become its first "bishop."

The Trinity

When we were discussing the Jewish concept of God we said that the Jews thought of God as being One, the Creator of heaven and earth. The Christians would agree with this. The Jews believe God is omniscient, all-knowing and omnipotent, all-powerful, and the Christians would agree with this. Where then do Jews and Christians disagree?

In order to answer this question we must understand the basic foundation of Christianity, which is the belief in Jesus as the Christ, the Messiah, the only Son of God and Savior of mankind. Christians believe that God contains three aspects or "persons," the Trinity of Father, Son, and the Holy Spirit, and is yet one God. All three aspects of God are found in the Trinity and all are one, the same and equal. Thus, Catholics believe that Jesus is one aspect of God Himself.

To redeem man, according to Christian doctrine, God sent his divine son, Jesus, to earth in human form. This is called the "incarnation," the event of God's becoming true man even as He retained the nature of true God. Catholics believe that the birth of Jesus was a miraculous one and call it the miracle of the Virgin Birth. Through the power of the Holy Spirit, the Son of God was born to the Virgin Mary. And through another miracle, Mary was herself a completely pure woman. She herself was born *immaculate,* that is, untouched by sin and evil and was therefore able to be the "mother of God." This is called the doctrine of the *immaculate conception.*

The Crucifix

As soon as a Catholic child is old enough to notice things, he will see in his home a picture or image of Jesus upon the cross. This is called a *crucifix.* The child will also see a statue of the mother of Jesus. When the child is held up to the statues, his mother makes the sign of the cross over his head, heart and shoulder, saying the words that were said at his baptism: "In the name of the Father and of the Son and of the Holy Ghost." When the child is old enough to talk he will learn to say: "Hail Mary, full of Grace. The Lord is with Thee. Blessed art thou among women; and blessed is the fruit of thy womb, Jesus; Holy Mary, Mother of God, pray for us sinners now and at the hour of our death. Amen."

The years pass and the child is given a rosary. This is a string of beads, alternating one large and ten smaller ones, with a crucifix at the end. By this, he can count his prayers. The first is called the *Paternoster,* from the first two Latin words:

Our Father, who art in heaven, hallowed be Thy name.

Thy Kingdom come. Thy will be done on earth as it is in heaven.

Young Catholic girls are adorning the statue of the Virgin Mary, whom they venerate, and to whom they pray for intercession with Jesus.

Give us this day our daily bread

And forgive us our trespasses as we forgive those who trespass against us

And lead us not into temptation, but deliver us from evil.

Amen.

The child counts his prayers, saying a Paternoster for each big bead and a Hail Mary for each smaller one. There are five groups. He says the whole three times to complete the rosary, but not necessarily all in one day.

The mission of Jesus

Catholics believe that Jesus came to earth to save man. By the example of his righteousness he demonstrated to man the life of holiness. And by his suffering and death on the cross he redeemed the souls of sinning mankind. This sacrificial death is called the Crucifixion. By sending His only Son to suffer and die for the sake of mankind, God expressed His love for His creatures. It is up to man to accept this love of God by having faith in Jesus.

Catholics also believe that three days after the crucifixion, Jesus rose from the dead in the miracle called the "Resurrection." He appeared to his chief followers, the twelve apostles. These men, empowered by the experience of seeing the Risen Lord, went out and preached His message of salvation to other men. Together, the believers in Christ organized churches. The Church administers the sacred rites of Christianity and teaches Christian beliefs. By obeying the truths of the Church, partaking of its sacred rituals, and imitating the life of Christ in his own life, a person may achieve salvation.

The seven sacraments

We have already discussed the major beliefs of Christianity—the Incarnation, Crucifixion and Resurrection. Now we will examine the central rituals of the Church. These rituals, which are called *sacraments,* are very important to Catholics. They represent the life and saving work of Jesus. In receiving the sacrament the Catholic participates in the reenactment of the life and redeeming power of Jesus. The sacramental ritual is an act, an external sign of the deep personal relationship which the believer feels towards Christ and the Church.

The word *sacrament* comes from a Latin translation of the Greek word for "mystery." It is not the kind of mystery you see on television. It is a sacred mystery, or a rite, which confers or gives God's "grace," or favor, upon the soul of the believer.

The first and most important of all the sacraments, the Eucharist, is the climax of "the Mass." It reenacts the "Last Supper" of Jesus when Jesus and his disciples ate together just before his trial and crucifixion, and it uses the symbols of wine and bread. Catholics believe that during the Last Supper Jesus took the bread and said, "This is my body, given for you," and raising a cup of wine said, "This is my blood, shed for you," and then added, "Do this in remembrance of me." Jesus thus commanded his followers to perform this same act and thereby join him in his sacrifice on the cross. Catholics believe that when Jesus said, "This is my body," and "This is my blood," a miracle took place, that the bread became the actual body of Jesus, and the wine became his actual blood.

During the latter part of the Mass the priest lifts up the "chalice," a cup made of silver or gold, which contains a mixture of water and the wine that is regarded as transformed into the blood of Christ. Then the priest takes a rounded bread wafer, called the "Host." He holds both high above his head and then proceeds with the Mass. He distributes the wafer to the worshiper, who has fasted for four hours before this. Kneeling at the altar rail, the Catholic receives the Host upon his tongue. This is known as "receiving Communion." It means that the Catholic partakes of, shares, or has in common the body and blood of Christ, and unites with Jesus and the Church. Only the priest partakes of the wine in the Catholic Church.

There are seven sacraments to remove sin or to impart "sanctifying grace" to the soul and "leave an indelible character. They are:

1. *Baptism.* Baptism takes place when the

infant receives his Christian name and is initiated into Christian life. The priest pours water on the head of the child (or adult) in the name of the Father, and of the Son and of the Holy Ghost. This act symbolizes the washing away of the original sin in Adam and unites the individual with the Church, the body of Christ. This means that he has received the grace of God.

2. The *Eucharist*. The Eucharist is the partaking of the Host (as often at Mass) and is begun by the child at "First Communion."

3. *Confirmation*. Confirmation gives spiritual maturity to the individual and strengthens him for the practice of his Catholic faith. It usually takes place when the child is around twelve years of age. Before Confirmation, instruction is given in the doctrines of the Church. The ceremony consists of the individual's being anointed with oil and being blessed by the bishop.

4. *Penance*. Penance means the confession of sins in the presence of the priest. The priest then grants *absolution,* or forgiveness. The person must first examine himself to determine whether he is free of serious sin before he may receive holy communion.

5. *Holy Orders*. Holy orders for the clergy is the ritual by which Catholic men are ordained as priests and receive the spiritual power of the Catholic Church. The bishop places his hands on the priest's head as a sign of ordination into the priesthood. Nuns do not receive holy orders but take their vows and are married symbolically to Jesus.

6. *Holy Matrimony*. As the name suggests, matrimony is the marriage of two baptized persons. Marriage is a sacred contract to be maintained until death. The Catholic Church does not permit divorce.

7. *Extreme Unction*. Extreme unction is given when the person is dangerously ill,

Confirmation is an important day in the lives of Catholic boys and girls, already instructed in their faith.

	Roman Catholic belief	**Jewish belief**
God	God is three in one, a Trinity.	God is one in one, indivisible.
Jesus	The Christ, Son of God, born of the Holy Ghost and Virgin Mary. Sent by the Father to earth to teach religious truths and redeem man by His own death.	A Jew who taught Jewish ideals and beliefs. Some believe he went astray by claiming he was God's physical son. Others insist that he never claimed to be anything but a man and a Jew.
Incarnation	The event of God's assuming human form once in history.	God is spirit and can never become man.
Virgin Mary	Conceived Jesus through the Holy Ghost. Revered by Catholics as Mother of God.	No belief in Virgin Birth. Mary had other children and all were naturally born.
Immaculate Conception	Mary born without taint of original sin.	No such belief.
Hail Mary	Mary is revered and pleads for a Catholic to Jesus.	Jews pray directly to God. No intermediary.
Original Sin	The belief that man became sinful because of the disobedience of Adam. All who were born thereafter were born in original sin.	No such belief. The soul is born pure.
Crucifix and Images	Symbols used to worship Jesus, Mary and the saints.	No images of Jewish heroes or teachers to be revered or worshiped.
Paternoster	A sacred prayer to be recited with rosary, at morning and evening prayers, and during Mass.	Nothing objectionable about this prayer, but it is regarded as Christian.
God's Grace	God's free gift of His love and favor to man. Through faith in Jesus man accepts the gift of grace and is thus purified of sin and sanctified.	Forgiveness is obtained through repentance, prayer and making amends through a righteous life. God's love is given to all people.
Salvation	Being saved from Hell and for Heaven through faith in the redeeming acts of Jesus Christ and participation in the Church, his representative on earth.	Three different aspects in Jewish belief: (1) reward of individual soul with immortality, (2) redemption of Jewish people, (3) establishment of justice and peace in a renewed society.
Communion	The commemoration of the Last Supper in which Christians share in or partake of the bread and wine, as the body and blood of Christ.	No equivalent ritual.
Baptism	The washing away of the original sin of Adam. Unites person with Church.	No equivalent. Every soul is born pure. A related ritual is the *mikvah* practiced among traditional Jews.

	Roman Catholic belief	Jewish belief
Hereafter	Souls of the dead go to Heaven or Hell, depending on whether they died in a state of grace. In purgatory souls may be purged of sins, then go to Heaven.	The soul returns to God and enters into eternal life.
Sacraments	Sacred rituals that confer God's grace.	There are *mitzvot* in Judaism but no *sacraments*.
Confirmation	At age of 12.	Jewish confirmation and Bar or Bat Mitzvah are similar, but they are not sacraments.
Penance	Sacrament involving confession of sins, forgiveness for those confessed, and a punishment to atone for them.	Repentance is the resolve to right the wrong and follow God's way. No man can absolve another.
Confession	Sins acknowledged to the priest who grants forgiveness, as a representative of God.	Sins acknowledged privately and publicly in prayer. Forgiveness granted directly from God.
Holy Orders	The sacrament which confers sanctity and divine power to those who serve Christ as priests.	Rabbis are preachers, teachers and judges. After study are declared qualified, but have no divine power.
Holy Matrimony	Marriage of two baptized persons. Divorce is not permitted but occasionally annulments are granted.	Marriage performed in religious ceremony. Divorce is discouraged but permitted.
Extreme Unction	Ritual anointing and prayers—and, if possible, confession and Communion to the dying to prepare man for the hereafter and to forgive his sins.	Judaism has prayers for the dying, including a *viddui,* confession of sins. However, these are not a sacrament and do not confer grace.
One True Religion	Because it embodies the message of Christ, the Roman Catholic Church is God's truest representative on earth.	All religions and all men who promote morality and seek truth can earn God's favor. Israel is a holy people, selected to promote monotheism and morality throughout the world.
Scripture	Old and New Testaments. In addition, some Apocryphal books. The New Testament's authority displaces that of the Old.	The Hebrew Scriptures include only what is called Old Testament books. In addition, the Oral Law is regarded by Orthodox as authoritative.
The Pope	Spiritual head of the Church of Rome. Supreme authority in religious matters.	There is no one spiritual head of the Jewish religion. Jews choose a rabbi to act as teacher and authority in matters of Jewish law.
The Church	The representative of God on earth, through which God's grace is given to all believers.	Israel has been chosen by God for a special mission on earth. The synagogue or temple is a Jewish House of Prayer, Study and Assembly.

actually on the threshold of death. It involves the anointing of the five senses of the dying person with oil. If the person is able, he is to make confession and a last Communion. These rites help to prepare the person for the hereafter. Extreme unction may be administered right after death because it may be assumed that the person is still alive in some way.

QUESTIONS AND ANSWERS

Imagine that a Catholic priest came to your class to discuss Catholicism. Here are some questions and answers about Catholic beliefs.

Question: What do Catholics believe about God?

Answer: Catholics believe that God created the world, and that the Almighty is just, merciful and most holy.

Question: What is meant by "God's grace"?

Answer: Since man isn't able to live without sinning, he needs the gift of God's love to save him. This is known as "God's grace," and it is made possible through the Church.

Question: Saved from what and for what?

Answer: Saved from Hell and saved for Heaven, to live in bliss eternal.

Question: Is it true that the Pope can do no wrong, and that every Catholic must do whatever he says?

Answer: About the fourth century the title of *"Pope"* came into being. The word means "father," and the Pope is the spiritual head of the Roman Church. Catholics believe in the "infallibility of the Pope." This doesn't mean that he is perfect and can do no wrong. It means that in terms of Church doctrine or dogma, what he says is prompted by the spirit of God, and he must be obeyed by all Catholics in religious matters.

Question: Is it true that you have to be a Catholic to be saved and go to Heaven, and do you believe that Roman Catholicism is the only true religion?

Answer: Some Catholic authorities have maintained that no one outside the Church can be "saved," except the "invincibly ignorant." This exception applies to those who have not been able to know the true teachings of the Church. Not all Catholics believe that there is no salvation outside of the Catholic Church. Catholics do believe that theirs is the only true religion, but this does not mean that they do not respect other peoples' differing beliefs.

Question: What is the Greek Orthodox Church?

Answer: This Church is officially called the Holy Orthodox Catholic Apostolic Eastern Church, but its members are often called Greek Catholics to distinguish them from the Roman Catholics. It really started at the Council of Chalcedon in 451. The Greek and Latin Christians had agreed that they believed "in the Holy Ghost who proceedeth from the Father." Some of the Church leaders wanted to add that the Holy Ghost proceeded also from the Son. This was accepted by the Western Catholics. The Eastern Catholics refused to accept it. However, the real break between the two groups did not occur until July 16, 1054, when the Roman Pope excommunicated the Patriarch of Constantinople, spokesman for the Eastern church. After a series of quarrels the two finally divided. The Church in the West was known as the Roman Catholic Church and the Church in the East, the Greek Orthodox Church.

Question: Do the Greek Orthodox Catholics believe the same as the Roman Catholics?

Answer: Basically they do, but there are some important differences. The Greek Orthodox believe in the virgin birth of Christ but reject the doctrine of the immaculate conception. Orthodox priests may marry.

Monks and bishops, however, may not marry.

(To find out more about the Greek Orthodox Church, its beliefs and its practices and how it differs from the Roman Catholic Church read Chapter 11 in *The Faiths Men Live By,* Charles Francis Potter.)

LET'S COMPARE

In the beginning of this chapter we asked where do Judaism and Christianity disagree. We then went on to discuss Catholic beliefs about the Trinity and especially about Jesus, for it is the Christian belief that God sent His Son to be the Messiah of mankind. That is a basic difference between the two religions. Judaism could not accept the idea that God had a son and that this son assumed a human form at a specific moment in history. Now reread the chapter and wherever you think that Judaism doesn't accept a Catholic belief, jot down the difference. After you have completed your own list, compare it with this one.

II. WHAT PROTESTANTS BELIEVE

The original Protestants were those who joined with a monk named Martin Luther in *protest* against some of the teachings and practices of the Roman Catholic Church. Luther's revolt began in 1517. He was followed by others who separated from the Catholic Church in a movement known as "the Reformation." The followers of Luther formed a church called the Lutheran Church. The Reformation spread throughout Europe so that before long there arose the Protestant churches of Presbyterians, Methodists, Baptists, and others. Today there are at least 255 Protestant denominations with differing beliefs and practices. That is why it is difficult to present the Protestant belief about God, since there are so many different interpretations. What we will do here is summarize the beliefs about God that are held by many Protestants, using the *Lutherans,* a major Protestant sect, as the example.

In order to understand how many different types of Protestant churches there are in your community, open the phone book to the yellow pages and look under "Churches—Protestant." Make a list of the various Protestant churches in your city.

THE CREATOR OF ALL

Almost all Protestants believe that God is the Creator of all, that He is Eternal, All-powerful, All-knowing, and that He is everywhere. Very much as the Catholics believe, the Protestants believe that God is a Trinity: the Father and the Son and the Holy Ghost. They believe that God became flesh (incarnate) and came to earth. God gave His only begotten Son, Jesus, to die upon the cross to save mankind from being destroyed. This shows God's love for man.

Salvation comes through God and not through the Church. It comes as a gift from God when man realizes his sinfulness and puts his trust in God through Christ. It is only through faith in Christ that a person can come to God and be redeemed from sin.

The Lutherans believe in what is called "justification by faith." This means that since man is essentially sinful, his salvation comes through believing in God through Christ—but without rites, sacraments or righteous deeds. Of course Lutherans teach that man should be righteous, but without the belief in Christ, righteous deeds will not save him.

Protestants believe that God is the giver of all blessings and good gifts. This belief is shown in what is called the Doxology, or "Praise to God." The Doxology is sung.

Praise God from whom all blessings flow:
Praise Him all creatures here below:
Praise Him above, ye heavenly host,
Praise Father, Son and Holy Ghost.

At the end of the service, the minister will frequently use the blessing:

The Lord bless thee and keep thee;
The Lord make His face to shine upon thee
And be gracious unto thee;
The Lord lift up His countenance upon
 thee
And give thee peace.

This is borrowed from the Jewish priestly benediction found in Numbers 6:24–27.

Sometimes the service ends with this prayer:

The grace of the Lord Jesus Christ, the love of God, and the communion of the Holy Spirit be with you all.

According to the Protestants, salvation comes directly to the individual from God. The Church is not necessary as an institution which mediates God's love to man. Salvation comes as a gift from God when man realizes his sinfulness and puts his trust in God and Jesus. It is only through faith in Christ that a person can come to God and be redeemed from sin.

The individual participates in worship. The prayer service is not in Latin as it is often in the Catholic Church, but in the language of the country in which the person lives. The minister, unlike the priest, does not worship almost entirely for his people. Pastor and congregation join in prayer and song.

Lutherans believe that God reveals His truth to man not through the Pope or the Church but through the Christian Bible. The Bible contains the Word of God and reveals His will. It is therefore the final authority in all religious matters.

Of the seven sacraments of the Catholic Church, most Protestants observe two: Baptism and the Lord's Supper or Communion. Some Protestants interpret the meaning of these sacraments as the Catholics do, while others interpret them more symbolically. The individual participates in worship mainly through prayer and song. The central part of

Martin Luther, called before a Church convention, or Diet, at Worms, staunchly refused to retract his writings against the Papacy.

the Protestant service is the Bible reading and the sermon based upon it, which transmit the Word of God to all participants.

Are there any beliefs held by almost all Protestants?

Dr. Henry P. Van Dusen, in the book, *Religions in America,* edited by Leo Rosten, says, "Yes."

Faith in Jesus Christ as Lord and Savior;

The Bible as the primary source of what is true and right;

The loving concern of God for every human being;

Direct and constant fellowship between God and each believer;

God's forgiveness in response to each person's penitence and faith;

PROTESTANT BELIEFS

Sacraments   There are two basic sacraments, baptism and the Lord's Supper or Communion.

Salvation   Comes through God and not from the Church. Salvation is through Christ.

Predestination   The state of being foreordained to earthly damnation or divine salvation by divine decree.

Bible   Protestants refer to the Bible as the record of God's revelation to man. God reveals his truth to man not through the Pope or the Church but through the Christian Bible.

Communion   Most Protestants regard the bread representing the body of Christ and the wine representing the blood of Christ as symbolic.

Baptism   The method and the age of baptism differ in Protestant churches. Some Protestant ministers sprinkle the water—some pour. Some churches, such as the Baptist, will require complete immersion.

Virgin Birth   Some Protestants accept the doctrine of the virgin birth of Christ. Others do not.

The Church   The church is the place of worship. It is not the means of salvation nor is it the absolute authority for religious practice or principle.

Heaven and Earth   Most Protestants believe that eternal life in fellowship with God is "Heaven." Permanent separation from God is "Hell."

Original Sin   Most Protestants believe there is a powerful inclination toward wrongdoing in every person. Some maintain that this inclination is an inheritance passed on from generation to generation. Others do not place emphasis upon original sin and regard the newborn child as born in innocence and purity.

Prayer   Most Protestants pray through Jesus the Christ. They believe he is the intermediary between man and God.

The church choir praises God in song. This part of the junior choir of a Methodist church in Baltimore, Md.

The Church as the community of followers of Christ;

The responsibility of every Christian for his faith and life (the "priesthood of all believers");

The duty to discover and do God's will in his daily work (the "divine significance of every calling");

The obligation to seek to advance the Kingdom of God in the world;

Eternal life with God in the "communion of saints."

On a separate piece of paper write out how Judaism agrees and disagrees with these Protestant beliefs.

Write out what beliefs you think almost all Jews would accept.

QUESTIONS FOR DISCUSSION

1. In the next chapter we will discuss the Jewish view of Jesus. Before reading it, discuss in class what you think the Jewish view of Jesus is. To what extent do you agree and disagree with the view of Jesus presented by Catholicism?

2. If Judaism claims that God is One, why is God's name sometimes given in the plural? For example, in the Bible, *Elohim* is used as a name for God. This is in the plural. How would you explain this?

3. What is the attitude of Judaism toward "original sin"? Reread Genesis, Chapter 3. Christians call this event the "fall of man." Explain what this phrase means to you. Does Judaism believe that men are responsible for the sins of others?

4. What do you think of the Catholic and Protestant belief in "one God," who may be divided into three parts or aspects?

5. How does the Catholic idea of confession differ from the Jewish idea?

6. What is the Jewish belief in Heaven and Hell? Do you think the belief in Heaven and Hell would help to bring Jews closer to their religion? What about you?

7. What do you believe about the Catholic view that God became flesh and descended to earth as a man?

8. If according to the Catholic view, Jesus is part of God, what do they mean when they teach that Jesus is the only-begotten

Son of God? Who in Jewish belief is a "son of God"?

9. How did baptism arise from a Jewish practice? What are the differences between the use of the *mikveh* and baptism?

10. How does the Lord's Prayer differ in Catholicism and Protestantism? To whom does the word "Lord" refer?

11. What is a dogma?

12. To what extent do you think Judaism places an emphasis upon dogma?

13. What is your opinion of the statement made by Pope Pius XII when on November 1, 1950, the Catholic Church announced the dogma of the Assumption of Mary?

We, by the authority of Our Lord Jesus Christ, of the Blessed Apostles, Peter and Paul, and Our Own, pronounce, declare and define it to be a dogma divinely revealed that the Immaculate Mother of God, the ever Virgin Mary, when the course of her earthly life was run, was assumed in body and in soul to heavenly glory. Therefore, if anyone which God forbid shall willingly dare either to deny or to call into question what has been defined by Us, let him know that he has utterly abandoned divine and Catholic faith.

14. Are there dogmas in Judaism? Is a Jew permitted to disagree with the beliefs set forth by rabbinical conferences? Are there dogmas that Protestants must accept?

THINGS TO DO

1. Read a book that explains how Protestantism came into being and bring a report to class.

2. Make a chart showing the differences between the God idea of Catholics and Protestants. List other differences in belief.

3. Draw up a list of questions about Catholicism and interview a Catholic priest.

4. Write an essay on your opinion of why priests are not permitted to get married.

5. Look up the idea of "virgin birth" in James Frazer's *Golden Bough,* or in Hastings' *Encyclopedia of Religion* and write an essay on the virgin birth idea in early religions.

6. Write an essay on the Christian concept of "Sacraments" and the Jewish concept of *mitzvot.*

7. Write a one-page life of Martin Luther.

8. Debate in class the proposition: Resolved, There should be a Jewish Pope.

9. Look up the priestly blessing in Numbers 6:24–27 and compare it with the Protestant and Catholic versions. Are there differences?

SELECTED QUOTATIONS

"Sacraments" in Judaism

The moral life and human aspirations are the "sacraments" of Judaism. It recognizes no others.

There are no beliefs which "save" men. There are no ceremonial or ritual acts the very performance of which bestows supernatural grace and saving power.

There are visible symbols in Judaism, signs of the covenant, memorials of fidelity, but no sacraments.

From earnest and faithful quest of the good life, in all ways, great or small, flow all divine grace and favor.

—RABBI ABBA HILLEL SILVER

The Word became flesh

First, it must be emphasized that the "truth" of the Christian faith does not rest upon the originality or uniqueness of the teachings of Jesus or of any New Testament writer. Scholars have long known that there is little in them that is truly original. The Christian faith rests not upon the uniqueness of Jesus' teaching, but upon the belief in the incarnation, the belief that "the Word became flesh" in Jesus Christ.

—PROFESSOR J. PHILIP HYATT

The Lord, Jesus Christ

Believe in the Lord Jesus Christ, and thou shalt be saved."

—ACTS 16:31

Jesus saith unto him, I am the Way, the Truth, and the Life: no man cometh unto the Father, but by Me.

—JOHN 14:6

SELECTED READINGS

FACKENHEIM, EMIL L., *Paths to Jewish Belief*
FITCH, FLORENCE MARY, *One God*
MANWELL, REGINALD D., and FAHS, SOPHIA L., *The Church Across the Street*
MILLER, MILTON G., and SCHWARTZMAN, S. D., *Our Religion and Our Neighbors*

GLOSSARY

Baptism: Rite using water for purification from sin.

Catholic: Person who belongs to the universal Christian (Catholic) Church.

Chalice: Eucharistic cup (part of Roman Catholic sacrament) used in Mass.

Communion: Ritual eating of the wafer and drinking of the wine in commemoration of the sacrifice of Jesus' body and blood on the cross.

Confirmation: Christian rite admitting baptised person to full church privileges. Ceremony confirming Jewish youth in ancestral faith.

Crucifix: Representation of Christ on cross. Catholics use crucifix. Most Protestants use cross without the image of Jesus.

Dogma: Doctrine concerning faith formally stated and authoritatively proclaimed by Church.

Doxology: Expression of praise to God.

Extreme Unction: Roman Catholic sacrament in which priest anoints critically ill person and prays for his salvation, or possible recovery.

Grace: Virtue (or state of sanctification) given freely by God because of His love for man.

Holy Ghost: Third person of the Trinity, Holy Spirit.

Holy Orders: Rite or sacrament of ordination.

Host: Eucharistic bread, used in the Mass.

Immaculate conception: Mary born free of original sin by divine grace; held in Catholic dogma to be manner of conception of Virgin Mary by her mother.

Incarnate: Invested with bodily form.

Incarnation: The embodiment of the Deity in human form.

Invincibly ignorant: Not aware of the laws of the Church through no fault of one's own.

Last Supper: Supper of Jesus and his disciples on night of his betrayal.

Mass: Sequence of prayers and ceremonies, culminating in Communion.

Original sin: Sin held in Christian theology to be inherited as result of original sinful choice made by Adam.

Penance: A sacrament consisting in repentance or confession of sin.

Protestant: Christian not of the various Catholic churches.

Rosary: String of beads used in counting prayers.

Sacraments: Religious acts, sacred. Especially one instituted by Jesus as means of receiving grace.

Salvation: Saving of man from power or effects of sin.

Trinity: Unity of Father, Son and Holy Spirit in one Godhead.

Virgin birth: Theological doctrine that Jesus was miraculously begotten of God.

5

What Is Man?

THE STATUE AND THE BEGGAR

According to the Talmud, Rabbi Joshua ben Levi once took a trip to Rome. He beheld the wonders of the Roman civilization with astonishment. His guides showed him the bathhouses and the place where the Roman circus was held. They let him see the magnificent buildings and the costly statues of emperors and noblemen.

"Notice how the statues are covered with expensive tapestries to protect them from the cold of winter," said the guide.

The Rabbi nodded. "This is indeed a magnificent civilization," he said.

Just then he felt someone tug at his sleeve. He turned quickly and saw a man covered with torn rags. "Please," he begged, "give me a coin to buy a crust of bread. I'm starving to death."

The Rabbi looked again at the buildings and statues, and then at the sick old man.

"I was wrong," he said, as he handed the shivering old man a coin. "This is not a magnificent civilization. Here are statues of stone so carefully protected against the cold of winter, covered with costly tapestries—while human beings created in the image of God are covered with rags. A civilization that is more concerned with building statues and monuments than with the welfare of man shall surely perish!"

1. What does this Talmudic story teach?
2. How would this story apply to our civilization today?
3. What does this story tell us about the Jewish belief about man?

ORIGINAL SIN

To understand one of the main differences between the Jewish and the Christian belief about man we must understand what is meant by *original sin*.

But before we consider what Christians teach about original sin, we should first think about the word *sin* and what it means.

Webster's Dictionary defines *sin* (noun) as:

1. Transgression of the law of God.
2. An offense in general.

It defines the verb *sin* as:

1. To break the divine law.
2. To violate human rights or law.
3. To do or commit wrongly.

Many pointed stories, such as that of the statue and the beggar, crowd the pages of the Talmud, rousing the minds of young readers, teaching lessons for today.

List what you think are some sins that people commit.

Who or what determines whether something we do is a sin?

The Hebrew word for sin is *ḥet,* which means to "miss the mark." To "miss the mark" is to go astray from God's teachings, to do things that hurt yourself or others. The Jewish point of view is that when we disobey the teachings of God and refuse to follow the ways of God, we are missing the mark and committing sins.

In the Book of Genesis, Chapter 3, we find the story of the first sin committed by man. The serpent tempted Eve to eat of the fruit of the tree of the knowledge of good and evil, although God had commanded both Adam and Eve not to eat of it. Eve tasted the fruit and then gave some of it to Adam to eat.

After this we read, "And the eyes of them both were opened, and they knew that they were naked; and they sewed fig-leaves together and made themselves girdles."

God was angry because Adam and Eve had disobeyed Him, and they were punished and driven out of the Garden of Eden. Judaism and Christianity differ in the interpretation of this story of the first sin.

Christianity teaches that the sin which Adam and Eve committed in the Garden of Eden is transmitted to every child at birth. It isn't anything that the individual has done. The sin was there when he was born and he is made impure by it. This concept is called *original sin.*

Judaism does not believe this. It does not accept the idea that the sin of Adam and Eve is passed on to every man and makes every man impure at birth. Why should someone who didn't have anything to do with the sin be blamed for what happened, and be born guilty? Even if Adam and Eve committed a sin, Judaism does not believe that all future generations should suffer.

Modern Christians think of the sin of Adam and Eve as disobeying God and they interpret original sin as the sin of disobedience. Roman Catholics, Baptists and Lutherans believe that a child is born not pure, because of the original sin of Adam and Eve, and the way to cleanse a person of this sin is through the ritual of baptism in the name of Jesus Christ. Then the person becomes pure and clean.

Judaism believes that the story of Adam and Eve and the Garden of Eden is a poetic myth and a way of teaching moral and religious lessons, but it is not historically true.

We do not really believe that Adam was the first man, nor do we believe that Eve was the first woman. The Hebrew word *Adam* means mankind. *Ḥavvah,* the Hebrew word for Eve, means "life" and represents "womankind."

Not all Protestants believe the same way about original sin. Most Protestants, however, do believe that man is sinful unless and until he is redeemed by the sacrifice of Jesus, who gave his life to save mankind.

Judaism does not believe in baptism or the necessity of being saved through the belief in Jesus or in original sin. We think the story of Adam and Eve teaches an important lesson. The lesson is that man moves away from God when he disobeys God's teachings.

The fall of man

The act of Adam and Eve whereby they brought sin into the world is known in Christian thought as the "fall of man." Paul, one of the founders of Christianity, wrote:

> By one man sin entered the world. (Rom. 5:12)

> By the offense of one, judgment came upon all men to condemnation. (Rom. 5:18)

> By one man's disobedience, many were made sinners. (Rom. 5:19)

This idea was summarized in a book called *New England Primer.* In it we find these lines:

> *In Adam's fall,*
> *We sinned all.*

Paul, one of the founders of Christianity, taught that all human beings were unclean and sinful because of the sin of Adam, and because of the sinfulness of the body. He believed that only God's nature and Jesus' nature were pure and completely righteous because they were everlasting "spirit."

Paul did not believe that fulfilling the commandments of Judaism could take away man's sinfulness—not even worship on the Day of Atonement nor the observance of the laws of the Torah. Man could become clean only by becoming one with Jesus, believing in him as the son of God, and by participating in the sacraments.

Is it fair to believe and say that Christianity sees man as sinful and evil and that only Judaism believes and sees man as good and holy? No, this would not be fair to Christianity.

Christianity also believes that man has to choose between good and evil. Christianity too believes that man is sacred, created in the image of God.

Judaism declares that while man can be, and is often, inclined to sin, man is not born sinful, and therefore baptism is unnecessary. Some Christian groups accept this Jewish view, and use baptism as a symbol of inner purification and holiness, and not as a means of purifying the individual from original sin.

Judaism does not believe in the fall of man or that people are born with original sin.

Judaism teaches that every individual is born innocent and pure. As he grows up, he has to make a choice between good and evil. If he chooses the good, he comes closer to God in holiness. If he chooses evil, he departs from the ways of God and will live a life of selfishness and evil. In other words, man may commit sins, but he is not essentially evil or sinful. Even if a person does commit sins, he may change his ways through atonement and repentance so that God will forgive him in His love for all His children: Christian, Jew and Moslem, white, black and brown. All people are created in the image of God, and through their deeds they can all move closer to God.

HOW MUCH ARE YOU WORTH?

If you were asked to designate an amount of money, estimate:

> How much are you worth?
> How much are your parents worth?
> How much is any human being worth?

Foolish questions? Perhaps not when we are told that the human body is made up of the following chemicals: oxygen, carbon, hydrogen, nitrogen, calcium, phosphorus, potassium, sulphur, iodine, sodium, chlorine, magnesium and iron. A magazine reports that a noted chemist said that today a human being is worth $33.54 in terms of chemicals. Twenty-five years ago, a human was worth 98c.

A world-famous physician, Dr. Charles H. Mayo, once said: "The ingredients of the human body might be commercially figured as follows: he has enough potassium for one shot of a toy pistol; a product value of seven bars of soap; enough iron for an eight-penny nail; enough sulphur to keep fleas off a dog; enough lime to whitewash a chicken coop; enough magnesia to make a single dose for a person with a sour stomach, and enough phosphorus to cover 2200 matches."

Won't you agree that a human being must be worth more than the cost of the chemicals in his body? If you do agree, then what makes him worth more than that?

In the image of God

The Bible says that "man is created in the image of God." It also teaches us that "man is but little lower than the angels" (Ps. 8). This tells us a great deal about both the Christian and the Jewish belief in man.

Judaism and Christianity teach us that man is more than chemicals. Man is more than a wondrous robot, more than a super IBM machine, more than flesh and glands and organs that may be X-rayed or examined under a microscope, because God has given to each of us a soul.

This is what Judaism and Christianity mean by the "image of God" within man. This is what makes man different, and this is why there isn't enough money in the whole world to pay for a human life.

Everyone has a soul. We don't know exactly what it is. No one has ever seen a soul. We can't examine it with a microscope, but we believe that the soul is part of God within us. Though the body dies, the soul lives on forever. It is like energy that can never fade away. The soul can never die. It is a part of God.

You may wonder: What does the soul do? A body can walk and talk and hear and see. A soul can't do any of these things, but a soul can help us talk with God and listen to God. The soul is the source of our conscience, which helps us to choose between right and wrong. To have a soul means to have a capacity to seek truth, to find beauty, goodness and holiness. The soul is a portion of God within man.

Let us examine more closely Judaism's ideas on the soul and the value of man. Judaism believes that the soul is good and the body is good. The soul was given to us by God, and a body was given to us by God. Both are good, if we choose good.

Maybe you're thinking: "If the body is good, and the soul is good, why is it that people do wrong? Why do people sometimes choose to be evil and act mean and disobey God?"

Our teachers explained it in this way:

The two inclinations

Man is free to choose good or evil. Something within him encourages or discourages him. That something is called an *impulse,* or an *inclination.* Judaism teaches that everyone has two inclinations. The good inclination is called *Yetzer ha-Tov.* The bad or the evil inclination is called *Yetzer ha-Ra.* Both are at work all the time. When we are tempted to do something wrong, the evil inclination, the *Yetzer ha-Ra* says: "Go ahead. I dare you. Don't be a square. What's the difference? Do what you want to do. You can get away with it, and if you get caught, so what?" The good inclination, the *Yetzer ha-Tov* says: "No, it's not right. You can resist temptation. Don't bring sadness to your parents. Be what they want you to be, and do right. It is not God's way. Be strong and choose the right way."

What would the rabbi have said about permitting poverty like this? Would he call it sin? Do you? This picture was taken during a severe cold spell in Dallas.

Which inclination urged men and nations to work together to raise the United Nations headquarters in New York? What would the other inclination urge? What is the alternative?

The evil inclination urges us to do what is wrong. The good inclination urges us to do what is right and reminds us that we are created in the image of God. The point is that the body isn't evil, and we don't have to do everything we are tempted to do. We have freedom of will to listen to the *Yetzer ha-Tov* and do what is right and kind and good.

The prison guard and the clown

The rabbis taught through a story that the true worth of man may never be judged by outer appearances. This is the story:

Once Rabbi Baroka walked through the crowded market place of his town and met Elijah, the wandering spirit of prophecy in Jewish lore. "Who of all this multitude has the best claim to heaven?" asked the rabbi. Elijah pointed out a rough looking man who was a prison guard. "That man!" exclaimed the rabbi. "Yes," said Elijah, "because he is considerate to his prisoners and treats them with kindness. His hope is to convince the prisoners to give up their evil ways and obey God's commandments."

Looking at the people rushing through the market place, the rabbi asked: "Who else is worthy of eternal life?" Elijah then pointed to two motley-dressed clowns who were cavorting and jumping around before an amused and delighted audience. The rabbi was astonished: "These foolish clowns," he said.

"Do not scorn them," said the prophet.

"They go around and cheer the sick, the depressed and the sorrowful. Whenever they see a sufferer they join him and by merry talk they help him to forget his grief." Therefore, we are taught: The heart ennobles any profession or work. A kindly guard or a clown may be first in the Kingdom of Heaven.

Bricks or people?

The rabbis taught that every human life is sacred, and human beings must be more precious to us than buildings or bricks. They illustrate this by telling what happened when the people were building the Tower of Babel.

According to the Midrash, the Tower of Babel reached so great a height that it took a whole year to climb to the top. It took many bricks to make this tower, and to the builders, a brick was more precious and valuable than a human being.

If a man fell down and met his death, no one took notice of it. Human life wasn't very important. But if a brick dropped, the builders wept because it would take a while to replace it.

We are also told that women who were working on the tower were not permitted to interrupt their work even to take care of their children.

Because the builders of the Tower of Babel had no respect for human life or human feelings, God destroyed the Tower, and the people were scattered throughout the world. The strangest part of the story is that God confused them so that each spoke a different language, and people couldn't understand what others were saying.

The rabbis taught that those who have no regard for the holiness and the sanctity of human life and put more emphasis on the value of bricks, buildings or things will find themselves in trouble, and even worse, they will destroy themselves and their civilization.

What we should remember is that every human being is scared no matter whether he is rich or poor, no matter what the color of his skin or his religious belief—because every man and woman is a child of God. And because man is a child of God he has been given a wonderful gift called "freedom of will."

MAN ISN'T A ROBOT

According to Judaism man isn't a robot or a machine or a computer, reacting mechanically without freedom of will to choose the better way.

A computer may choose between facts, but a computer can't choose between good and evil, right and wrong. A computer does not have a conscience, and a computer can't hear the still small voice of God urging it to be just, merciful and kind.

Judaism maintains that God has given to man freedom of will and the privilege of choosing between good and evil. The Torah tells us in the Book of Deuteronomy, Chapter 30:

See, I have set before thee this day life and good, and death and evil, in that I command thee this day to love the Lord thy God, to walk in His ways, and to keep His commandments and His statutes and His ordinances . . .

I call heaven and earth, to witness against you this day, that I have set before thee life and death, the blessing and the curse; therefore choose life, that thou mayest live, thou and thy seed . . .

Judaism teaches us that God gives each of us a choice. We have the power to choose our own way of life.

This interior view of the control tower at Wichita, Kans.,
airport shows banks of machines that man has made to help
him guide his planes in safety. But man is more than
a machine. The Maker of man must guide him.

Climbing ladders

The Midrash tells of a lady who asked what God has been doing since he created the world. Rabbi José ben Halafta replied: "He has been building ladders for some to ascend and for others to descend."

This teaches that man is given the freedom of will to ascend or descend the ladder of divinity. Since he needs a map or a guide, he turns to the Torah to show him the way.

In case you are thinking: Will I be able to follow the way of the Torah: Will I know what to do? Will it be too difficult for me? Then listen to the words of Deuteronomy, Chapter 30, beginning with verse 11:

For this commandment which I command thee this day, it is not too hard for thee, neither is it far off. It is not in heaven, that thou shouldest say: "Who shall go up for us to heaven, and bring it unto us and make us to hear it, that we may do it?" Neither is it beyond the sea, that thou shouldest say: "Who shall go over the sea for us, and bring it unto us, and make us to hear it, that we may do it?" But the word is very nigh unto thee, in thy mouth, and in thy heart, that thou mayest do it."

No one expects us to be perfect. This is one of the teachings of Judaism. The only perfection is God—not Moses, not Isaiah, not Jesus—no human being can be perfect —but we can be better than we are. We have the power within us to be the best that we can be. That's why you should know what Rabbi Zusya taught when he was very sick and about to die.

When Zusya meets God

Before his death Rabbi Zusya wept. His pupils asked: "Our Rabbi, why do you weep?"

Rabbi Zusya said: "I am afraid to meet my God."

The students were surprised. They said: "But, Rabbi, haven't you always told us that God is love, and that we should never be afraid of death, or of meeting God?"

"You don't understand me," said the Rabbi. "I am not afraid of death, and I know God is love, but what I'm afraid of is this: In the coming world God will not ask me: 'Why were you not as Moses?' because I am not Moses. God will not ask me: 'Why were you not as Isaiah?' because I am not Isaiah."

"Then of what are you afraid?" asked his perplexed pupils.

Rabbi Zusya sighed as he answered: "I'm afraid that God will ask me, 'Zusya, why were you not, Zusya, the best that Zusya could have been?' And what then shall I answer?"

THE CHILDREN OF GOD

One of the differences between Judaism and Christianity is our belief that man does not become a God and God does not become a man. Christianity believes that God became flesh, and that He came to earth as a man in the body of Jesus. Judaism can never accept this because we believe that God doesn't have a body. God is a spirit, a spirit that we can never see or touch or feel. God is invis-ible although His presence is always with us. God is everywhere—in the skies above, on the earth beneath, and even within man him-self.

As Jews we believe in the One, Eternal, Invisible God. Judaism cannot agree with Christianity that God had a son, and that Jesus is God's only child and son.

Paul, one of the great founders of Chris-tianity, thought of Jesus as more than human or even more than a Messiah. He taught that Jesus was the "son of God." God had caused Mary to bear His son so that God might ap-pear as a human being to save mankind. It should be clearly understood that to Paul, Jesus was not just an ordinary man or even a man, but rather Jesus *was* God in human form.

Judaism could never believe this. We could never think of God as becoming a man or ever coming to earth in human form. We also could never believe that Jesus was God in human form, or that Jesus was an only child of God.

However, there is a sense in which Juda-ism and Christianity do agree. They both believe that *all* people are children of God, and that we are *all* created in the image of God. God loves all of His children, no mat-ter what their nationality, no matter what their religion, no matter what the color of their skin.

Once we begin to really think of God as the Father of all His children, then we also have to think of all people as being related to each other as brothers and sisters with the same Heavenly Father.

An amazing discovery

Modern rabbis like to tell the story of a man who was lost in a jungle. He tried des-perately to find his way out, but to no avail. Suddenly fear clutched at his throat as he beheld coming toward him from a distance what seemed to be a wild and ferocious beast. He wanted to run, but terror held him rooted to the spot. As the beast came closer, he noticed with considerable relief that it looked like a tame animal. As the beast came still closer, he could see the figure of a man. Summoning all of his courage, he advanced to meet the man. When he extended his hand in fellowship and looked into the man's eye with understanding, he made an amazing discovery. It was not a ferocious wild beast. It was not a domesticated animal. It was not an ordinary human being. It was his brother!

How would you explain the meaning of this story? What does it teach us about what our feelings should be about other religions, nationalities and races?

At first the man thought it was a wild beast and he was frightened. That's the way people of other faiths and other races seem to us when we look at them or think of them from a distance.

When the beast came closer, it turned out to be a tame animal. This could mean that when people of other faiths and races come closer to us we find out that they are not so wild or dangerous.

When the tame animal came closer, it turned out to be a man, a human being. That's what happens when we get to know other people. We find out that they are human, too, and that they have the same fears and the same hopes and the same ideals that we have.

If we will only stop talking about religious faith, and begin to *live* by our faith—by taking a few steps in the direction of our fellow-man, by looking into his eyes with understanding, by extending our hands and our hearts in fellowship—we, too, may find that he is our own brother.

MAN IN COPARTNERSHIP WITH GOD

In the Talmud we find the question: "Why did God begin the creation of man with only one couple? Why not with several couples?" The rabbis answer: "To teach us that all human beings are descended from one common ancestor, so that no man may ever be able to say: "My family is better than thine," or, "My tribe is better than thine."

The Ḥasidic Rabbi Shelomo asked, "What is the worst thing that the evil inclinations can achieve?" He answered: "To make man forget that he is the son of a King." Just as a son of a king must live up to high ideals of conduct, we are all sons and daughters of God, the King of all kings, and therefore we must be pure, clean and righteous in all our doings.

The Talmud tells us of a favorite saying of the scholars of Yavneh:

I am a creature of God
My neighbor is also a creature of God;
My work is in the city,
His work is in the field;
I rise early to my work,
He rises early to his.
Just as he is not overbearing in his calling,
So I am not overbearing in my calling,
Perhaps thou sayest:
"I do great things and he does small
* things!"*
We have learned:
It matters not whether one does much or
* little,*
If only he directs his heart to heaven.

Rabbi Akiba taught: "Beloved is man, for he was created in the image of God; but it was by a special love that it was made known to him that he was created in the image of God."

This means that since all men are created in God's image, there is a divine relationship that makes us brothers and sisters. No man must think that he is above another, or better than another, because all share in God's love.

Throughout our history we have learned

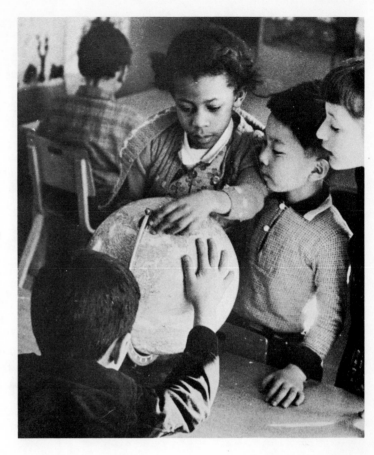

Students from Africa, Asia and Europe, in the UN International School, study the problems of man's common globe.

from our Torah and from the teachings of the rabbis that we must look upon every human being as a child of God.

It is because man is a child of God that he must act and live in a manner pleasing to his Heavenly Father. Just as people judge our own fathers by what we do, by our actions and our behavior, so, taught the rabbis, people who are not Jews will judge our Heavenly Father by the way we act.

Just as man needs God, so God needs man to help Him build a better world. God needs man to fulfill His Divine plan for the future — and that plan is to bring about the Messianic age of universal justice, brotherhood and peace on earth. Judaism teaches that each of us must try to be a copartner with God and do our share to help make this a better world for all of God's children.

QUESTIONS FOR DISCUSSION

1. Do you believe that you have control over your own choices and decisions? Explain.

2. In your opinion is man basically good or evil? What are your reasons?

3. What is meant by man being created in the image of God?

4. How must a Jew act toward his fellow

man if he really believes that man is created in the image of God?

5. What do you think the psalmist meant when he said "man is but little less than divine"?

6. How should your belief in God affect your actions and behavior?

7. Consider the meaning of the Midrash that teaches that human beings mint coins bearing the picture of one original (a king or prince) and all coins are the same. However, the King of kings, the Holy One, blessed be He, patterned all human beings after the image of Adam, the symbol of the first man, and yet no two human beings are exactly alike. Because of all these reasons every individual is privileged to declare, "For my sake was the entire world created." Explain the last statement.

8. What did Rabbi Akiba mean when he said that, "Everything is foreseen, yet freedom of choice is given"?

9. If Jews have a responsibility to be co-partners with God, how can you help to make this a better world?

THINGS TO DO

1. Write out the following verses from the Bible and discuss in class: Genesis 1:27; Genesis 2:7; Deuteronomy 30:15–16; 19–20.

2. Write an essay on the meaning of Psalm 8, verses 5–6.

3. Write an essay on what Maimonides believed about man's freedom of will.

4. Write an essay on the modern meaning of Psalm 133:1

Behold, how good and how pleasant it is
For brethren to dwell together in unity.

When planning your essay look back to Chapter 2, pages 28–30, and recall the difference between *unity* and *uniformity*.

5. Interview a priest, a minister and a rabbi asking: "What is your belief in man? Is man good or evil? Is Jesus the son of God? How can those of us who have differing religious beliefs but the same hopes and ideals for mankind work together as copartners of God in the building of a better world?

This statue of Justice may be seen in front of the United States Supreme Court building in Washington, D.C.

SELECTED QUOTATIONS

A religious duty

Once Hillel, the gentle teacher, concluded his studies with his students and walked forth with them. They asked him, "Master, where are you going?" He answered, "To perform a religious duty." "What is the religious duty?" they asked. He said to them, "To bathe." Said they: "Is this a religious duty?" "Yes," he replied, "if the statues of kings in theatres and circuses are showered and washed by the man who was appointed to look after them, how much more should I bathe my body, which is the temple of the soul, as it is written, 'In the image of God made He man.' "

—MIDRASH

A Christian view of evil

Christianity says: "Evil is a terrible and wide-spread fact in life; man was made potentially good; yet all individuals are liable to evil, and actually do sin against God, against other persons, and also against their own best self."

—ROBERT ERNEST HUME,
The World's Living Religions

Original Sin

Original Sin has been interpreted in many ways in Christian theology, some of which are unacceptable to many Christians today . . . "For all have sinned," says St. Paul, "and come short of the glory of God." Jew and Gentile; white man and black man; British, Americans, Russians, Chinese—you and I—are sinners. The sin is ours: we are responsible.

—DAVID H. C. READ,
The Christian Faith,
Charles Scribner's Sons

Are we sinners?

In Christian doctrine there is no group, or individual, who is regarded as sinless. The one immaculate (without sin) is Christ: all else are sinners. It follows therefore that in the Christian view, however much may and should be done in the psychological, economic, social, and political fields for the betterment of mankind, no fundamental solution of our problem can be reached from within the human situation. Help must come from beyond.

—*Ibid.*

Wherein Christianity and Judaism differ

Christianity starts with one idea about man; Judaism starts with another. The idea that Judaism starts with is that man is created in the likeness of God. You don't have to go far to discover that it is possible to bring forth the divine within you and the divine in other men. There is always the opportunity to do a *mitzvah* [good deed]. It is with that opportunity that I begin as a Jew.

Christianity begins with the basic assumption that man is essentially depraved and sinful—that left to himself he can do nothing. He has to be saved. Man starts with despair. To the profoundest minds in Christian theology it is inconceivable that man should ever be able to do anything good. He is involved in evil.

This is not the Jewish way of thinking. When I walk through the streets of a city and a Christian missionary meets me, the first question he asks me is: "What do you do for the salvation of your soul?" I have never thought of salvation. It is not a Jewish problem. My problem is what *mitzvah* can I do next. Am I going to say a *b'rachah* [blessing]? Am I going to be kind to an-

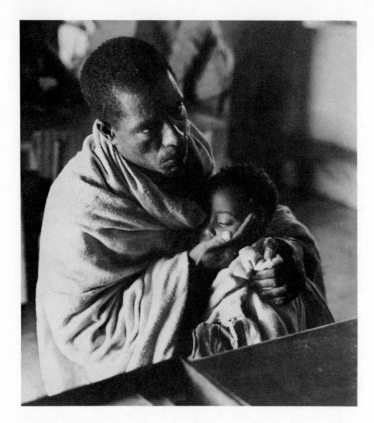

A father at Kolla Duba health center, Ethiopia, listens intently to instructions about the care of his sick child. Mankind's compassion, channeled through UNICEF, WHO and other groups, helps support the rural health center.

other person? To study Torah? How am I going to prepare for the Sabbath? Those are my problems. The central issue in Judaism is the *mitzvah,* the sacred act. And it is the greatness of man that he can do a *mitzvah.* How great we are that we can fulfill the will of God!

—PROFESSOR ABRAHAM J. HESCHEL

The love of man

A learned but ungenerous man said to Rabbi Abraham, "They say that you give people mysterious drugs and that your drugs are effective. Give me one that I may attain to the fear of God."

"I don't know of any drug for the fear of God," said Rabbi Abraham, "but if you like I can give you one of the love of God."

"That's even better," cried the other. "Give it to me."

"It is the love of one's fellow man," answered the Rabbi.

—ḤASIDIC LITERATURE

Only man

Now we are in a position to understand

fully why man is the crown of creation and why all men are entitled to equal rights. Only a man—not an animal—can know truth, do good, create beauty and worship God. But, too, only a man can speak lies, do evil, pervert beauty into ugliness and commit idolatry. . . .

—RABBI EMIL L. FACKENHEIM

We are all God's children

According to the religious consciousness of modern Israel man is made in God's image, and is thus a child of God. Consequently Jew and non-Jew, saint and sinner have the same claim upon God's paternal love and mercy. There is no distinction in favor of Israel except as he lives a higher and more godlike life. Even those who have fallen away from God and have committed sin remain God's children.

—RABBI KAUFMANN KOHLER

Man will prevail

I believe that man will not merely endure; he will prevail. He is immortal, not because he alone among creatures has an inexhaustible voice but because he has a soul, a spirit capable of compassion and sacrifice and endurance.

—WILLIAM FAULKNER
(from his Nobel Prize Speech)

SELECTED READINGS

FACKENHEIM, EMIL L., *Paths to Jewish Belief*, Chapters 6–9
GITTELSOHN, ROLAND B., *Little Lower Than the Angels*, pp. 206–208
SILVERMAN, WILLIAM B., *The Jewish Concept of Man*, Judaism Pamphlet Series, B'nai B'rith Youth Organization
———, *The Still Small Voice*, Chapter 6

6

The Jewish View of Jesus

WHAT DO JEWS BELIEVE ABOUT JESUS?

Many years ago, a noted Christian scholar of the Bible, Julius Wellhausen, wrote:

> Jesus was not a Christian. He was a Jew, and as a Jew, his life-story is that of the prominent men of the Jews of his time, while his teaching is Jewish teaching.

Before we go on to learn about the Jewish view of Jesus, how would you answer the following questions?

1. Do you agree or disagree with Professor Wellhausen? Give your reasons.
2. Do you think that Jesus was a prophet, a rabbi, a Jewish teacher, a saint, the only son of God, or a god? Explain why you believe as you do.
3. In the Midrash we read:

> The rabbis say: God said to Israel: "My children, all that I have created I have created in pairs; heaven and earth are a pair; Adam and Eve are a pair; this world and the world to come are a pair; but my Glory is One and unique in the world. Therefore: Hear, O Israel, the Lord our God, the Lord is One."

What do you think the rabbis who said this would believe about Jesus?

CHRISTIANITY'S DEBT TO JUDAISM

When the Reverend Dr. John Haynes Holmes was minister of Community Church of New York, he paid tribute to the contribution of Jews to the Christian religion in a famous sermon called "Christianity's Debt to Judaism—Why Not Acknowledge It?"

Dr. Holmes began in this way:

> In the first place, I would remind you that Jesus' parents were Jews. Whether his father, Joseph, was of 'the stem of Jesse,' and thus of the royal house of David, as the Bible states, is altogether unknown and quite improbable . . . As a matter of fact, we know very little about Joseph—only that he lived in Nazareth in Galilee, that he was a carpenter by trade, and that he died, in all probability, before Jesus came to manhood. In much the same way, we know little about Mary, the mother of Jesus. She is a shadowy figure who emerges into the light only in the last few hours in the career of her eldest born. But amid

all this obscurity, there remains the in-dubitable truth that these two persons, who are so venerated by the Christian church, were both of them Jews.

The second fact is of course that Jesus, as the oldest child of those parents, was thus himself a Jew . . . If we know anything about Jesus at all, it is that he was a child of Jewish parents born in a Jewish home as the first-born of a large family, and thus himself a Jew.

The Jewishness of Jesus

The third thing to be said about the Jewishness of Jesus is that he was reared and trained in the Jewish faith. His parents were pious Jews; they went each year to Jerusalem to keep the feast of the Passover! They taught Jesus, by precept and example, to attend the synagogue where he became acquainted with the Bible of his race. In his early manhood, it was his custom to go to the synagogue on the Sabbath day, which is more than a good many Jews do today; and he began his public ministry, so the record tells us, by standing up in the synagogue in Nazareth and reading from the prophet Isaiah. In spirit as well as in blood, this Nazarene was a son of Israel.

It is from these three points of view, his parents, his birth, and his religious training—that we must agree that Jesus was a Jew. It is to the Jews that the Christians

The Damascus Gate leads into the old walled city of Jerusalem.
Twin domes of the Church of the Holy Sepulchre
rise on the skyline.

owe this peerless leader and founder of their faith.

It is only fair to recognize, it seems to me, that the New Testament is throughout a Jewish book. Every word of it, from the first chapter of Matthew to the last chapter of Revelation, was written by Jews, and thus is saturated with the Jewish spirit and ideals.

SOME QUESTIONS FOR DISCUSSION

1. If Jesus was reared and trained in the Jewish faith, do you think he regarded himself as a Jew? If the answer is "yes," then was it correct for Dr. Holmes to say that he was the founder of the Christian faith?

2. If, as Dr. Holmes says: "he became acquainted with the Bible of his race," did that Bible include the New Testament? Why is it incorrect for Jews to refer to their Scriptures as the "Old Testament"? Do you think that Jews are a race? What do you think Jews are: a race, a culture, a nationality, a people, a civilization, a religion? What are your reasons?

3. Why do you think Jesus was in the synagogue?

   a. To attend a Sabbath Service with his parents.

   b. To attend a Festival Service with his parents.

   c. To participate in his Bar Mitzvah.

   d. To participate in weekday worship.

Read Luke 2:41–52 before you give your answer.

4. What is the meaning of the word: "Nazarene"? Look up the word in the *Universal Jewish Encyclopedia,* Vol. 8 p. 134.

5. Dr. Holmes said: "In spirit as well as in blood, this Nazarene was a son of Israel." Do you think he was correct in using the word "blood"? Is there such a thing as Jewish blood? If, in ancient times, the land where Jews lived was called Judea, why did Dr. Holmes refer to Jesus as a "son of Israel"? What if Jesus lived in the State of Israel today, would it be correct to refer to him as a "son of Israel"?

WHAT JESUS BELIEVED ABOUT GOD

What if Jesus did live today, do you think he would regard himself as a Jew or a Christian?

Before you try to answer study the following incident as described in the New Testament:

According to the New Testament, a scribe once asked Jesus to summarize his main teachings and what he thought were the most important commandments of his religion. This is what happened.

And one of the scribes came, and . . . asked him: Which is the first commandment of all? And Jesus answered him, The first of all the commandments is, Hear, O Israel; the Lord our God is one Lord: And thou shalt love the Lord thy God with all thy heart, and with all thy soul, and with all thy mind, and with all thy strength: This is the first commandment. And the second is like, namely this, thou shalt love thy neighbor as thyself. There is none other commandment greater than these.

And the scribe said unto him, Well, Master, thou hast said the truth: for there is one God; and there is none other but He. And to love Him with all the heart, and with all the understanding, and with all the soul, and with all the strength, and to love his neighbor as himself, is more than all whole burnt offerings and sacrifices. And when Jesus saw that he answered discreetly, he said unto him, Thou art not far from the kingdom of God. . . .

This passage is from the Gospel according to St. Mark, 12:28–34. Now open your Bible to Deuteronomy 6:4—5 and compare.

What are the similarities?

What are the differences?

What does the passage in Mark, Chapter 12, tell us about Jesus' belief in God?

Where did the verse "Thou shalt love thy neighbor as thyself" first appear? In the Jewish Scriptures or the New Testament? (Before answering, look up Lev. 19:18.)

It happened in Duluth, Minnesota, that a rabbi was invited to speak to a group of Christian ministers. After his lecture on Judaism one of the ministers began to discuss the sermon topic he was preparing for the next Sunday. He said that the title of his sermon would be, "If Jesus Came To Duluth." One of the ministers turned to the rabbi and asked, "And what do you think about this, rabbi?"

"Instead of answering, let me ask you some questions," the rabbi said.

"Suppose Jesus did come to Duluth. Where would he worship? In the Catholic church? They didn't have any Catholic churches when he lived because Catholicism had not yet come into being. Would he worship in the Lutheran, Episcopal, Presbyterian, Baptist, or Methodist church? We know that the Protestant churches didn't come into existence until the sixteenth century. No, he wouldn't have worshiped there. He would probably go to the synagogue where he always worshiped.

"On what day would Jesus observe the Sabbath? Wouldn't it be Friday evening and Saturday, which was and is the day of the Jewish Sabbath, and not Sunday?

"What prayer book do you think Jesus would know? Wouldn't it be the order of Jewish prayers that he knew as a boy and a young man? Even the New Testament tells us that Jesus worshiped in the synagogue and read from the scroll of the prophet Isaiah.

"What Holy Days and festivals would Jesus observe? The same Holy Days and festivals he always observed: Rosh Hashanah, the Jewish New Year; Yom Kippur, the Day of Atonement; Sukkot, the Feast of Booths; Passover, the Feast of Unleavened Bread; and Shavuot, the Feast of Weeks.

"Don't most Christians observe Communion, the holy wafer and the wine because Jesus told them to do so at the Last Supper?" asked the rabbi.

"Scholars do not all agree, but many believe that the Last Supper was a Passover Seder where Jesus held up the *matzah* and said, 'This is my flesh, and the wine is my blood.'

"We really don't know a great deal about what Jesus observed. We can only guess. It is my opinion that he observed Shavuot, but I'm not so sure that he ever observed Purim or Hanukkah. But if Jesus lived at the time the Christians say he did, then surely he must have kept the Jewish Holy Days and festivals together with other Jews.

"At the time he lived, Jesus wouldn't have known about Christmas, Easter or the other Christian Holy Days and observances, because they came into being years later.

"Speaking of the Law, in Matthew 5:17 Jesus said, 'I am not come to destroy but to fulfill.' He also said, 'I come to preach to the lost sheep of Israel' (Matt. 15:24). He was preaching to and teaching his people, the Jews.

"Even when he died, the New Testament tells us that he said, *Eloi Eloi lama sabachthani,* which means 'My God, My God, why hast Thou forsaken me?' This is the Aramaic of the original Hebrew of Psalm 22:1. Read this for yourself and compare it with the statement in Mark 15:34.

"It is believed that Jesus spoke Aramaic, which is very similar to Hebrew. If Jesus did come to Duluth, I guess we would have to call on a rabbi to speak with him. Jesus didn't speak English, German, French or even

Greek. He spoke Aramaic and knew the Sacred Scriptures in Hebrew.

"There is another statement that Jesus is supposed to have made before he died. It is found in the New Testament. The statement is: 'Into Thy Hands, O God, I commit my soul.'

"This is found in a Jewish hymn, the Adon Olam, which we sing in the synagogue. These are the words:

Into Thy hands, O God, I yield my soul,
Both when I wake and when I sleep.
And with my soul, my body too,
The Lord is with me. I shall not fear.

Before the meeting was over, one of the ministers said to the rabbi: "If Jesus did come back to Duluth or even to our city, I really believe that he would know more about Judaism than about Christianity." And then he added: "As Jews and Christians, we share a great and holy heritage together. We should really respect and love each other as brothers."

SOME GREAT DIFFERENCES

While we both, Jews and Christians, agree that Jesus was a Jew, there are some very great differences.

We may believe that Jesus was a teacher and a holy and God-loving man, and we may agree with many of his teachings because they were Jewish teachings, but we cannot accept what some of the later Christians taught about him.

They taught that Jesus was more than a great teacher and a man. They said that he was the only Son of God, and that he *was* God who became flesh and had a body. Later they taught that he was part of the holy Trinity, a more than human God who had come to earth. This Judaism could never believe and never accept. If Jesus lived, he was a

man and not a God, and not part of any Trinity. There is but one God, and there is none else. Judaism says Jesus was a human being, a great and good teacher. Here is where Judaism and Christianity disagree and part company.

Was Jesus the Messiah?

We can understand the difference between the Jewish and Christian views of Jesus by discussing the idea of Messiah. The word Messiah is taken from the Hebrew word *mashiah,* which means "the anointed one." That same word in Greek is *Christos* or *Christ*. Christ means the anointed one and it also means the Messiah.

Since Christ means Messiah, then you can see that the term "Christian" means a follower of or believer in the Messiah.

Many Christians believe that the Jewish Bible tells all about the coming of the Messiah, and predicted exactly what would happen to Jesus. According to Jewish belief, it is true that the Bible predicts the coming of the Messiah, but it does not predict that Jesus is the Messiah.

The Messiah idea in Judaism is old and the Jews awaited the coming of the Messiah for many, many years before Jesus was born.

The Messiah idea in Judaism

Let's trace the development of the Messiah idea in Judaism. We can trace three steps or stages. We will begin here with the first two:

1. In early Jewish history priests and kings were anointed with holy oil. Since they were the anointed ones they were in a sense messiahs. They were filled with God's power and were to lead the people in His ways. This concept of the king is still held today. At the coronation of a king or queen, holy oil is poured on his head. The belief has persisted

that a special holiness is instilled through the oil.

2. Then there developed the belief in Judaism that the Messiah would be a special man, a messenger of God. He would be preceded by Elijah the prophet, and as soon as Elijah came back to earth the people would know that the Messiah would soon come.

The pangs of the Messiah

For many years Jews believed that Elijah would announce the arrival of the Messiah. But the Jews also believed that before the Messiah came there would be terrible suffering and misery in the world. This is called *Ḥevlei Mashiaḥ,* or the pangs of the Messiah. They believed there would be war, starvation, disease and oppression, and then the Messiah would come, and there would be "the days of the Messiah."

What is supposed to happen in "the days of the Messiah?" That question has to be answered from two points of view. One is the supernatural and the other is the natural. Both viewpoints are found in the Bible, in rabbinic teachings and in other Jewish sacred literature.

This eighteenth-century Russian goblet is an Elijah cup, to be placed on the Seder table. Engraved on it is a picture of the Messiah, on a donkey.

The resurrection of the dead

The supernatural view says that when the Messiah comes there will be many miracles: the blind will see, the deaf will hear, the lame will walk straight. Those righteous ones who have been buried outside of Israel will roll underground through subterranean paths to the Holy Land of Israel and will live again. They also believe that there will be no more suffering, no more poverty, and no more death. But even more important, there will be the resurrection of the dead, when all the dead people will come to life again.

Isaiah wrote in Chapter 11:

And the wolf shall lie down with the lamb,
And the leopard shall lie down
* with the kid;*
And the calf and the young lion and the
* fatling together,*
And a little child shall lead them.
And the cow and the bear shall feed;
Their young ones shall lie down together,
And the lion shall eat straw like the ox.
And the sucking child shall play on the
* hole of the asp,*

And the weaned child shall put his hand
  on the basilisk's den.
They shall not hurt nor destroy
In all My holy mountain;
For the earth shall be full of the
  knowledge of the Lord,
As the waters cover the sea.

According to tradition, when the Messiah comes all the Jews will go back to the land of Israel, the Temple will be restored, and all mankind will live in peace and happiness forever.

Another prophet named Isaiah is called

A portion of the book of Isaiah in one of the Dead Sea Scrolls, of parchment. Its prophecies of a Messianic era are still the hope of mankind.

Deutero-Isaiah, Second Isaiah, or the Prophet of the Exile. His is the third step in the development of the Messiah idea.

3. Deutero-Isaiah believed that the Messiah was not a king, or a priest or a man, but rather a *people,* and Israel was the Messianic people, the suffering servant of God. Israel was the anointed of God, chosen to bring about a Godly world for all mankind.

To accomplish this Deutero-Isaiah believed that Israel would have to suffer and take upon itself the sins of the world. In Chapter 53, he wrote about Israel, the people, as if he were talking about a man:

He had no form nor comeliness,
  that we should look upon him. . . .
He was despised and forsaken of men,
A man of pains, and acquainted
  with disease,
And as one from whom men hide
  their face;
He was despised and we esteemed him not.
Surely our diseases he did bear and
  our pains he carried;
Whereas we did esteem him stricken,
  smitten of God and afflicted.
But he was wounded because of
  our transgressions,
He was crushed because of our iniquities;
The chastisement of our welfare
  was upon him.
And with his blows we were healed.

Vicarious atonement

This passage from Isaiah has been interpreted to mean that Jesus is the one who suffers, and that he takes the sins of mankind upon himself. This belief in Christianity is called Vicarious Atonement, and it means that someone takes others' sins upon himself and suffers.

Many Christians believe that Isaiah predicted the coming of Jesus. According to Jewish views, the first Isaiah predicted the coming of an individual, personal Messiah, and the second Isaiah predicted that the entire people of Israel would be the Messiah. Let us finish reading the verses from Isaiah 53:

And the Lord hath made to light on him the iniquity of us all.
He was oppressed, though he humbled himself
And opened not his mouth. . . .
By oppression and judgment he was taken away.
And with his generation who did reason?
For he was cut off out of the land of the living,
For the transgression of my people to whom the blow was due.
And they made his grave with the wicked, and with the rich his tomb;
Although he had done no violence,
Neither was any deceit in his mouth.

Many scholars believe that the New Testament writers wrote their story of Jesus, using Isaiah 53 as a guide to make the prediction come true. They didn't understand that Isaiah was referring to a messianic people. What's more, even if Isaiah were referring to a man who would be the suffering Messiah, this doesn't mean that he was predicting the coming of Jesus.

The Messianic Age

There is a fourth point of view that may be termed the natural view. This is called the belief in the Messianic Age or Messianic Era.

4. The first Isaiah voiced this belief in Chapter 2. He probably believed that the Messiah would be a man, but he gives a vivid description of the Messianic Age.

And it shall come to pass in the end of days,
That the mountain of the Lord's house shall be established as the mountains,
And shall be exalted above the hills;
And all nations shall flow unto it.
And many peoples shall go and say:
Come ye, and let us go up to the mountain of the Lord,
To the house of the God of Jacob;
And He will teach us of His ways, and we will walk in His paths.
For out of Zion shall go forth the Torah, and the word of the Lord from Jerusalem.
And He will judge between the nations, and shall decide for many peoples;
And they shall beat their swords into plowshares, and their spears into pruning-hooks;
Nation shall not lift up sword against nation,
Neither shall they learn war any more.

According to the natural belief man shall achieve a good world in the Messianic Age. Through science, education and religion there will be no more poverty, no more sickness, no more hatred, no more war. People will live by the teachings of God and dwell together in justice and peace, and then God will rule over His Kingdom on earth.

There were many different ideas about the Messiah and the Messianic Age. Almost all agreed that the Messiah would be a descendant of King David and that he would bring about a new society where people would live in harmony and peace. Many times in Jewish history people thought that the Messiah had come, but they were always disappointed.

Jesus wasn't the only one thought to be a Messiah. As you study in your Jewish history books you will find a number of men who claimed that they were the Messiah: Shabbetai Tzevi, Solomon Molcho, David Reubeni, Jacob Frank and many others. But they were shown to be ordinary human beings.

The Jewish Jesus and the Christian Christ

There is a great difference between the Jewish Jesus and the Christian Christ. According to Judaism, Jesus was a man, a teacher who taught the ideals of his Jewish faith. He was not the Messiah, because he did not fulfill the messianic expectations. He did not bring an end to Roman tyranny. He did not bring an end to poverty and hatred and ignorance. He did not bring an end to war. He was a rabbi, a Jew, touched by the messianic fervor of his time. He lived as a Jew. He died a Jew.

According to Christianity, Jesus was and is the Messiah, the anointed one, the Christ, the savior who took upon himself the sins of mankind and died so that humanity would be saved. Years after his reported death, there crept into Christianity another belief that was completely un-Jewish. That belief is that Jesus was the only begotten Son of God, that Jesus *was* God incarnate, made flesh, God come to earth as a man. In time he was made part of the Trinity, which means God in three parts: the Father, the Son and the Holy Spirit or Ghost.

After the crucifixion of Jesus, the Christians had a real problem if they were to believe that Jesus was the Messiah. If Jesus was the Messiah, then what happened to all the miracles that were supposed to occur when the Messiah came?"

The early Christians tried to solve the problem by saying that Jesus showed himself the first time to make himself known and to provide a means of salvation for his followers. It would be in the second coming of Jesus that the world would become a Kingdom of God.

Judaism does not accept the belief that Jesus was the Messiah the first time, or that he was the Christ, or that there will be a second coming of Jesus.

TO SUM UP

Now we can see the various and differing beliefs about the Messiah.

Christianity believes that Jesus was the Messiah and will come again.

Orthodox Judaism believes that the Messiah is yet to come some day in the future.

Reform Jews and many who follow Conservative Judaism believe in a Messianic Age in this life, hoping that some day people will live by the teachings of God and make of our world a real and wonderful Kingdom of God on earth.

While Judaism and Christianity agree in many things and share great hopes and ideals, it is obvious that they do not at all agree when it comes to the idea of Jesus as the Messiah.

Judaism and Christianity disagree on other beliefs, too, besides the belief that Jesus is the Son of God, or part of the Trinity.

There are also many beliefs that Jews and Christians share. That is why we are going to consider the Jewish and Christian beliefs about man, prayer, miracles, salvation, and what happens to us in the next world.

WHAT DO YOU THINK?

News item:

Worcester, Mass.—A letter from Rabbi Joseph Klein to Superintendent of Schools Thomas F. Power resulted in the substitution of the word "God" for Jesus in a prayer taught to kindergarten children here.

Rabbi Klein wrote to Power after receiving a letter from a Jewish parent whose child reported he had learned a song whose lyrics included mention of Jesus.

Mr. Power ordered that the word "God" be substituted for the word "Jesus."

"What if Jesus came back today?" Christian imagination is caught by the question. This wood carving in the Methodist Temple Sky Chapel, Chicago, depicts him as overlooking that city, much as Matthew described him compassionately overlooking Jerusalem.

1. Do you think the Rabbi should have objected to the use of the word "Jesus" in the lines used by the kindergarten children? What are your reasons?

2. Do you think that such lines should be used in the public schools?

3. If you were a Christian, how do you think you would react?

4. Does it make any difference to Christians whether the word "God" or "Jesus" is used in prayer? Why?

If Jesus came back today

. . . He would be invited to appear on television. Children would gather around Him, as of old . . . He would address crowds in the open air . . . He would be extremely unpopular in certain parts of the world wherever one people oppressed and exploited another . . .

—ETHEL MANNIN

If Jesus appeared on television, what do

you think he would speak against? What would he be for? Would he regard himself as a Jew or a Christian?

1. Read the article in the *Universal Jewish Encyclopedia,* Vol. 8, pp. 473–475 on the "Pharisees." Write an essay on "The Pharisees and why this group was so despised by the Christians."

2. Discuss in class the subject: "If Jesus was a Jew, should he not be accepted by Jews as a great teacher and prophet?"

3. Read the Lord's Prayer found in Matthew 6:9–13. Compare with the English translation of the Kaddish prayer. What are the differences? What are the similarities? Do you think it is proper for Jewish boys and girls to repeat the Lord's Prayer in their public schools? Should it be used in Jewish religious schools? Is it proper for Jews to call it the *Lord's* Prayer?

4. Norman Cousins, editor of *The Saturday Review,* writing in American Judaism magazine, *Rosh Hashana,* 1960, asked: "Should not the fact of Jesus as Jew serve as the holiest of bonds between Christian and Jew?" Discuss in class your opinion on whether the Jewishness of Jesus has helped, or will help, to bring Christians and Jews together in greater friendship and understanding.

5. *The National Jewish Post and Opinion,* February 20, 1959, reported that a prominent rabbi said: "Jesus would feel very much at home in a Reform Jewish Congregation today." This opinion was expressed by Dr. Maurice N. Eisendrath, President of the Union of American Hebrew Congregations, in an interview with George W. Cornell.

Discuss in class: Do you agree or disagree with Rabbi Eisendrath? If Jesus came to earth today do you think he would be a Christian or a Jew? If a Christian, would he be a Catholic or a Protestant? If a Jew, would he be an Orthodox, Conservative or Reform Jew? State your reasons.

Rabbi Eisendrath also believes that we should reconsider the Jewish attitude toward Jesus and consider including him as one of our great Jewish teachers. What do you think?

SELECTED QUOTATIONS

Jesus the Jew

Jesus did not found a new religion. He was Jewish in his faith throughout all his life. He was a reformer more than an initiator. He advocated a righteousness that exceeded legalism and a godliness more vital than that of ritual. Like the greatest Jewish prophets before him, he protested against turning piety into the saying of prayers and the offering of sacrifices in the temple. Like Rabbi Hillel, his older contemporary, Jesus emphasized the humble, contrite heart and the forgiving spirit.

—REGINALD D. MANWELL and
SOPHIA LYON FAHS

Was Jesus the Messiah?

The real and inescapable difference between the two religions is the Christian claim that Jesus was the Messiah and even the Son of God.

Since the days of the prophets, the Jews had been waiting for a man, endowed by God with extraordinary powers, who would unite all men in love and brotherhood. This longed-for figure was called the Messiah. The hope for the Messiah has been a part of Judaism since then. Jews have believed that through his coming, good eventually will triumph over evil. But while in some ages the Jews have envisioned the Messianic age as a period in the far future, at other times the entire Jewish people believed that the Messiah's coming was near. And in such times it often happened that an individual became sincerely convinced that he was the Messiah. If such an individual was a powerful and impressive personality, he often convinced others of the truth of his claim.

—EMIL L. FACKENHEIM

A faithful son of Israel

It is in the light of this outreach of spirit which has characterized the counsels of the Catholic Church that I would have my fellow Jews likewise agonizingly reappraise their present attitude toward the man, the Jew, Jesus. I would have them recognize that Jesus was in truth a faithful son of Israel who sought, as he himself phrased it, "not to destroy but to fulfill the Torah of Judaism." Jesus absorbed the ethical ideals and moral values which were an integral part of his Hebraic environment. At no time did he himself profess that he was saying anything that had never been said before. How could he, in view of what

he had read in, and what he so frequently quoted from, the Prophets and the Psalms?

—RABBI MAURICE N. EISENDRATH

A gifted teacher

Very well then, says the Christian, let it be conceded that Jesus is neither God, nor uniquely His son, nor the Messiah, nor a moral prophet, nor even an impeccable human being. Certainly he was, despite his defects, a great man, a gifted and exalted teacher. Will not the Jews accept him as such? To which the answer of Jews runs: Have Jews, except under the extremest provocation, ever quarreled with such a presentation of him?

—RABBI MILTON STEINBERG

SELECTED READINGS

BERNSTEIN, PHILIP, *What the Jews Believe*, pp. 65–70

COHON, BERYL D., *Introduction to Judaism*, Part IV, Judaism and Jesus

FACKENHEIM, EMIL L. *Paths to Jewish Belief*,

7

Who Killed Jesus?

Is it true that the Jews of ancient times crucified Jesus? This is a question that has been asked for almost 2,000 years, and is still being debated.

In the past, Jews have been persecuted and even killed because of this false accusation. Even today there are some narrow-minded people who believe that all Jews were responsible for the crucifixion of Jesus.

That is one reason why it is important for us to know more about the period of history when Christianity was born. It is also essential for us to solve the mystery of "who killed Jesus?" and what his crucifixion meant to Christians, Romans and Jews. To do this we must learn more about Jewish and Roman law. We must also find out how the scholars answer the question: Who was responsible for the death of Jesus, the Jews or the Romans?

A Christian scholar, Joel Carmichael, gave his answer when he wrote:

The crucifixion ... was a characteristic Roman execution and was never used as a capital punishment by Jews. The capital sentence that the Jewish authorities would have been authorized to carry out was strangulation, stoning, burning at the stake, or decapitation. The mere fact of Jesus' crucifixion thus involves the direct authority of the Romans ... He was executed as King of the Jews, that is, as a contender for power. This was not a religious matter at all, but it was of direct concern to the Roman state.

—*The Death of Jesus*

Before we study this further, we will have to think about still another question, and that is: "Did Jesus ever live?"

Did Jesus ever live?

Christian and Jewish scholars do not all agree that Jesus ever lived. Jesus never wrote anything—he left no books, no letters, no sermons. Everything that he is supposed to have said and done is what others have written about him—particularly in the four Gospels, Matthew, Mark, Luke and John, and by the apostle Paul.

Some scholars say that Jesus is not historical because there is no real proof that he ever lived. Two historians of that period, Josephus and Tacitus, have some vague reference to him, but scholars believe that these references are forgeries.

When the Dead Sea Scrolls were discovered in a cave in Qumran in 1947, there was great excitement because the Christian scholars thought surely there would be historical proof of the existence of Jesus. They were very disappointed to find that there were no references to Jesus even though the scrolls were written from about 100 B.C.E. to 200 C.E., the time that Jesus is supposed to have lived and died, and the time when Christianity began and developed.

This is all very perplexing, especially when Jesus is supposed to have had such influence upon the followers of Christianity who lived at that time.

The argument between the scholars who believed that Jesus lived and those who say that he did not live has been going on for many years. We must, however, continue to search for the real truth.

What happened to Jews under Roman rule?

Let us assume that Jesus did live and look back at the time in which he lived and taught and died.

After the Maccabees defeated the Syrians, a series of Hasmonean kings, descendants of the Maccabees, ruled Judea. When the Roman armies conquered most of the known world, little Judea became a vassal state of Rome and a Roman governor ruled the Jewish people.

Jesus was born in what were troubled times for the Jews. Roman rule was tyrannical, taxes were very high, and the Romans struck down anyone who objected or rebelled against the rigid Roman laws. The Roman military leaders scoffed at Jewish beliefs and made fun of Jewish worship. Only those Jews who were friendly to Rome were given positions of leadership among their own people, and

the Hasmonean kings became puppets of the Roman masters.

As the Roman rule became more and more cruel, the Jews longed to be free and they became impatient. Some of the younger Jews joined a group called the *Zealots* and vowed that they would resist Roman tyranny and fight back even at the risk of their lives.

But how could they fight back against the mighty Roman Empire with its legions of soldiers, with its wealth and its power? Some Jews said that they would be free only when the Messiah came. Others said that they couldn't wait such a long time, and if they were to be free, they would have to rebel against Rome at once.

It was extremely dangerous for anyone to talk this way because the Romans had their

Herod's Temple, from a model at Harvard University. Its magnificence did not blind the people to Herod's cruelty or his disregard of Jewish tradition and values.

spies everywhere, and anyone who was thought to be an enemy of Rome was crucified. This was the cruel way Romans put rebels to death. Crucifixion meant nailing a person to a high wooden cross as a public spectacle, until he died a slow and horrible death. Only the Romans had the power to put anyone to death by crucifixion.

Even though the Roman law forbade Jews to carry weapons, some of the Jews were members of an organization called the *Sicarii* —which means dagger-men. They secretly carried daggers and sometimes killed Roman legionnaires. The most serious opposition came from Galilee, where the Zealots became the leaders. There were many clashes between the Jews and the Romans, and the country seethed with rebellion.

The Roman governors, called *procurators,* crucified thousands of Jews, who were thought to be political rebels against the power of Rome. Just before Jesus was born there was a king who ruled Judea. His name was Herod. Herod was half Jewish and half Idumean. His lust for power and his desire to appease Rome were dominant in his life. He killed his wife and even his own sons because he thought that they were plotting against him. Herod thought that by being cruel to the Jews he would find favor with Rome. At first he tried to get the Jews to like him and even rebuilt the Temple. But then he spoiled it all by setting up the image of a huge Roman eagle over the principal gate. When some young men tried to pull the eagle down, Herod had them burned alive. No wonder the Jews refused to honor him. Then Herod became even more cruel, and murdered thousands of Jews, crucifying not only rebels, but the innocent as well. The people groaned under the oppression.

Herod, the friend of the Romans, died and was succeeded by his son Archelaus, a weak ruler. Archelaus was soon exiled, and the Roman procurators took his place and ruled with even greater power in Judea. One was called Pontius Pilate. He ruled for ten years and made laws that were more strict and cruel, as he resolved to crush the spirit of the Jews. Pilate used the Temple treasure, which made the Jews angry. Roman soldiers killed Jews on the slightest provocation. Jewish leaders were crucified. Jewish villages were burned to the ground.

JESUS OF NAZARETH

Historians have asked: Was Jesus a rebel, too? Did he protest and fight against the tyranny of Rome?

Actually, Jesus was not a political rebel, although later the Romans put him to death, not for religious reasons, but because they thought he was an agitator and was setting himself up as King of the Jews.

We must remember that according to the Jewish tradition, the Messiah was thought to be the King of the Jews, and when Jesus was acclaimed as the Messiah, the Romans thought of him as a political menace.

The Gospel according to Luke relates that Jesus was born in Bethlehem, in Judea, where Mary and Joseph had gone to be taxed in obedience to a decree issued by Caesar Augustus, the Roman Emperor. They later returned with the child to their home in Nazareth, in Galilee. According to the Gospel accounts of Matthew and Mark, Jesus had four younger brothers and also younger sisters, children who were born later to Mary and Joseph. Catholics, however, in order to worship Mary, Jesus' mother, as perpetually pure, deny that he had any brothers and sisters and call them his cousins, Protestants accept the Gospel story of Mary's large natural family.

Galilee was a province in which many political agitators and zealots lived. It was regarded as the hotbed of rebellion, and anyone who came from Galilee was suspected of being dangerous. As we will see a little later, this fact influenced the Romans and made them suspect Jesus all the more.

The boy Joshua (Jesus is the Greek form of the name) became a carpenter like his father Joseph. He had received no formal education but he learned the Bible and the interpretations and sayings of the Jewish sages.

At the age of thirty, Jesus began his career as a preacher, teacher and miracle worker. According to the Gospels, Jesus was baptised in the River Jordan by his cousin, John the Baptist, who proclaimed that all should repent because the Kingdom of God was near, and the end of the world would soon come. When John (or Johanan, in Hebrew) was decapitated by a Herodian ruler, Jesus decided to take his place.

Jesus wandered about speaking in parables, stories which taught a moral lesson. He gathered about himself some devoted disciples who followed him wherever he went.

Jesus was a Jew and taught the best and the noblest that was in the Jewish tradition. He proclaimed the *Shema,* and asked the people to love the Lord their God with all their heart and soul and might, and to love their neighbors as themselves. He cured the sick and crowds gathered whenever he appeared in a village or town to hear him speak about God's love.

Jesus preaches a dangerous doctrine

According to the Gospels, Jesus began to preach a new doctrine. When he spoke, he did not speak in the name of God as all the other prophets did, or in the name of his teachers as all the other teachers did. He would say: "It has been said in olden times, but I say unto you."

Annunciation scenes are one of the gentler subjects in Christian art. This painting of Mary and the angel was made by Jan Van Eyck, in fifteenth-century Flanders.

This shocked many of the Jews, and they were even more shocked when it was reported that Jesus thought of himself as the Messiah, the Son of God. Whether this was true or not, we do not know.

The week before Passover, Jesus went to Jerusalem, where he caused great excitement. He drove the money-changers and the dealers in animals for sacrifice out of the Temple precincts, even though the priests had set them up there for the convenience of pilgrims from foreign lands. He taught there, disputing, arguing with other teachers, insisting that the Kingdom of God would soon be, and final judgment was near. Some Jews hailed him as the Messiah and believed that he would deliver them from the oppression of the Romans. They believed that at last God had sent His servant the Messiah to save them.

Trouble begins

The Jewish leaders, however, did not believe that Jesus was the Messiah, and some of them worried about how the Romans would react, and what they would do to the Jewish people if Jesus would be hailed as King of Jews. They thought, surely the Romans would murder, burn and bring about terrible days of suffering if they believed that the Jews were planning to revolt against Rome and set up their own king.

While the Jewish leaders worried about this danger, they were equally worried about what would happen if Jesus continued to teach the people that they didn't have to obey all the laws of the Torah. What was more he spoke blasphemy when he let others acclaim him as the Messiah, the Son of God. The Jewish leaders met and decided to summon Jesus to answer the charges against him.

Jesus knew that there was trouble in the air. He realized how much he had antagonized the leaders and he was prepared to meet with them and defend his beliefs.

The Gospels say that on the eve of the Passover he sat with his disciples for the last time at supper. Some believe that this was the Last Supper—the Passover Seder, when Jesus told the disciples that the *matzot* would represent his flesh, and the wine his blood. However, we can't be sure because there were so many differing reports and versions of what Jesus believed and what he said and what he did.

According to the Gospels, Jesus was arrested that night, betrayed by one of his disciples, Judas of Kirioth. Judas was paid thirty pieces of silver and identified Jesus to the High Priest's police.

Many wonder: If Jesus was so popular, and had created such a sensation, with great multitudes gathering around him, surely he must have been well known. Why was it necessary for one of his disciples to point him out?

Actually we don't know because the Gospels were not written until 65 to 100 years after the death of Jesus—and the Gospels don't agree as to really what happened. Therefore, it is very difficult to know for sure who took Jesus prisoner and what occurred at the trial.

Jesus on trial

The Gospels tell us that Jesus was brought before the High Priest and the scribes, but they couldn't find anyone to testify against him. Some false witnesses spoke up, but they contradicted each other. All this time, Jesus said nothing.

Finally the High Priest stood up and asked Jesus, as we read in the Gospel of Mark: "Art thou the Christ, the son of the blessed?"

And Jesus said, "I am: And ye shall see the son of man sitting on the right hand of power and coming in the clouds of heaven."

Then the High Priest tore his clothes and said: "What need we any further witnesses?

Ye have heard the blasphemy: what think ye? And they all condemned him to death."

The next morning the Chief Priests held another consultation with the elders and scribes and the whole council, and bound Jesus and delivered him to Pilate. The Gospel according to St. Mark, 15:2 reads:

"And Pilate asked him, 'Art thou the King of the Jews?' And he answering said unto him, 'Thou sayest it.' "

For almost two thousand years, people have been arguing about that statement. Some have believed that Jesus regarded himself as the Messiah by agreeing: "You have said it," meaning, "You are right. It is so that I am the Messiah." Others have insisted that what Jesus meant was "*You* have said it, not *I*. So you may believe as you wish."

There are verses in the Gospels that lead us to believe that Jesus really did regard himself as the Messiah, and there are other verses that lead us to believe that Jesus did not regard himself to be the Messiah.

We have to constantly remember that we actually don't know what Jesus believed and said since he left none of his own writings. That is why some scholars make a distinction between "the religion *of* Jesus, and the religion *about* Jesus." There are many differing conclusions and opinions recorded in the New Testament.

Jesus stands before Pontius Pilate

In all the Gospel accounts except John, Pontius Pilate is made out to be a merciful and tender judge, eager to save Jesus, but powerless when the Jewish mob howled for the blood of the innocent man.

According to the Gospels, and specifically Mark, Chapter 15, Pontius Pilate offered to release Jesus and let him go free in honor of the Feast of Passover. But the Chief Priests incited the mob to call for the release of another prisoner, Barabbas, a political rebel who had revolted against the Romans as had many other Galileans.

In Mark 15:12, we read: "And Pilate answered and said again unto them, 'What will ye then that I shall do until him whom ye call the King of the Jews?'

"And they cried out again, 'Crucify him.'

"Then Pilate said unto them, 'Why, what evil hath he done?' And they cried out the more exceedingly, 'Crucify him.'

"And so Pilate, willing to content the people, released Barabbas unto them, and delivered Jesus, when he had scourged him, to be crucified."

Another Gospel, Matthew, tells a different story of what happened. In his story the wife of Pontius Pilate wants him to release Jesus, but the Jewish mob would not hear of it. Pilate pleads with the mob to permit Jesus to be saved, but the mob cried out: "Let him be crucified."

In 27:24–26, we read: "When Pilate saw that he could prevail nothing, but that rather a tumult was made, he took water, and washed his hands before the multitude, saying, 'I am innocent of the blood of this just person, see ye to it.'

"Then answered all the people and said, 'His blood be on us, and on our children!'

"Then released he Barabbas unto them: and when he had scourged Jesus, he delivered him to be crucified."

Difficult to believe

It is difficult to understand why Pontius Pilate should change his whole character all of a sudden, and out of kindness want to save Jesus, who was supposed to be the King of the Jews. Wasn't Pilate the one who crucified rebels and those who were against Rome? Wasn't Jesus thought to be a political agitator? What's more, why would he want to release Barabbas, who murdered one of his own Roman soldiers in a revolt?

Another puzzling problem for scholars is the incident of Pilate washing his hands of the whole thing, as if to say, "I want to let this enemy of Rome go free and you won't let me."

It is perplexing because according to Roman law, the procurator had to put to death those who rebelled against Rome. The whole land was seething with rebellion, and it is fantastic to believe that Pontius Pilate, who was known for his cruelty, would want to treat any Jewish rebel so kindly.

Most scholars agree that when the Gospels were written, the writers regarded it as dangerous to blame the Romans, and so they put the blame on the Jews. From everything the historians tell us about the Roman procurators, it is difficult to believe that things happened the way the Gospels say they did.

Let us bring the matter closer to our own time and consider what happens when a political enemy of a tyrant government is brought to trial. Imagine under the Nazis in Germany, that a Jew accused of setting up a revolt and calling himself King of the Jews is brought before the Gestapo or before a Nazi kommandant, and the Nazi leader says to the Jewish multitude: "He's innocent. Let him go." Can you imagine the Jews, who were persecuted and massacred by the cruel Nazis, turning one of their own people over to the hated enemy and crying for his blood? The Romans were almost as cruel to the Jews as the Nazis and were equally cruel when their political power was at stake.

Or, let's consider a country that has been taken over by the Communists—perhaps Poland, and a Pole is accused of plotting against the Communists and is called King of the Poles or King of Poland, and the Communist Commissar says: "He's innocent. Let him go," as the Polish people, who were being oppressed by the Communists, cry: "No! Kill him! Execute him! Torture him!" And then the Communist washes his hands of the whole thing as the Poles say: "Let his blood be on us, and on our children." Can you even imagine the Poles turning over one of their own people to the hated Communists?

If Barabbas murdered a Roman soldier, do you think that Pilate would let him go free? It is extremely unlikely that a Roman governor would have freed Jesus or Barabbas or anyone else charged with political rebellion against Rome.

Jesus of Nazareth, King of the Jews

Pontius Pilate wasn't at all interested in the local problems of the Jews or their religious disputes. He wasn't at all concerned about those who kept the Jewish ritual or ignored it. He wasn't interested in the religious arguments of the Pharisees or Sadducees—but he was very interested and very much concerned about any hint of a political revolt against the power of Rome.

As we continue reading in Mark 15, it becomes all the more certain that the Romans regarded Jesus as a political agitator and a man who was considered as King of the Jews and, therefore, dangerous to the welfare of the Romans.

As we read from the Gospel, we see what happens to Jesus, who was hailed as King of the Jews.

> And the soldiers led him away into the hall, called Praetorium; and they called together the whole band.
>
> And they clothed him with purple, and plaited a crown of thorns, and put it about his head.

Notice that the Romans were ridiculing and mocking Jesus. "You are a king?" they said. "Here is your royal robe of purple, your majesty. Oh, yes, you will need a crown. Well, we have a very nice crown to place on your head. Here it is, a beautiful crown of thorns."

Scoffing and laughing the Romans paid homage to the Jewish king,—"and began to salute him, hail, King of the Jews."

The more we read, the more clear it becomes that the Roman concern about Jesus wasn't religious, but political. The famous or rather infamous *Pax Romanus*, which means Roman Peace, meant that any political rebellion would be put down immediately with crushing force so that the people of the rebellious province never again would consider resisting the mighty power of Rome. Let us continue:

And they smote him on the head with a reed, and they spat upon him, and bowing their knees worshipped him.

The reed was supposed to be a royal sceptre, but not only the sceptre, but the robe and the crown of thorns, were royal symbols that they bestowed in mockery to ridicule one who was supposed to be the King of the Jews.

And when they had mocked him, they took off the purple from him, and put his own clothes on him, and led him out to crucify him.

And they compel one Simon a Cyrenian, who passed by, coming out of the country, the father of Alexander and Rufus, to bear his cross.

And they bring him unto the place Golgotha, which is, being interpreted, the place of a skull.

And they gave him to drink wine mingled with myrrh: but he received it not.

And when they had crucified him, they parted his garments, casting lots upon them, what every man should take.

And it was the third hour, and they crucified him.

And the superscription of his accusation was written over, the King of the Jews.

My God, my God, why hast Thou forsaken me?

This makes it all very clear that Jesus was crucified for political reasons and not because of any religious differences. There were always differences of opinion among the Jews, with many opposing factions, groups and sects, but the Jewish authorities never turned opponents over to the enemy to be killed.

Crucifixion was a horrible method of execution that the Romans used to punish criminals and political enemies of Rome. The Gospels tell us that Jesus was first scourged, then fastened to the cross at Golgotha outside of Jerusalem. For hours he hung there in agony. He cried out in the words of the Psalms: "My God, my God, why hast Thou forsaken me?"

Late in the afternoon he died. His body was put in a nearby tomb and a stone was placed at the entrance. Only a few women faithful to their teacher even unto death stood by weeping.

On Sunday, some of the women came to his tomb to mourn for him. To their amazement, they found the stone rolled away and the tomb empty. Then there were visions in which the women and then the disciples saw Jesus again. This is called the resurrection of Jesus. They believed that he would return again soon to establish the Kingdom of Heaven. This would be the second coming of Jesus.

No matter how people may try to twist the facts around, even the Gospels say that the Romans crucified Jesus. It is one of the most unfair and unjust accusations of history to blame the Jews for something they didn't do. For almost 2,000 years, Jews have suffered because of the false charge of "deicide," which means killing God. Not all Christians have felt this way, and most Christians today do not hold all the Jews responsible for the

Christian artists have often depicted scenes from Jesus'
life in terms of their own land and era. This is a detail
from "Road to Calvary," by the sixteenth-century
Flemish painter, Peter Breughel.

death of Jesus, but history records that ever since Jesus died, Jews have been persecuted because of this accusation.

Anyone who studies Jewish law soon is convinced that the Jews couldn't possibly be guilty of the charge of crucifying Jesus. That's why we are going to take a few minutes now and consider what the Jews of Jesus' time believed about capital punishment.

The Jewish attitude toward capital punishment

The crucifixion of Jesus, was clearly conducted in accordance with Roman law. The whole description of the procedure, the mock crowning, the beating, the bearing of the cross to the place of execution, and the crucifixion itself, were typical of the Roman government's punishment of those who rebelled against its authority. This plainly shows that Jesus died not as a heretic, but as a political rebel.

It was against Jewish law to have a trial on a Jewish festival, or to execute anyone on or the day before a holiday. Many scholars believe that no Jewish court at any time had the power to sentence anyone to death or use capital punishment. Some believe that the court had the right to punish Jews with death if they were disobedient over religious matters. Others disagree. Almost all, however, agree that it is extremely unlikely that a Jewish court would turn a Jew over to the Roman courts to be put to death.

In the Bible, a person could be sentenced to capital punishment for murder, blasphemy, Sabbath breaking, idolatry, witchcraft, kidnaping and disrespect for the authority of parents, rulers or religion. The usual method of capital punishment in the Bible is by stoning.

The Mishnah Sanhedrin gives a description of capital punishment. Four different types of capital punishment are given: stoning, burning, beheading and strangulation. Crucifixion is not even mentioned.

The Talmud teaches that the law of "Thou shalt love thy neighbor as thyself" must be applied even to a criminal. In the few cases where the death sentence was carried through, the criminal was always given a drug to deaden his senses before the execution.

The Pharisees established so many safeguards as law that it was difficult ever to bring about the death penalty. A Sanhedrin that put even one person to death in seven years was regarded as bloody. Eleazar ben Azaryah said that if it should happen even once in seventy years, the Sanhedrin was bloody. Rabbi Akiba and others were opposed to capital punishment at any time or for any reason.

Circumstantial evidence was ruled out, and only on the testimony of two reliable witnesses could a person be sentenced to death. This was after a long trial, many delays, and every effort made to save the life of the accused to be sure that an innocent man did not receive unfair punishment. And no man was ever burned to death.

The Sanhedrin

The Jewish Grand Council known by the Greek name of *Sanhedrin* was composed of seventy-one members. The Sanhedrin met in the famous Chamber of Hewn Rock. It was the rule that the court could not meet until after the morning sacrifice in the Temple. No trial was started with an accusation. Nothing was permitted to be said against an accused person until one of the judges had urged something in his behalf. The first argument was always in favor of mercy, fairness and acquittal.

Following arguments for and against the accused, the discussion became general among the judges. When the entire case had been reviewed, the balloting started on the guilt or innocence of the accused. The youngest members of the Sanhedrin were required to vote first, so that they would not be influenced by the decisions of their seniors.

Each member voted by standing up and giving a brief explanation of his decision. If the vote were for acquittal, the prisoner was immediately released. If the vote were for conviction, then sentence could not be pronounced until the next afternoon. The judges went home in pairs discussing the case. In the evening they met again for further deliberation.

In the night that followed, the judges fasted and prayed. In the morning they attended the sacrifice in the Temple and again assembled in the Chamber of Hewn Rock where the trial resumed from the beginning. At the close of the deliberations, they voted again. If the prisoner was declared guilty, then the execution was to follow.

An important book, called *Trial of Jesus,* written by a non-Jew, Walter Chandler, after he studied the Talmud and the Jewish literature available, offers this explanation of how an execution was carried out under Jewish law.

Before the execution

As the culprit was led away to his doom, a man carrying a flag was stationed at the entrance of the Sanhedrin Hall. A herald . . . made proclamation to the gazing multitude along the way that the person was about to be executed. He cried out, "AB is to be put to death on the testimony of CD and XY on such and such a charge. If any man knows anything favorable to the accused, in the name of God, let him come forward and speak, in order that the prisoner may be led back to the Sanhedrin Hall to be again confronted and tried by his judges."

If any witness came forth to furnish new evidence in favor of the condemned man, the procession was halted and the accused was led back to the Sanhedrin Chamber. If any member of the court still sitting in the hall of judgment bethought himself of any new argument in behalf of the accused that had not been offered at the trial, he rose quickly in his place and stated it to his fellow judges. The flag at the gate was then waved and the mounted messenger galloped forward to stop the execution.

The culprit himself could delay or prevent the accomplishment of the death sentence if he could give the rabbis any valid reason why he should not be put to death. He was led back (for a new trial) as often as he gave any good excuse, not exceeding five times. If no new witness appeared and if the prisoner made no further plea for life, the procession proceeded to within a short distance of the place of execution.

Human life is sacred

According to this, it would be almost impossible for someone to be executed. Surely, his friends would try to save him and offer evidence, and the trial might go on for months, or possibly for half a year. That is exactly what the Jewish judges had in mind. Human life is so sacred they wanted to make

certain that no innocent person would be executed. They looked for reasons and excuses to find him innocent, or to delay the trial hoping that new evidence would be found in favor of the defendant.

If that same kind of a trial had been given to Jesus it would have been impossible for the Sanhedrin to meet the night of Passover, go through all this and hand Jesus over to the Romans to be crucified.

That is why it is so bewildering that the Gospels read the way they do. According to Jewish law, it would have been impossible for the Chief Priests and the Sanhedrin to have acted in the way described by the Gospels.

The drug of mercy

But what happened according to Jewish law if no one came forward with evidence to save the convicted man? Walter Chandler tells us:

. . . he was then led to the ground of execution. The death draught, consisting of a mixture of frankincense and myrrh, poured into a cup of vinegar or light wine, was then given him. This was a powerful drug that made the prisoner unconscious. As soon as the draught had been administered the execution took place.

It is horrible when anyone is put to death, but we must remember that very few were put to death by the Sanhedrin's police. In those days the Jewish method was the most merciful and humane. Other people laughed at the Jews because they were humane to those convicted. All other peoples made a public show of executions and prolonged it as a warning to the people.

The reason we have considered so much of Jewish law and in such detail is to make it clear to you how ridiculous it is to ever believe that the Jews were responsible for

Prelates in Vatican City for the Ecumenical Council attended a Solemn Pontifical Mass marking the fourth anniversary of the coronation of Pope John XXIII.

the crucifixion of Jesus. It is important that you know the facts about the Jewish attitude toward capital punishment.

WHY BLAME THE JEWS?

We may wonder why, in view of all this, intelligent people would blame the Jews for the crucifixion of Jesus. It is difficult to understand, if the Jews did crucify Jesus, which they didn't, why modern Jews who had nothing to do with it should be blamed and sometimes hated.

Christians of good will are trying to change this situation. Pope John XXIII will long be remembered for his efforts and for his part in the ecumenical movement. The word *ecumenical* means "worldwide." Many Protestant, Greek Orthodox and other Christian bodies have been seeking greater understanding and unity among themselves. The Pope was concerned for the unification of all Christians, but he also sought better understanding of the Jews in the interests of world brotherhood.

Pope John called together a Vatican Council in Rome, and one of the points discussed was a *schema*, or resolution, to remove the accusation against the Jews of crucifying Jesus. The Catholics have removed offensive statements about the Jews from their literature and from the textbooks used in Catholic schools.

The forgiving and the forgiven

Some people think that instead of the Catholics and others forgiving the Jews, it is the Catholics and the Protestants who persecuted and killed so many Jews over these many years, who should be begging for forgiveness.

While it is true that the Catholics and Protestants need forgiveness, and while it is true that we shouldn't go around begging for forgiveness or lose our dignity, it is always better to have good will and understanding, rather than hatred, ill will, resentment and anti-Semitism. We should favor any good cause that will help Catholics, Protestants and Jews remove hatred from their hearts, and enable them to understand each other and live together as brothers.

Anti-Semitism—the ugly ghost

Anti-Semitism means prejudice against Jews and unfortunately it exists. It is an ugly ghost that has been haunting us for a long time. But great progress is being made, and it is unfair to judge all Catholics or all Protestants by those who are petty and prejudiced. Let us think of the Catholics and Protestants who are not anti-Semitic, and who want to understand and appreciate Jews and their faith.

Anti-Semitism is unfair and against the teachings of most sects of Christianity. However, not all people practice what their religion teaches. There are many reasons and theories that are given for anti-Semitism.

One is that some Christians still blame the Jews for the crucifixion of Jesus. That is a factor, but there are many more causes. Some people don't like others who are different. The Jews were easy to blame when things went wrong and they became scapegoats. During depressions and economic crises, when people are out of jobs and are hungry, they look around for someone to blame for their misery and sometimes they blame the Jews—even though they have no reason to.

Then again, there have been dictators, rulers and governments that encouraged anti-Semitism, to take the minds of the people away from their real troubles. And in every

land and in every age there are sick people, sick emotionally or mentally, who feel that they have to hate someone, and they think up all sorts of stupid and silly reasons why they hate Jews.

The Nazi holocaust

In 1933, when Adolf Hitler came to power in Germany, the Jews of Europe faced the greatest threat and danger of their entire history. Hitler and the Nazis resolved to destroy the Jews, and offer a "final solution" of what they called the "Jewish problem." What happened is a horrible period in the history of mankind. Jews were gathered together, and transported to concentration camps to die of disease and starvation. Millions of Jews were forced into crematoria and gas chambers and killed without mercy. As the Nazi army marched into nation after nation, the Jews were first deprived of their rights, then imprisoned in terrible camps and finally put to death. Over 6½ million Jews were cruelly murdered in what has come to be known as "the holocaust."

Many Jews went like sheep to the slaughter. Sometimes Jews resisted, as in the Warsaw Ghetto where they fought back and died fighting bravely and heroically. Today, Jews throughout the world have resolved that never again will they permit themselves to be helplessly exterminated as their people were in Nazi Europe.

It is true that some Jews were saved by Christians. There were noble examples of Christians who endangered or gave up their lives to protect and save Jews from the Nazis. Unfortunately, however, while many Christians deplored mass murder and were sorry for what was happening, they were too frightened or too indifferent to take action, protest, or make significant efforts to save the Jews from the terror of Nazism. Today, many Christians feel a sense of guilt and shame for

Many Danish Jews, like those in this little fishing boat, escaped to Sweden. Friendly Danes row this group to safety at night.

what was permitted to happen to the Jews. Some Christians have tried to make atonement through word and deed because of regret for the weakness of the Catholic and Protestant churches and the "terrible silence" that permitted millions of Jews to die. They realize now that hatred of the Jews results in hatred of other groups, and ultimately is a danger to Catholics, Protestants and free people everywhere.

Anti-Semitism still exists in Europe and throughout the world. Responsible and dedicated clergymen and laymen of the Catholic and Protestant churches are fighting this prejudice against the Jews and are trying to remove prejudiced statements from their religious literature and religious teachings.

The lesson of history must be learned, and hatred and prejudice against Jews or any other people or religion must be resisted and eradicated wherever and whenever it occurs.

Anti-Semitism is the ugly ghost that has not yet been driven away, but it is not tolerated by most of the Catholic and Protestant churches. It is regarded as un-Christian to be guilty of prejudice against Jews.

Understanding each other

Through organizations such as the National Conference of Christians and Jews, through dialogues in which Catholics, Protestants and Jews get together to discuss and talk out problems and questions, and through working together for great and noble causes, Catholics, Protestants and Jews have come to know each other better through the years.

Although there may always be some anti-Semitism on the part of stupid, ignorant and malicious people, we believe that as time goes on anti-Semitism will decrease and some day there will be a true brotherhood of man and a partnership of faiths working together for a brighter and better tomorrow.

QUESTIONS FOR DISCUSSION

1. Some Christians say that Jesus was sent to earth to die and be crucified so that he could take the sins of the world upon himself and save the world from destruction. If they believe that this is the will of God and Jesus was sent to earth to be crucified, why do they blame the Jews or anyone for doing something that saved the world? What do you think? Ask or write to a Catholic priest or a Protestant minister and request an answer to this question.

2. How important is it for the Christian religion to prove that Jesus was historical and really lived? How important is it for Jews and the Jewish religion?

3. Suppose it could be proved that Moses never lived. How would this affect Jews and Judaism?

4. Christianity is based on the birth, life, teachings and death of Jesus. What happens to Christianity if it is proved that Jesus never lived? Is the Jewish religion based on the birth or death of any of its great teachers?

5. What is the significance of the statement: "Pilate also wrote a title and put it on the cross; it read: 'Jesus of Nazareth, the King of the Jews'" (John 19:19)?

6. Do you think that Jesus regarded himself as the Messiah? What are your reasons?

7. Pope John XXIII said that it is wrong to accuse the Jews of *deicide,* which means killing God, for, he continued, even though the Romans put Jesus to death, the whole world denied him and the whole world rejected him, and it is for the whole world that he wished to die as redeemer. What do you think?

8. Some people think that instead of the Catholics forgiving the Jews for deicide, it is the Catholics and Protestants who persecuted and killed so many Jews who should be begging for forgiveness. Do you agree?

9. What do you think about the Jewish attitude toward capital punishment?

10. When Jesus disagreed with some practices of Jewish Law, did this mean that he was no longer a Jew? To what extent do Reform and Conservative Jews disagree with some of the traditional practices of Jewish law? Are they still Jews? Are they turned over to the authorities for punishment?

11. If we had a Sanhedrin today, what do you think this court would do about Reform and Conservative Judaism? What would it do with Jews who didn't wish to remain Jews?

12. Jewish law does not accept circumstantial evidence, but insists upon the testimony of at least two witnesses in criminal cases. What do you think about this?

13. What can Jews do to drive out the ugly ghost of anti-Semitism from the world? What can Christians do?

THINGS TO DO

1. When Jesus died he said: "My God, my God, why hast Thou forsaken me?" Compare Mark 15:34, Matthew 27:46 with Psalm 22. Does the Psalm answer Jesus' cry?

Jesus also said: "Into Thy hands I commit my soul." Compare Luke 23:46 with the last verse of Adon Olam. Do you think Jesus knew that he was quoting?

2. Look up the references in Matthew 27:37; Mark 15:26; Luke 23:28; John 19:19, and then write a brief essay on the reasons the New Testament gives for the crucifixion of Jesus. Might these reasons absolve the Jews for the crucifixion?

3. Read these verses and then write an essay on Capital Punishment in the Bible: Exodus 21 and 22; Leviticus 18, 20, and 24; Nos. 15; Deuteronomy 13, 17, 18, 21, 22.

4. Look up the articles in the *Universal Jewish Encyclopedia* and write a paragraph on each of these factions: the Pharisees, the Sadducees, the Essenes and the Zealots.

5. Do some library research and then write an essay on the attitude of the State of Israel toward capital punishment today.

6. Interview a Catholic priest and a Protestant minister and write up their views of the ecumenical movement and the hope of greater inter-faith understanding in the future.

7. Reconstruct the trial of Jesus in class. Select a prosecuting attorney, a defense attorney, a judge and jury, and determine what the charges were against Jesus, what the defense, and what you think the verdict should have been. Then put the Christian people on trial for the persecution of the Jews throughout history. Select a prosecuting attorney, a defense attorney, a judge and jury and present the case for and against the Christians.

8. Just as there is anti-Semitism, there is anti-Gentilism or anti-Christianism. To what extent are Jews prejudiced unfairly against Christians? Write an essay on this subject.

9. Write to the Anti-Defamation League, 315 Lexington Avenue, New York, New York 10016, and inquire about materials they have on books that contribute to anti-Semitism. Discuss in class.

10. Discuss in class the meaning of the following statement:

The Second Vatican Council's Declaration on the Jews

Although the Jewish authorities and those who followed their lead pressed for the death of Christ, nevertheless what happened to Christ in His Passion cannot be attributed to all Jews, without distinction, then alive, nor to the Jews of today.

Although the Church is the new people of God, the Jews should not be presented as rejected by God or accursed, as if this follows from Holy Scriptures.

SELECTED QUOTATIONS

Jesus crucified again and again

Ever since his death Jesus—the symbol of love and human brotherhood—has been crucified again and again, often by those who profess to revere him as Lord and Master. He was crucified in the bigotry of the Middle Ages when Christian fought against Christian and both persecuted the Jew. He was crucified when six million Jews were done to death in Nazi concentration camps and crematoria. He is crucified every time brother slaughters brother in war, every time a man raises his hand against his brother man in hate whether he be white or black or yellow or brown, or denies him his unalienable human rights as a child of God.

—RABBI RAPHAEL H. LEVINE

What the Gospel writers didn't know

Obviously the Gospel writers are completely in the dark regarding the real circumstances of Jesus' trial and death.

They do not know that a preliminary hearing of any kind, such as they allege to have taken place at the residence of Annas, or of Caiaphas, could not possibly have been held.

They do not know that a formal session of the Sanhedrin could not open until the morning service at the Temple was terminated.

They are not aware that the Sanhedrin never met on a Friday, nor on the eve of the Passover.

They are perfectly oblivious of the unalterable tradition that sentence was not to be passed on the same day a trial was held.

Jesus never appeared before and hence never was convicted by any Jewish court.

The New Testament stories of his condemnation by the Sanhedrin are pure fantasy.

—PIERRE VAN PAASSEN

In the name of justice

I demand in the name of justice . . . that the representatives of the Church openly admit and proclaim henceforth in all houses of worship and in their parochial schools, that the Jews are innocent [of the crucifixion of Jesus] and begin now to right the deadly wrong which they have committed against the Jews. Let them cease inciting their followers against the Jew with their Passion Plays before the approach of Easter. I demand in the name of justice, that they revise those chapters in the Four Gospels that tell of the trial of the Nazarene, and delete from the New Testament texts all accusations against the Jews, and thus forever exonerate the Jewish people of a crime they never committed. I demand these things . . . not only in the name of . . . Jewry, but in the name of all that is decent in Christianity, in the name of the conscience of mankind.

—HYMAN E. GOLDIN

Those who believed in Jesus were Jews

Some historians maintain that all we know of Jesus is that He died a deliberate death at the hand of disbelievers; perhaps we do not know who killed Him, but we do know who believed in Him.

The only ones who believed in Him were the Jews. Not all of them, to be sure, but those who sat at his feet and listened

were Jews, and Jews only, and those who carried His message across the world were Jews, and Jews only.

—DAGOBERT D. RUNES

Spiritual Semites

At the beginning of the Nazi persecutions, Pope Pius XI wrote in a famous encyclical: "Spiritually we are all Semites." Now the Reverend W. Gleason, Chairman of Fordham University's Department of Catholic Theology says that "the man who looks down on Jews is apostate from the Christian faith. I can only describe it as Christian spittle on the face of our Jewish Savior." He said in a sermon given at New York's famous St. Patrick's Cathedral: "As a gentile, I speak to you as gentiles and as a Jew, I speak to you as Jews. By virtue of natural descent I am a gentile, by virtue of super-natural descent, by the grace of God, I am also a Jew. I trace my spiritual lineage to Abraham." Speaking of Jesus, he emphasized that "his mother was a Jewess, his fosterfather was a Jew until his death, and he reigns in heaven as a Jew, and all his memories of earth are memories of Israel and Palestine."

SELECTED READINGS

LEVINE, RAPHAEL H., *Two Paths to One God*, pp. 189–193

MILLER, MILTON G., and SCHWARTZMAN, S. D., *Our Religion and Our Neighbors*, pp. 80–82

UNIVERSAL JEWISH ENCYCLOPEDIA, Vol. 3, *Crucifixion; Capital Punishment;* Vol. 6, *Jesus of Nazareth*

8

Prayer: The Service of the Heart

THE SCHOLAR AND THE PEASANT

Naḥman of Bratzlav was a Ḥasidic rabbi, and he used to pray for all the peoples and nations of the world. Then he would conclude in this way:

May it be Thy will, O God, to extend peace, great and wondrous, in the universe. Let all the peoples of the earth recognize and know the innermost truth; that we are not come into this world for quarrel and division, nor for hate and jealousy, contrariness and bloodshed; but we are come into this world to recognize and know Thee. Be Thou blessed forever.

—Ḥasidic literature

In Ḥasidic literature, we read about an ignorant Jew who entered the synagogue for worship. He listened to the scholars and sages offer their beautiful prayers to God. Since he, too, wished to express his love of God, he ascended the pulpit and stood before the Holy Ark. The worshipers were astonished to hear him just repeat the letters of the Hebrew alphabet over and over again.

They laughed at him because he didn't even know the simplest prayers of the Jewish service. Then the simple man began to speak,

and the congregation stopped laughing. Their mockery turned to shame as they heard him say:

Lord of the universe, I am a simple man —an ignorant man. Oh, how I wish that I had the words to fashion beautiful prayers to praise Thee! But, alas, I do not know these words. So please listen to me, O God, as I recite the letters of the alphabet and You, dear God, form the words that express the love for You, that is in my heart.

Having said this, he continued to repeat the letters of the alphabet over and over again.

WHAT DO YOU THINK?

1. What are your reactions to the prayers of the learned and the prayer of the simple Jew? Which do you think is the better prayer? Why? Or do both have validity?

2. What kind of prayers do you think God answers?

3. Do you think God hears you when you pray?

4. Does God hear bad people's prayers?

5. What kind of prayers do you think God will not answer?

6. Will there be a better chance that your prayer will be answered if a rabbi, minister or priest prays to God for you? What are your reasons?

Here are some questions. Don't answer too quickly, but give them some thought.

DO WE HAVE TO BE TAUGHT TO PRAY?

Before discussing in class the reasons why people pray, imagine that a young boy has been cast ashore on an uninhabited island. He manages to find berries and fruit to eat and survives. His home is a cave that protects him from the rain and storms. He lives on this island for many years without talking to a single human being. He has no books, no Bible, and no one to tell him about religious prayer. The question is: do you think he will ever pray? If so, what kind of a prayer do you think he will pray? Since he doesn't remember anything he has been taught about God, to whom will he pray?

Discuss in class some of the reasons why you think people pray. Make a list of the reasons you believe are the most important.

Why do we pray?

We pray when we are frightened, when we are grateful, when we want something, when we are sad and when we are happy. We pray when we are in the synagogue or church, when we are alone in our room, when we go to sleep, when we wake up. We pray on the Sabbath, on festivals and Holy Days. We pray when we are outside looking at the stars. We pray when we are sorry and want forgiveness. We pray when we want to be better than we are. We pray when we want God to tell us the right way to act, and the right thing to do.

What kind of prayer do you think is the most childish prayer, and what kind of prayer do you think is the most mature or grown-up type of prayer?

Where do we pray?

We pray in our own room when we are alone. We pray when we are outside in the fields or in a forest. We pray when we are in a church or in a synagogue. Where do you think is the best place to pray? Do you think it makes any difference to God where we are when we pray? Do you think God listens to us more when we pray in our temple or synagogue than when we pray in our own room?

Praying alone and with others

Most of the prayers in our Jewish prayer book are "We" prayers rather than "I" prayers. Very seldom do we read "My God" in our prayer book. Most of the time we read "Our God." When we pray to God we usually start with "Our God and God of our fathers. Even the blessings are in the plural, such as "Blessed art Thou, O Lord, our God, King of the Universe."

Why do you think that most of the prayers in the Jewish prayer book are plural rather than singular?

Do you think it is better to pray alone or to pray with others?

What are the advantages and disadvantages of praying with others?

How does praying with others help us to be more concerned with the problems and the troubles of other people?

Try an experiment. Bring to class some prayer books from the Catholic, Episcopal, Methodist, Presbyterian and Baptist churches. Look through these prayer books and then decide what prayer books emphasize the "we" more than the "I"—the Jewish

Jews once again pray together in the Pestalozzistrasse Synagogue, destroyed by Nazis in 1939 and rebuilt ten years later.

or the Christian prayer books. Which type of prayer do you think makes us more concerned with the welfare of others: the "we" prayer or the "I" and "me" prayer?

Different ways of praying

In Judaism, there are different ways of praying and different kinds of prayers.

There is the prayer that is said aloud.
There is the prayer that is said silently.
There is the prayer that is said alone.
There is the prayer that is said with others.

You may be surprised to know that in Judaism the study of Torah is regarded as prayer. Why do you think Judaism regards study as an equivalent of prayer? Is this also true in Christianity? Ask a Christian minister if study is accepted as a kind of prayer.

Worship without words

Strangely enough, there is another kind of prayer that is offered without saying a single word. Judaism teaches that when you do good deeds, *ma'asim tovim,* or acts of kindness, *gemilut ḥasadim,* helping others, this too is a form of prayer. It is worship without words. It is prayer in action.

Which kind of prayer do you think God loves the best? Which kind of prayer do you think is better for you, and does you the most good?

When do we pray?

Is it better to wait until we feel like praying before we pray, or should we pray regularly, whether we feel like it or not—let us say in the morning when you wake up and at night when you go to bed?

Even though your mind isn't on your

Embroidered Hebrew initials and embroidered headband distinguish this nineteenth-century Russian tallit.

The language of prayer

Do you think that God understands prayers in all languages or does God have a favorite language for prayer?

Will God pay more attention to a prayer and answer it if it is in Hebrew, English, Latin, Greek, French, Spanish, German?

Why do Jews pray in Hebrew? Has tradition any true force in prayer?

Is it better to have someone else pray for you or to do your own praying?

Is there a right and wrong kind of prayer?

The Talmud teaches us that there are certain prayers that are not proper. An example of an improper prayer is when a person prays: Let the baby that is going to be born be a girl. Why is this a meaningless prayer? Is it right or wrong to pray when you hear a fire alarm: "Dear God, don't let the fire be at my house"? What are your reasons?

Do you think God will answer your prayers for—

> rain or sunshine?
> for a new bike or a new dress?
> for a good grade in your studies?
> for a boy friend or girl friend to like you?
> for you to get over your cold sooner?
> to heal a broken arm or leg in a hurry?
> to let your favorite team win the baseball or football game?

What are wrong prayers and right prayers?

What are childish prayers and mature or grown-up prayers? We say that praying for a bike is childish, yet praying for sustenance or for peace is mature. Why?

If God is the father of all people, do you think that God loves the prayers of Jews more than Christians, Catholics more than

prayer, is it better to say a prayer before eating than not to say any prayer at all?

Is it better to wait until we feel like brushing our teeth or taking a bath or studying our lessons, or just go ahead and do these things regularly whether we feel like it or not? How would this apply to prayer?

Should we wait until we feel like it before going to synagogue, before we go to the dentist or physician or to school?

Protestants, Protestants more than Moslems, Moslems more than African tribes who dance and scream their prayers to God?

It has been said that prayer is talking to God. What do you think this means?

It has been said that prayer is listening to God. What do you think this means?

PRAYER IS LISTENING TO GOD

We have spoken of prayer as a conversation with God. In a true conversation we must not only speak but also listen. If we never listen then our prayer ceases to be a conversation and becomes a monologue. We often forget this most important element in prayer, namely, that we not only speak to God, we also listen to Him. If we could only sit still and think of God, our religious life would become much more sincere and deep. That is the meaning of the Bible verse: "But the Lord is in His holy temple; let all the earth keep silence before Him" (Hab. 2:20).

—RABBI SOLOMON B. FREEHOF

The following prayer was written in a little booklet for the Universal Day of Prayer for Christian students:

Prayer is so simple.
It is like quietly opening a door, and
  slipping into the very presence of God;
There in the stillness to listen to His
  voice—
Perhaps to petition,
Or only to listen;
It matters not;
Just to be there
In His presence
Is Prayer.

1. Explain what you think is meant by "listening to God."
2. How does God speak within us?

3. How can the study of Torah help you to hear God speaking within you?

4. Do you think God speaks in the same way to Catholics and Protestants? What are your reasons?

5. How can prayer bring us nearer and closer to God?

THE DIFFERENCE BETWEEN JEWISH AND CHRISTIAN PRAYER

The "Lord's Prayer" is found in the Gospel according to St. Matthew, 6:9–13.

Our Father which art in heaven, Hallowed
  be Thy name,
Thy Kingdom come. Thy will be done on
  earth, as it is in heaven.
Give us this day our daily bread.
And forgive us our debts, as we forgive
  our debtors.
And lead us not into temptation, but deliver us from evil;
For thine is the kingdom, and the power,
  and the glory forever. Amen.

The "Lord's Prayer" is in the New Testament and in Christian prayer books. It is the prayer which Jesus taught to his followers and as such it is regarded as a Christian prayer. We may ask what is the difference between a Jewish and a Christian prayer?

The main difference is that when the Christian prays to God, he is praying to the Father, Son, and Holy Ghost. To the Christian God is one, but made up of three that are joined as one. When Jews speak of the Lord or pray to the Lord, they pray to the one God and not to a Trinity. The Jews respect the teachings of Jesus, but do not believe that Jesus is God or should be called Lord.

Another difference is that when Jews pray, they pray directly to God. They say, "O Lord our God" or "Our Heavenly Father." Since all men are children of God, there is no need to call in anyone else to aid our prayers. If our prayers are truthful and sincere they go directly to God. Christians, however, often direct their prayers to God through Mary or Jesus.

WHAT DO YOU THINK?

1. Must Catholics pray through the Holy Mother instead of through Jesus? May they pray to and through Jesus instead?

2. What makes a prayer a Christian prayer or a Jewish prayer?

3. The "Lord's Prayer," from beginning to end, is derived from Jewish sources. A famous Christian authority, Theodore Keim, referring to the Lord's Prayer wrote, "Not only the address of God, together with the first two petitions, but pretty well all of it in detail, appears here and there in Jewish talmudic prayers." The great Jewish scholar, Joseph Klausner, of the Hebrew University in Jerusalem, whose *Jesus of Nazareth* is regarded as the ablest biography of Jesus ever written by a Jew, says of the Lord's Prayer that it is "a remarkable prayer, universal in its appeal, earnest, brief and full of devotion. Every single clause in it, however, is to be found in Jewish prayers and sayings in the Talmud."

Rabbi Joseph Krauskopf, in his five discourses on "Jesus—Man or God?" wrote: "The following are supplications contained in the prayers of the rabbis of that age:

Our Father who art in heaven, hallowed and glorified be Thy name. May Thy unity be everywhere proclaimed, and Thy kingdom be established forever. Thine is the greatness and the power, Thine the glory and the majesty. May Thy will be done; what seemeth best in Thine eyes that do Thou do. Give us bread to eat and raiment to put on. Save us from the power of sin,

keep us from yielding to temptation. May the peace of Heaven be the reward of those who reverence Thee on earth.

Compare this prayer of the rabbis with the Lord's Prayer. What are the differences? What are the similarities?

The Episcopal prayer book

Have you ever looked inside a Christian prayer book? If you opened an Episcopal prayer book you would read at the beginning of the service: "The Lord is in His holy temple; let all the earth keep silence before him." This is also a hymn that is sung in synagogues and temples: "The Lord is in His Holy Temple. Let all the earth be silent now!"

Many other Christian prayers come from the Bible. For example:

Let the words of my mouth and the meditation of my heart, be always acceptable in Thy sight, O Lord, my strength and my redeemer.

There are prayers based on the Psalms, and prophets but there are also prayers that are different from Jewish prayers, such as "Grace be unto you, and peace, from God our Father, and from the Lord Jesus Christ."

Here is a typical Christian prayer, called *Te Deum Laudamus:*

We praise thee, O God; we acknowledge thee to be the Lord.
All the earth doth worship thee, the Father everlasting.
To thee All Angels cry aloud; the Heavens, and all the Powers therein.
To thee Cherubim and Seraphim continually cry,
Holy, Holy, Holy, Lord God of Sabaoth;
Heaven and earth are full of the Majesty of thy glory.

The glorious company of the Apostles
praise thee.
The goodly fellowship of the Prophets
praise thee.
The noble army of Martyrs praise thee.
The holy Church throughout the world
doth acknowledge thee;
The Father, of an infinite Majesty;
Thine adorable, true, and only Son;
Also, the Holy Ghost, the Comforter.

Thou art the King of Glory, O Christ,
Thou art the everlasting Son of the Father,
When thou tookest upon thee to deliver
man, thou didst humble thyself to be born
of a Virgin.

When thou hadst overcome the sharpness
of death, thou didst open the Kingdom
of Heaven to all believers.
Thou sittest at the right hand of God, in
the glory of the Father.
We believe that thou shalt come to be our
Judge.
We therefore pray thee, help thy servants,
whom thou hast redeemed with thy precious blood.
                  —*Book of Common Prayer,* p. 10

1. Are there any portions of this prayer
which might well be spoken by a Jew? Do
you recognize some of this prayer as also
being in the Jewish prayer book? How does
our prayer book translate the word *sabaoth?*
2. To whom does this prayer refer when
it uses the words apostles, prophets, martyrs,
Church, Holy Ghost? Do Jewish prayers ever
refer to prophets or martyrs?
3. What does the prayer mean when it
speaks of Christians being "redeemed with thy
precious blood"? Redeemed from what? Are
Jews in danger if they are not redeemed according to Christian standards? Is there anything from which Jews really must be redeemed by Jewish standards?

A collect for aid against perils

Here is another, shorter, prayer:

Lighten our darkness, we beseech thee,
O Lord; and by thy great mercy defend
us from all perils and dangers of this night;
for the love of thy only Son, our Saviour,
Jesus Christ. Amen.
                              —*Ibid,* p. 31

1. To whom is this prayer addressed?
Might Jews use this prayer, that is, all of
it except the last phrase? Almost all Christian prayers end with this phrase or a similar
one: "for the love . . . ," "for the honour of
. . .", "through our Lord . . .", "and this we
beg for Jesus Christ's sake," etc.
2. Why do almost all Christian prayers end
this way? Can a Christian pray without ending his prayer with a reference to Jesus as
the Christ? Would it be invalid for him to
leave it out?
3. Do Jews ever pray in the name of anyone? When we say: "Blessed art Thou, O
Lord, God of our fathers, God of Abraham,
God of Isaac, and God of Jacob," is that
the same as ending a prayer: . . . "in the name
of Jesus Christ, our Lord?"
4. Do Christians believe that God would
forgive them for their sins if Jesus had never
lived, never sacrificed himself? Do Jews believe that God will forgive Christians for their
sins if they come in sincerity, even though
they pray as though a man was God? Do
Christians believe that God will forgive Jews
for their sins if they come in sincerity, because they do not pray to be redeemed
through the power of the sacrificial blood of
Christ?

Many Christians pray in this way. From
the time of childhood they have been taught
about Jesus as Lord and the Son of God.
We haven't been taught that way. It is im-

portant for Jews and Christians to learn more about each other's religion, even though we may not believe the same way or think the same way. The more we learn about each other's religion, the more we begin to understand each other better.

THINGS TO DO

1. The students should borrow copies of the prayer books used by Catholics, Episcopalians, Baptists, Methodists and Presbyterians and bring them to class. Compare them in class and discuss how they are different, and how they are the same.

2. Compare the *Book of Common Prayer* used by Episcopalians with the Orthodox Jewish prayer book. Make a list of similarities and differences.

3. Compare *The Union Prayerbook* used by Reform Jews with the Conservative and Orthodox prayer books. How do they differ? How are they the same?

The Catholic prayer book (missal)

To you, Lord, I have lifted up my soul. My God, I put my trust in you, let me not be put to shame, nor let my enemies laugh at me; for none of them who wait on you shall be confounded.

O Lord, show me your ways and teach me
   your paths.
Direct me in your truth and teach me, for
   you are my God and my Salvation. For
   you I have waited all the day long.
Do not remember the sins of my youth;
   remember me according to your mercy,
   for the sake of your goodness, O Lord!
Glory be to the Father, and to the Son,
   and to the Holy Spirit.
As it was in the beginning, is now and ever
   shall be, would without end. Amen."

              —Saint Andrew Bible Missal

1. How does this prayer compare with Psalm 25:4–7?

2. Would this prayer be acceptable to a Protestant?

3. How much of this prayer would be acceptable to a Jew?

The Presbyterian prayer book

Our help is in the name of the Lord, who
   made heaven and earth.
O come, let us worship and bow down:
   let us kneel before the
Lord our Maker. For He is our God, and
   we are the people of
His pasture, and the sheep of His hand.

        —The Book of Common Worship
        approved by the General Assembly
        of the Presbyterian Church in the
        United States of America

1. Compare the first line of this prayer with Psalm 121, and the rest with Psalm 95:6–7.

2. Compare the next lines with the Alenu in *The Traditional Prayer Book* (Orthodox) and the Adoration in *The Union Prayerbook*.

The Methodist Hymnal

The Minister: O Lord, open Thou our lips.
The People: And our mouth shall show
   forth Thy praise.
The Minister: Praise ye the Lord.
The People: The Lord's Name be praised.
The Minister: Hear, O Israel, the Lord our
   God is one Lord:
   And thou shalt love the Lord thy God
with all thy heart, and with all thy soul, and with all thy mind, and with all thy strength.

              —Methodist Hymnal

1. Can you find the first two lines of the prayer in a Jewish prayer book?

2. How do the next two lines compare with the Barchu?

3. Where in a Jewish prayer book will you find an equivalent version of the last paragraph of the above selection? Where in the Jewish Bible will you find it?

4. Read through the Responsive Readings in your prayer book and make a list of how many are taken from the Jewish Bible.

The Orthodox Jewish prayer book

The Morning Service begins:

How goodly are thy tents, O Jacob, thy dwelling places, O Israel! As for me, in the abundance of thy lovingkindness will I come into thy house: I will worship toward thy holy temple in the fear of thee. Lord, I love the habitation of thy house, and the place where thy glory dwelleth. I will worship and bow down: I will bend the knee before the Lord my Maker. May my prayer unto thee, O Lord, be in an acceptable time: O God, in the abundance of thy lovingkindness, answer me with thy sure salvation.

—*The Authorized Daily Prayer Book*
by DR. JOSEPH H. HERTZ

1. Compare this prayer with Numbers 24:5, Psalm 26:8 and Psalm 69:14.

2. What words would you have to change to make this prayer acceptable to a Christian?

The Conservative Jewish prayer book

O Lord,
Guard my tongue from evil and my lips
  from speaking guile,
And to those who slander me, let me give
  no heed.
May my soul be humble and forgiving unto
  all.

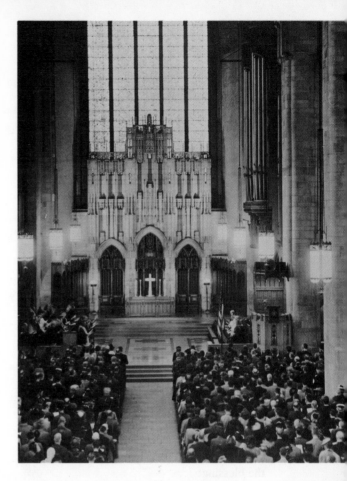

Members of thirty Christian communions joined in prayer at an ecumenical service in the University of Chicago Chapel.

Open Thou my heart, O Lord, unto Thy
  sacred Law,
That Thy statutes I may know and all Thy
  truths pursue.
Bring to naught designs of those who seek
  to do me ill;
Speedily defeat their aims and thwart their
  purposes
For Thine own sake, for Thine own power,
For Thy holiness and Law.
That Thy loved ones be delivered,
Answer us, O Lord, and save with Thy
  redeeming power.

May the words of my mouth and the meditation of my heart be acceptable unto Thee, O Lord, my Rock and my Redeemer. Thou who establishest peace in the heavens, grant peace unto us and unto all Israel. Amen.

—*Sabbath and Festival Prayer Book*
The Rabbinical Assembly and
The United Synagogue of America
Edited by MORRIS SILVERMAN

1. Would this prayer be acceptable to an Orthodox Jew?
2. Could this prayer be offered by a Reform Jew?
3. Could a Christian use this prayer in his worship service?

The Reconstructionist Jewish prayer book

In the Sabbath Morning Service, the blessing before the reading of the Torah is not the same as it is in the Orthodox, Conservative and Reform prayer books. This is the blessing:

Blessed be Thou, O Lord our God, King of the universe, who hast brought us nigh to Thy service and hast given us Thy Torah. Blessed be Thou, O Lord, giver of the Torah.

—*Sabbath Prayer Book*
The Jewish Reconstructionist
Foundation

1. How does this blessing differ from the usual blessing given before the reading of the Torah?
2. What does this blessing tell us about the Reconstructionist's belief that Jews are the Chosen People?
3. Make a study of what the Reconstructionist movement believes and how it differs from Orthodox, Conservative and Reform Judaism.

The Reform Jewish prayer book

O Lord, how can we know Thee? Where can we find Thee? Thou art as close to us as breathing and yet art farther than the farthermost star. Thou art as mysterious as the vast solitudes of the night and yet art as familiar to us as the light of the sun. To the seer of old Thou didst say: Thou canst not see my face, but I will make all My goodness pass before Thee. Even so does Thy goodness pass before us in the realm of nature and in the varied experiences of our lives. When justice burns like a flaming fire within us, when love evokes willing sacrifice from us, when, to the last full measure of selfless devotion, we proclaim our belief in the ultimate triumph of truth and righteousness, do we not bow down before the vision of Thy goodness? Thou livest within our hearts, as Thou dost pervade the world, and we through righteousness behold Thy presence.

—*The Union Prayerbook*

1. Do you think this prayer would be acceptable to all groups within Judaism: Orthodox, Conservative and Reconstructionist as well as Reform Judaism? Give reasons for your answer.
2. Analyze the prayer and explain what it teaches us about God and Jewish belief.
3. What does it mean when it says: "I will make all My goodness pass before thee"?
4. How can we through righteousness behold God's presence?
5. Would this prayer be acceptable to a Christian?

QUESTIONS FOR DISCUSSION

There is a quotation at the bottom of the church bulletin of the Country Club Christian Church of Kansas City, Missouri:

O God, make the door of this house wide enough to receive all who need human love and fellowship; narrow enough to shut out all envy, pride and strife. Make its threshold smooth enough to be no stumbling block to children . . . make the door of this house the gateway to Thine eternal kingdom.

1. Do you think those of the Jewish faith could accept this prayer?

2. What do you think Isaiah meant when he declared: "My house shall be called a house of prayer for all peoples"? (Isa. 56:7)

3. Where do you think it is best to pray: at home or in the synagogue? What does Judaism teach about public and private prayer?

4. Do you think that prayer can heal sickness? Are there ways that prayer can strengthen a person who is ill? Explain.

5. In *The Union Prayerbook* there is a prayer that reads: "Give us the grace to fulfill this mission with zeal tempered by wisdom and guided by regard for other men's faith."

What is the Mission of Israel?

How important is it in Judaism to have regard and respect for other men's faith?

6. In the Jewish tradition, prayer has been called "The service of the heart." What do you think this means?

7. The story is told of a father who listened to his son's prayers and suggested quietly: "Son, don't bother to give God instructions; just report for duty." What do you think the father meant?

8. The Talmud tells us that when Rabbi Eliezer was visited by his pupils during his last illness, they asked him for some final advice. He said, "When you pray always realize before whom you stand." This statement is often engraved over the Ark in the synagogue. Sometimes it says: "Know Before Whom You Stand." What do you think Rabbi Eliezer meant? What does this statement mean to you? How can it help you to pray and act reverently and sincerely?

THINGS TO DO

1. Look up in the *Universal Jewish Encyclopedia* the meaning of the *Kaddish* prayer. Write a brief essay on why this prayer has always been so important and sacred to the Jewish people.

2. Compare the English translation of the *Kaddish* prayer with the Lord's Prayer. What similarities do you find?

3. Read in Rabbi Freehof's book, *In the House of the Lord,* how the synagogue, as a house of prayer, came into being. Ask a Christian religious school teacher how the church, as a house of prayer, came into being.

4. Arrange for the class to visit a Quaker prayer service to find out more about "listening to God."

5. Recently there was an advertisement about a faith healer:

YOU'VE SEEN HER on television, read about her in the papers, now see her in person. REV. SISTER WILLIAMS—God sent. All prayers and healing free. Touch of her hand will heal you. REV. SISTER WILLIAMS has the God-Given Power to Heal by Prayer. Everyone welcome, white or colored, at REV. SISTER WILLIAMS' home. What you see with your eyes, your heart will believe. Are you suffering? Are you sick? Do you need help? Bring your problems to REV. SISTER WILLIAMS today and be rid of them tomorrow. REV. SISTER WILLIAMS invites you to her home. A free LUCKY CHARM WILL BE GIVEN WITH EACH READING. REV. SISTER WILLIAMS guarantees to restore your lost nature. Bring this card. Her prayers are FREE by donation. Open from 8 in the morning till 10 at night. Open all day Sunday. 519 Minnesota Ave., Kansas City, Ks. For information and directions call FA 1-7673.

Interview a rabbi, a minister and a priest and ask about their opinions of faith healers and faith healing.

6. In Chapter 6 of the Book of Isaiah, the prophet describes a vision or a dream that he had. Read this chapter carefully and then write an essay on the meaning of the verse: "Holy, Holy, Holy is the Lord of hosts; the whole world is filled with His glory." What is meant by holiness? How can prayer help us to live a life of holiness?

7. The following Christian prayer goes back to the year 451 c.e.; from the Council of Chalcedon:

Holy God,
Holy and mighty,
Holy and immortal,
Have mercy upon us.

In the Scottish Prayer Book there is this prayer:

Holy, Holy, Holy, Lord God of hosts.
Heaven and earth are full of thy glory.
Glory be to thee, O Lord most high.
Hosanna in the highest.
Blessed is he that cometh in the name of
  the Lord.
Hosanna in the highest.

How do these two prayers differ from Isaiah 6:3? Do they reveal any differences between Judaism and Christianity? What is the meaning of the word *hosanna?* Is there a difference in the Christian meaning of the word?

8. In some school systems children once said this brief prayer before drinking their milk:

God is great. God is good.
Let us thank Him for our food.

Do you think there is anything wrong with children saying such a prayer in the public schools? What are some objections? If the students are permitted to say it or not to say it, do you think it is proper for younger children to say this prayer? If there is a child of an atheist who doesn't believe in God and the child is told that he doesn't have to say the prayer, but the others say it, do you think this will affect the child in any way? Is it possible to work out something in the public schools so that Christians and Jews will learn about each other's religion? What are the advantages and disadvantages?

9. Write an essay on: "How prayer can help me become a better Jew."

10. Consider the following news item:

Vatican City (AP)—The official Vatican weekly yesterday approved the introduction of jazz into the newly-reformed Roman Catholic liturgy. It also endorsed decoration of churches with modern art.

Do you think jazz, modern music and interpretive dancing in the church and synagogue can make worship more meaningful?

SELECTED QUOTATIONS

Decalogue of the Art of Prayer

1. When you cannot pray with proper concentration, try your utmost to speak the words in a spirit of belief in their truth.

2. Let your heart hear what your mouth speaks if you wish to offer proper prayer.

3. The prayer of an individual is not heard unless he concentrates upon it, but the prayer of the many is heard, even if not all of them are wholehearted.

Orthodox Jewish males over thirteen still wear phylacteries, prescribed by Biblical injunction, at all morning prayers except on Sabbath and holidays.

4. Do not ask that God change the laws of nature for you.

5. Limit your request for your material need, but ask for all you wish in Torah and spirit.

6. Clothe the words of your prayers in grace; namely, pronounce them carefully and with sincerity. Would you mumble your words and ignore their meaning when addressing a superior?

7. Every word of your prayer is like a rose which you pick from its bush. You continue until you have formed a bouquet, a complete blessing. From them you form new bouquets of blessings until you have completed a wreath of glory unto the Lord.

8. Forget everybody and everything during your worship. Forget yourself and your needs. Forget the people of whom you have need. Turn not to the side of you to see who's near or far—not in back to observe latecomers. Then in truth you may be able to worship the Lord.

9. When you offer prayer, imagine yourself as one who is newly-born; without achievements of which to be proud; without high family descent to make you arrogant. Forget all proud dignity and self-esteem. Remember only the Creator.

10. Make every effort to pray from the heart. Even if you do not succeed, the effort is precious in the eyes of the Lord.

—NAḤMAN OF BRATZLAV

The Prayer of Peace

Lord, make me an instrument
  of Thy peace.
Where there is hatred, let me
  show love;

Where there is injury, pardon;
Where there is doubt, faith;
Where there is despair, hope;
Where there is darkness, light;
And where there is sadness, joy.
O Divine Master, grant that I
    may not so much seek to be
    consoled as to console;
To be understood as to understand;
To be loved as to love;
For it is in giving that we receive,
It is in pardoning that we are pardoned,
And it is in dying that we are born to
    eternal life.

—ST. FRANCIS OF ASSISI

The Modern Shema

Now hear this Israel:
The Lord our God is the Only One!
Blessed be His Kingship forever!

You shall love the Lord your God
With all your mind,
And with all the strength
Of your whole being.

And these words I command you today
Shall remain in your heart.

Repeat them:
Over and over
To your children.

Talk about them:
When you sit in your house,
When you travel,
When you lie down to sleep,
When you get up.

Wear them proudly;
Like an insignia on your shoulder,
Like a crown upon your head.

Write them:

On the doorway of your private dwelling.
And upon the entrance
To your courts of public law.

—RABBI SHAMAI KANTER

Do we need a mediator?

To find God (according to Christianity) man needs the mediator in the person of Jesus. This is of course the reason why Christians end their prayers with the expression, "through Jesus Christ, our Lord."

It is this answer which the Jew must reject with all the emphasis at his command. According to Judaism, there is no need for a mediator between God and man. Every man can always find Him, if he only seeks Him with all his heart (Deut. 4:29).

—EMIL L. FACKENHEIM

Making prayers come true

The British statesman, Gladstone, used to tell friends about a neighbor's little girl who really believed in prayer. When her brother made a trap to catch little sparrows, she prayed that it might fail.

Suddenly her face became radiant as she pondered the problem, and for three days she prayed hard. Her faith was so absolute that her mother asked one morning, "Julia, why are you so sure your prayer will be answered?"

Julia smiled. "I know that my prayer will be answered," she said, "because I went out three days ago and kicked the trap to pieces."

—*United Mine Workers Journal*

A Jewish prayer for all faiths

For the blessing of all and the hurt of none.
For the joy of all and the woe of none.
For the life of all and the death of none.

—*The Union Prayerbook*

Atomic power and soul power

After a few minutes of general conversation about a scientific problem, the man asked the scientist, Steinmetz, where we need the greatest emphasis in research today. Steinmetz thought a moment and replied that he considered it to be in the realm of the spirit. He said that when men turned over their laboratories to the study of God and prayer and spiritual forces, the world would see more advance in one generation than it has seen in the last four.

—A Temple Bulletin

What prayer teaches us

Where should one learn the eternal wisdom of compassion? The fear of being cruel? The danger of being callous? Where should one learn that the greatest truth is found in contrition? Important and precious as the development of our intellectual faculties is, the cultivation of a sensitive conscience is indispensable. We are all in danger of sinking into the darkness of vanity; we are all involved in worshipping our own egos. . . .

Everyone has a sense of beauty; everyone is capable of distinguishing between the beautiful and the ugly. But we also must learn to be sensitive to the spirit. It is in the Temple where we must try to acquire such inwardness, such sensitivity.

—PROFESSOR ABRAHAM J. HESCHEL

Grant us peace

As a result of discussion on prayer, a student in the Confirmation Class undertook a "revision" of "Grant us Peace," found in a Jewish prayer book:

Grant us the inspiration and ability to achieve world peace, Thy most precious quality, O Thou eternal source of inspiration, and enable Israel to be its messenger unto the peoples of the earth. Bless our world that it may ever be a stronghold of peace and unity. May contentment reign throughout the globe, health and happiness within every dwelling. Strengthen the bonds of friendship and fellowship among all the inhabitants of the earth. Plant virtue in every soul, and may the love of Thy name hallow every home and every heart. Praised be Thou, O Lord, who gives man the ability to achieve for himself the sacred quality of world peace.

SELECTED READINGS

BARTLETT, ROBERT MERRILL, *With One Voice*

FACKENHEIM, EMIL L., *Paths to Jewish Belief,* Chapter 8

FREEHOF, SOLOMON, *In the House of the Lord,* UAHC

————, *The Small Sanctuary*

HARNER, NEVIN C., *A Christian Faith for Youth*

JONES, JESSIE ORTON, *This Is the Way, Prayers and Precepts from World Religions*

WOLF, A., and GAER, J., *Our Jewish Heritage*

9

The Bible

DIGGING INTO THE PAST

In *The Bible As History,* written by Werner Keller, we read:

"Now the weight of gold that came to Solomon in one year was six hundred threescore and six talents of gold, . . ." (I Kings 10:14)

Doesn't it sound like a fairy tale?

Any man, even a king, about whom so much is told, is hard put to it to escape the charge of boasting. And any chronicler, telling such a story, easily gets a reputation for exaggeration. There are certainly stories in the Bible which are regarded by scholars as legends, such as the tale of Balaam the prophet and his talking ass (Num. 22) and the tale of Samson, whose long hair gave him strength (Judg. 13–16). But this most fabulous of all stories is really no fairy tale at all.

The archaeologists dug their way to the heart of the trustworthiness of these Solomon stories—and, lo and behold, Solomon became their unique showpiece.

When the "fairy tale" of King Solomon, as many still believe it to be, has been stripped of its frills, there remains a framework of sober historical facts. That is one of the most exciting discoveries of very recent times. It was only in 1937 that a wealth of surprising finds during excavations by two American expeditions produced proof of the truth of this Biblical story.

Packed high with the latest equipment, with drills, spades, and picks, and accompanied by geologists, historians, architects, excavators, and the photographer who is now indispensable on a modern expedition, a camel caravan left Jerusalem. Its leader was Nelson Glueck, who, like the others, is a member of the faculty of the American Schools of Oriental Research, and who later became the President of the Hebrew Union College–Jewish Institute of Religion.

Read Chapter 2 of *The Bible as History,* by Werner Keller, and explain how archaeology has revolutionized our thinking about the Bible. What has it done to your thinking?

Detectives of history

Once people thought that most of the stories were just ancient fables. Now we know that although some of the stories *are* ancient myths, most of the Bible is the history of the Jewish people with their laws, their writings and their religion. Many stories have been told about the reign of King Solomon. Through the archaeological discoveries of

Dr. Nelson Glueck and others, we now know facts about his reign that are even more impressive than the stories.

Dr. Glueck is not only a great Biblical scholar, but one of the greatest archaeologists of all time. Following clues in the Bible, Dr. Glueck came upon King Solomon's copper mines because he took seriously the description in Deuteronomy of the "land whose stones are of iron and out of whose hills thou mayest dig brass."

Just imagine! Digging down and coming across King Solomon's copper mines . . . discovering Eziongeber, King Solomon's port on the Red Sea.

Dr. Glueck is also one of the world's greatest authorities on the Negev, which is the southern part of Israel. He has found highways that the ancient Israelites used to travel, and ancient villages and wells dating back to the time of Abraham, and pieces of pottery that tell about the kings of Israel and Judah.

This sounds almost like a mystery story and, in a sense, archaeologists are detectives. They have to follow up clues and search for evidence. But they also have to be scientists and know about soil and rocks and be able to identify pottery and glass and relics by their color and their markings.

After many years of study and research, Dr. Glueck believes that most of the Bible is true. Not the myths and the fables, but the history is true. He once wrote that archaeology has demonstrated that the Bible can be believed and that most of what was meant to be history has been proved by archaeologists—and what's more, through Carbon 14 tests they can date many of the findings. Scientific tests show that most of the Biblical dates and stories are true.

Archaeology helps us find out how the Jewish Bible came into being, and the events and places in Scripture that can be proved factual. It also helps us learn more about the Christians' Bible, too, and what can be proved in their Bible and their history.

Almost every year there are new discoveries that tell us more and more about how the Christian religion developed, but because the history of the Jews is so much older, dat-

A modern reconstruction of Solomon's Temple, as shown in a model at Harvard University.

ing back almost 4,000 years, and because Christianity is based on Judaism, whenever new discoveries are made about Biblical events the Christian scholars are just as excited and interested as the Jewish archaeologists. What is more, we have to remember that some of the greatest discoveries in the archaeology of the Bible were made by the Christians.

You may be wondering: Did Noah ever live? Was there such a flood? Did ancient peoples really build a tower of Babel? Were the children of Israel slaves in Egypt? Did Moses ever live as a real person? Was David a real person and did he kill Goliath with a slingshot? Were the stories about prophets true? Did Jeremiah ever live, and Isaiah, and was Jonah swallowed by a whale? How did Christianity begin and was Jesus a real person who lived? Was Paul a Christian, a Jew, or both?

To answer these questions we have to do a lot more studying to find out what is historical and what is myth in the Bible. That's why we also have to learn more about the so-called New Testament in the Christian Bible, as well as our own Jewish Holy Scriptures.

WHAT DO YOU THINK?

1. Do you think that everything taught in the Bible is true?

2. Was the Bible revealed by God or written by man? Do you think there are parts of the Bible that are written by man, and parts revealed by God? What portions of the Bible do you think were revealed by God? Why do you think so?

3. Which of the following do you think were real people, and which were legendary: Adam, Cain, Noah, Abraham, Joseph, Moses, Joshua, Samson, Elijah, Saul, David, Solomon, Jeremiah, Isaiah, Jonah, Job, Esther, Jesus, Mark, Paul?

4. How can archaeology help us to find out which personalities really lived, and which personalities are legendary heroes in stories that teach us moral and spiritual lessons?

THE JEWISH BIBLE

In the early period of the Hebrews' history the Biblical tales were not written down, but were remembered and told from generation to generation. Later, however, the elders decided to put all the narratives into writing and preserve the written text so that no changes would be made at later times. There were many versions of the various Biblical tales and there were also new books being written about more recent Jewish history. Even later the rabbis had to set a limit to the number of books which would be included in the Holy Scriptures and they therefore had to choose between the various versions and also had to exclude most of the newer books. The Jewish version of the Bible contains only those books that the first century rabbis decided to include.

Those books which were not included are called the *Apocrypha*. Among them are the first and second books of the Maccabees, which tell the story of the war between Judah and Antiochus Epiphanes and of the celebration of Ḥanukkah. The Apocrypha is included in the Catholic version of the Bible, and also in the Lutheran and in some other Protestant Bibles.

The Jewish Bible may be divided into three parts. They are (1) *Torah,* the Law, or Pentateuch, or Five Books of Moses; (2) *Neviim,* the Prophets; and (3) *Ketuvim,* the Writings. All of these put together are spoken of as *TaNaKh.* Look at the first letter of the Hebrew words of each of the three divisions and you will see how this word came into being. Let us look at these three parts and see what books of the Bible are included in each part.

1. *The Torah*

The five books of the Torah are:
1. Genesis
2. Exodus
3. Leviticus
4. Numbers
5. Deuteronomy

2. *The Prophets*

These are divided into two parts:
1. Former Prophets
   a. Joshua
   b. Judges
   c. I and II Samuel
   d. I and II Kings

2. Latter Prophets
   Large books:
   Isaiah, Jeremiah, Ezekiel
   Smaller books: The Twelve—
   Hosea, Joel, Amos, Obadiah,
   Jonah, Micah, Nahum, Habak-
   kuk, Zephaniah, Haggai, Zech-
   ariah, Malachi

3. *The Writings*

Psalms, Proverbs, Job
The Five Scrolls or *Megillot:* Song of
Songs, Ruth, Lamentations, Ecclesi-
astes, Esther
Daniel, Ezra, Nehemiah, I and II
Chronicles

THE NEW TESTAMENT

The Christians' Bible is made up of what
they call "The Old Testament" and the "New
Testament." The Old Testament is the Jewish
Bible. The New Testament was so called because the Christians believed that it was God's
"new covenant" with the people in place of
the Hebrew Scriptures. The New Testament
tells us about the life and teachings of Jesus,
how Christianity came into being, and the
ideals and principles of Christianity.

The New Testament begins with the
Gospels. Gospel means "the good news." The
main theme is the appearance of the Messiah,
the Christ, Jesus, who is regarded as the
divine Son.

The Gospels tell the story of Jesus: his
birth, his life, his message, his crucifixion,
and his resurrection.

There are four Gospels, the Gospel—
According to Matthew.
According to Mark.
According to Luke.
According to John.

In the Gospel according to Matthew there
is the famous Sermon on the Mount. Read
Chapters 5 through 7 and write an essay
pointing out what you found to be most interesting and significant in the Sermon on the
Mount.

Read the story of the birth of Jesus in
Matthew, Chapter 1, verse 18, to the end of
Chapter 2. Compare with the story of the
birth of Jesus in Luke, Chapter 1, verse 5,
through Luke, Chapter 1, verse 80.

Matthew, Mark and Luke are called the
"Synoptic" Gospels. *Synoptic* means the
same point of view; general agreement. The
Gospel according to John is very different
from the other Gospels. John blames the
Jews much more than do the others for the
crucifixion of Jesus. John wrote in Chapter
3, verses 16 and 17:

God loved the world so much that he
gave his only Son, that everyone who has
faith in him may not die but have eternal
life. It was not to judge the world that
God sent his Son into the world, but that
through him the world might be saved.

What do you think John was trying to
teach? What is the attitude of Judaism toward
these teachings?

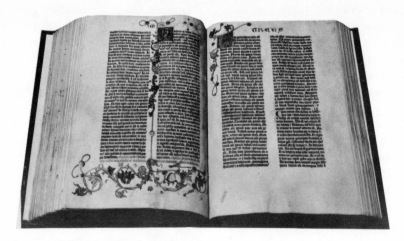

The Gutenberg Bible was the masterpiece of a fifteenth-century German printer, Johann Gutenberg. This richly illuminated copy is open at the beginning of the "New Testament." Gutenberg Bibles are now rare and valuable.

The Acts of the Apostles

Following the Gospels there is "The Acts of the Apostles," which tells the story of those sent forth to teach Christianity during the early years. The first part tells about Peter and the Church at Jerusalem, how Christianity developed and how the Church expanded. The second part tells about Paul and his mission of attempting to convert the Jews and the pagans to believe in Jesus. Peter, a disciple of Jesus, is regarded as the first Pope, or the Vicar of Christ.

As Jesus was a Jew, so Paul was a Jew. Originally, his name was Saul, and he lived in Tarsus. When he first heard about Jesus and those who followed him, he was very angry and resolved to travel to Damascus to punish the followers of Jesus. The New Testament describes what happened in Acts, Chapter 9:

While he was still on the road and nearing Damascus, suddenly a light flashed from the sky all around him. He fell to the ground and heard a voice saying, "Saul, Saul, why do you persecute me?" "Tell me, Lord," he said, "who you are." The voice answered: "I am Jesus whom you are persecuting. But get up and go into the city, and you will be told what you have to do." Meanwhile the men who were travelling with him stood speechless; they heard the voice but could see no one. Saul got up from the ground, but when he opened his eyes he could not see; so they led him by the hand and brought him into Damascus. He was blind for three days, and took no food or drink.

When he was restored to health and his sight returned, Saul changed his name to

Paul and determined to serve the new religion and convert the people to believe in Jesus as the Messiah and the only son of God. Paul's original intention was not to create a new religion, but to convince the Jews that Jesus was the Messiah. When he was not successful with Jews he turned to the non-Jews, the Greeks and Romans who worshiped pagan gods. It was Paul who made most of the significant changes in Christianity, such as the Sabbath on Sunday, the doing away with most of the laws of the Pentateuch, and the teaching that belief in Jesus as the Messiah is more important than observing the practices and laws of God's Torah.

The letters

Paul traveled from place to place teaching the people about Jesus as the Messiah. The letters that he wrote about his experiences, and the letters to the people and leaders form a large part of the New Testament. There are also letters that were sent to Paul, and letters written after he died. We find in the New Testament the following letters:

The Letter of Paul to the Romans
The First Letter of Paul to the Corinthians
The Second Letter of Paul to the Corinthians
The Letter of Paul to the Galatians
The Letter of Paul to the Ephesians
The Letter of Paul to the Philippians
The Letter of Paul to the Colossians
The First Letter of Paul to the Thessalonians
The Second Letter of Paul to the Thessalonians
The First Letter of Paul to Timothy
The Second Letter of Paul to Timothy
The Letter of Paul to Titus
The Letter of Paul to Philemon
A Letter to Hebrews

A Letter of James
The First Letter of Peter
The Second Letter of Peter
The First Letter of John
The Second Letter of John
The Third Letter of John
A Letter of Jude

The Book of Revelation

The New Testament ends with "The Revelation of John," sometimes called "Revelation." This important book of the New Testament deals with what is going to happen in "the end of days," at the second coming of the Christ, when the world as we know it comes to an end. Revelation discusses the apocalypse. An *apocalypse* is a vision of the future. John's vision foretells that the power of evil, namely Satan, who is now in control of this evil age is to be overcome by God. God will then create a new, perfect and eternal age that will be enjoyed by His righteous followers from among the living and the dead who will come to life.

Since Revelation is mainly concerned with the apocalypse, therefore most of the teachings are about the end of the world, death, and life in the age to come.

Read Revelation, Chapter 4, and compare with Isaiah, Chapter 6. What are the similarities? What are the differences?

In the story of the armies of the four horsemen of the Apocalypse we read:

This was how I saw the horses and their riders in my vision. They wore breastplates, fiery red, blue, and sulphur-yellow; the horses had heads like lions' heads and out of their mouths came fire, smoke and sulphur. By these three plagues, that is, by fire, smoke and sulphur that came from their mouths, a third of mankind was killed. The power of the horses lay in their mouths, and in their tails also; for their tails were like snakes, with heads, and with them too they dealt injuries.

—REVELATION 9:17

This is a vision of what the New Testament writer believed would happen in "the end of days," when the world comes to an end. What is your opinion of the vision of the four horsemen? How do you think Judaism would regard such a vision?

THE OLD AND THE NEW VERSIONS

The Hebrew Holy Scriptures have remained virtually unchanged for two thousand years. The discovery of the Dead Sea Scrolls allowed the scholars to prove this, for the differences between the ancient scrolls and our modern text were minimal.

Our Bible has been translated into just about every language of the world.

The English translation of the Jewish Bible that has been the most widely used was published by the Jewish Publication Society in 1916. Is is based on the 1611 English translation, but contains hundreds of more correct renderings from the Hebrew.

In 1962, the Jewish Publication Society printed a new translation of the Holy Scriptures called "The Torah—The Five Books

This famous painting by Titian is called St. John the Evangelist at Patmos. But it is not known whether the John who wrote Revelation was or was not the Saint of the Gospels.

of Moses." The language of this version is modern. It does away with archaic words and uses "You" instead of "Thou." There are other significant changes. Find some of these changes yourself.

1. Read Genesis 1: 1–5 in both versions and compare.

2. Read Exodus 15: 22–27 and compare.

Which version do you like better? What are your reasons? Which version is more scientific and accurate? What are your reasons? In praying to God, do you prefer to use "You" or "Thou"? Why?

THE ROMAN CATHOLIC BIBLE

The first Catholic Bible was St. Jerome's Vulgate, a Latin translation written about 400 C.E. The Douay Bible, the English version most accepted by Catholics, was translated 1582–1610. In 1952 the Catholics of the United States also accepted what is called the Confraternity Bible, a modern translation of the Vulgate.

WHAT DO YOU THINK?

1. If Jews, Catholics and Protestants have differing Bibles, do you think there is one true Bible? Do you believe that the Catholic and Protestant Bibles are also revealed by God? Are there parts of each Bible that help those of every faith to work together to build a better world?

2. How can an understanding of the Bibles of other faiths help us to understand each other, and contribute to a feeling of brotherhood?

3. Not all believing Jews accept every word of the Jewish Bible as true, or revealed by God. What is the attitude of a believing Protestant toward the Protestant Bible? Must he accept everything in it without questioning? What is the attitude of a believing Catholic toward the Catholic Bible? Must he accept everything in it as true?

4. Read the article on "The Apocrypha" in the *Universal Jewish Encyclopedia,* and write a paragraph or two telling why you believe the Catholics and Lutherans included seven books from the Apocrypha in their Bible.

5. Where will we find the story of Hanukkah?

6. Why is it not proper for a Jew to refer to his Bible as the Old Testament, but rather to call it Bible or Holy Scriptures or *TaNaKh?*

PUBLIC BURNINGS

The first English version of the Scriptures made by direct translation from the original Hebrew and Greek, and the first to be printed, was the work of William Tyndale. He met bitter opposition. The Church accused him of willfully perverting the meaning of the Scriptures, and his New Testaments were ordered to be burned as "untrue translations." He was finally betrayed into the hands of his enemies, and in October 1536 was publicly executed and his body burned at the stake. King Henry VIII tried to keep the Bible out of England and warned that anyone who read the Bible to himself or to another would be sent to prison for a month. Before this the Church had been even more strict. The laymen who owned a part of the Bible in any language risked flogging and even branding with a hot iron. Even the priests were not supposed to own a whole Bible. As recently as one hundred years ago Catholic priests in most of Europe were not allowed to possess an entire Bible.

It was the Protestants who fostered Bible translations and Bible reading. Martin Luther himself made a worthy translation into German.

THE OLD AND NEW VERSION
OF THE PROTESTANT BIBLE

The most widely known and used version of Holy Scriptures in English is the Protestant version called the King James Version, dated 1611. As it was written in the age of Shakespeare, it is not surprising that this translation should be majestic in language and in tone. It still has the greatest dignity of any English translation, but, alas, often its diction is unintelligible to modern ears.

To see the difference between the King James Version and the Revised Standard Version look up the verse in Isaiah 1:14.

What are the differences?

THE TEN COMMANDMENTS

Before we discuss the Ten Commandments, the Jewish version and the Christian version, give your answers to the following questions.

1. Do you think that Jews and Christians can accept the Ten Commandments without any dispute or differences of opinion? Why?

2. Would you favor or oppose public-school class sessions beginning with the reading of the Ten Commandments? Why?

3. What do you think of the Jewish organizations that oppose Bible reading, and the recitation of the Lord's Prayer and the Ten Commandments in our public schools?

4. Do you believe that opposition to religion in the public schools makes liberal Protestants and Jews appear to be atheistic and godless? State your reasons.

The Jewish version of the
Ten Commandments

There are slight differences in the Jewish version itself, as well as greater differences between the Jewish and Christian versions of the Ten Commandments. The Ten Commandments appear in two places in the Jewish Bible, and one is different from the other.

Turn to the Book of Exodus, Chapter 20. Write out these commandments. Then turn to Deuteronomy, Chapter 5, beginning with verse 6, and compare. Write out the differences between the two Jewish versions of the Ten Commandments.

The Protestant version of the
Ten Commandments

Compare the Ten Commandments in Exodus, Chapter 20, in the Jewish translation with that of the King James Bible. Write out the differences.

Compare the Ten Commandments of Exodus in the King James Version with that of the Revised Standard Version.

The Catholic version of the
Ten Commandments

Secure a copy of the Catholic Bible, which is called the Douay Version, and compare the Ten Commandments in Exodus 20 and Deuteronomy 5 with the Protestant King James Version. Then compare with the Ten Commandments in the Jewish Publication Society Bible.

We see that in the Catholic Version, the First Commandment is almost the same as the First Commandment in the King James Version and other versions:

King James Version: "Thou shalt have no other gods before me."

Newly Revised (Oxford) Protestant Version: "You shall have no other gods before me."

Catholic Douay Version: "Thou shalt not

have strange gods before me."
Jewish Publication Society Bible: "Thou shalt have no other gods before Me."
Jewish Publication Society, new translation of *The Torah:* "You shall have no other gods beside Me."

Which is the first commandment?

To Jews, the first commandment is not, "Thou shalt have no other gods before Me." Our first commandment is: "I am the Lord thy God Who brought thee out of the land of Egypt out of the house of bondage."

To help you understand why the Christians made our second commandment their first commandment, ask yourself a simple but obvious question: Our first commandment is, "I am the Lord thy God Who brought thee out of the land of Egypt out of the house of bondage." Then, what is the commandment? What are we to do, or what are we commanded not to do?

Here is a clue. The commandment is not expressed. It is implied, which means that we have to dig and search for the meaning.

God introduces Himself as the source and authority for these commandments. But what kind of a God does He declare Himself to be? The key word is "freedom."

God introduces Himself as the God of freedom, and the children of Israel are commanded to live in freedom, to love freedom and to make men free. If we were to put this in the form of a commandment how do you think we should word it?

What do you think? Write out your idea of the real meaning of the commandment.

What is the first commandment?

We can see why the Christians made our second commandment their first commandment. It seemed to them that our first com-mandment was just a statement of introduction. And until recently, neither Catholic nor Protestant Church appeared to be as concerned with freedom as were the synagogue and the Jews.

Now, if the Christians start with our second commandment, they should have one commandment fewer. But they have ten and not nine commandments. How did they find the other commandment?

Take a few minutes to read over the King James Version of the Ten Commandments and perhaps you will discover the answer. What is the second commandment of the Protestant version?

Now you see what they did. They took a part of our second commandment and made it into a third commandment in this way. Our second commandment begins: "Thou shalt have no other gods before Me," and then it goes on to state: "Thou shalt not make unto thee a graven image." What the Protestants did was to make this a separate commandment so that "Thou shalt not make unto thee a graven image" became their second commandment.

To summarize:

The Jewish first commandment is:
"I am the Lord thy God who brought thee out of the land of Egypt, out of the house of bondage.
The Protestant first commandment is:
"Thou shalt have no other gods before me."
The Jewish second commandment is:
"Thou shalt have no other gods before Me."
The Protestant second commandment is:
"Thou shalt not make unto thee any graven image."

Then, both the Jewish and the Protestant versions get together with the third commandment:

Thou shalt not take the name of the Lord they God in vain.

The Catholic version

The Catholic version begins with the Protestant first commandment, but continues with our third as its second commandment, "Thou shalt not take the name of the Lord thy God in vain." They do not make a commandment of the sentence banning graven images. To the Jews, this is considered part of the injuction against other gods. Catholics were obviously afraid that men might consider it a ban on the statues of saints and Mary that fill every Catholic church.

The Catholic numeration continues one behind the Jewish and Protestant versions, until it catches up by dividing our last commandment, "Thou shalt not covet," into two, and thus finishes with the same number. The Lutheran is the same as the Catholic except that it reverses the ninth and tenth commandments. The Lutherans follow the order of Exodus; the Catholics that of Deuteronomy.

When we started this discussion some of you may have believed that both Christians and Jews shared exactly the same Ten Commandments and that there was no reason why they shouldn't be recited in the public schools because they are exactly the same. Do you still feel that they are exactly the same?

THE HERITAGE WE SHARE

Even though we recognize the differences between Judaism and Christianity in beliefs, practices and in the teachings of the Bible, we must never forget that Jews, Catholics and Protestants share together a sacred Biblical heritage.

Truth isn't Jewish truth or Catholic truth or Protestant truth. Justice is the moral obligation of all peoples and all faiths. Mercy isn't the exclusive possession of any one religion. Love isn't the monopoly of the Jew, or Protestant or Catholic.

These are certain ideals and hopes that are part of the religious beliefs of many faiths. For example, think of Psalm 103:13–14—

Like as a father pitieth his children
so the Lord pitieth them that revereth Him.
For he knoweth our frame;
He remembereth that we are dust.

The belief in God's love for all His children was born among the Jews but it is shared now with our Catholic and Protestant brethren.

We think of the verse: "Love thy neighbor as thyself." Its origin is in the Jewish Bible, but it is also in the Catholic and the Protestant Bibles.

We should not forget that these ideas of God's love and mercy are also part of other religions too. We can find verses similar to this in the religion of Islam, in Hinduism and Buddhism. But right now we're discussing Judaism and Christianity, and that is why we seem to be neglecting the other religions.

What you should understand is that the Bible expresses hopes and great ideals that are shared by Jews, Catholics and Protestants as they work together to build a better world.

Both Judaism and Christianity teach that every human being is sacred. Psalm 8 reads:

When I behold Thy heavens, the work of Thy fingers.
The moon and the stars, which Thou hast established;
What is man, that Thou art mindful of him?
And the son of man, that Thou thinkest of him?
Yet Thou has made him but little lower than the angels,

Biblical injunctions of man's love for man brighten daily life. High school students of different faiths come to help at a home for elderly Jews in Riverdale, N.Y.

And has crowned him with glory and honour.

This is from the Jewish Bible, but this Psalm belongs to all men because it tells us of man who is the child of God. The teachings of the prophets of Israel summon all men to social action. The ideals of the prophets and psalmists as they call upon God's children to work together to build a better world, are these ideals really Jewish, or Catholic or Protestant? Don't they belong to all men and women everywhere?

Even the Lord's Prayer, or the Ten Commandments that we discussed, don't they, too, belong to all faiths? Doesn't the Sermon on the Mount speak to all people and all faiths? Certainly, we discussed differences, but are these differences so very important? Isn't the important thing for us to learn to practice and live by these teachings, not only as Jews or Catholics or Protestants, but as children of God?

Every time we read the magnificent utterance of the prophet, Malachi, we should say a silent prayer that God may help us to understand one another and love one another. Each of us should ask himself the same question that Malachi asked:

Have we not all one Father?
Hath not one God created us?
Why then do we deal treacherously
Every man against his brother?

1. When some Jewish leaders visited Pope Paul VI he said: "We have a common Bible and common God. Therefore, we pray together so that the Almighty guide, comfort and bless us." What did the Pope mean by a mon Bible and a common God?

2. Tell what you think Jesus meant when he said in Matthew 5:17–20: "Think not that I am come to destroy the Law or the prophets; I come not to destroy but to fulfill. For verily I say unto you, till heaven and earth pass away, one jot or one tittle shall in no wise pass away from the law, till all things be accomplished. Whosoever shall break one of these least commandments and shall teach men so, shall be called least in the kingdom of heaven; but whosoever shall do and teach them, he shall be called great in the kingdom of heaven. . . ." Did Paul contradict his own master? What is a jot and what is a tittle?

3. Read through the book of Jonah and explain what the last chapter teaches about God's love and mercy for all of His children. Explain what God meant in Jonah 4:10–11.

4. Which of the Ten Commandments do you think is the most important? Give your reasons.

5. God's love for the people of Israel is described in the second chapter of Hosea. Read the chapter and then discuss in class: Does God's love reach out to all His children: white, black, yellow and brown; Christian, Jew and Moslem?

6. There was one phrase which Jesus used a great deal, and that was "the Kingdom of Heaven." According to the fourth Gospel, John, Jesus meant an inward kingdom, born of the knowledge of the presence of God. What do you think John meant? What does the Kingdom of Heaven mean to you? What does Judaism mean by "the Kingdom of God on earth"? Look up the *Alenu* prayer in a traditional prayer book. What does it seem to mean? How can we help make this kingdom a reality?

1. The oldest Gospel text found is a papyrus fragment from St. John, 18:31–33 which probably dates from the early second century. Written in Greek, it was found in middle Egypt.

The oldest Hebrew text discovered so far is on leather fragments of a scroll which was dug from the dirt floor of a Dead Sea cave in 1952. The fragment dates back to 225–200 B.C.E. The text is from The First Book of Samuel.

Write an essay on "The Sources of the Bible," or "How the Bible Was Born."

2. Consult a Biblical encyclopedia and identify the Tyndale Bible, the Gutenberg Bible, the Geneva Bible and the Algonquin Bible.

3. Using a Biblical Concordance complete the following well-known quotations from the Bible:

a. Many are called, but few are . . .
b. A soft answer turneth away . . .
c. They shall beat their swords into . . .
d. Pride goeth before a . . .
e. The love of money is the root of all . . .

4. When St. Jerome did his Latin translation of the Jewish Scriptures and Apocrypha and the Christian New Testament, he divided the books into chapters and verses and he also arranged the books in the order in which they still appear in Christian Bibles.

The rabbis divided the books into chapters and verses just a little differently from the way Jerome did, so that sometimes if you look up a citation in our version of Scripture, you will find the desired line one or two verses away. The rabbis also arranged the

A Dead Sea Scroll, fragile with age, is carefully pieced together by the hands of a skilled archeologist.

books quite differently from the way Jerome did. Get a Christian Bible and compare its arrangement of the various books with that of our Holy Scriptures.

5. Compare: St. Paul's Epistle to the Romans, 12:20: "... if thine enemy hunger, feed him; if he thirst, give him drink: for in so doing thou shalt heap coals of fire on his head."

Proverbs 25:21: "If thine enemy be hungry, give him bread to eat; and if he be thirsty, give him water to drink. For thou shalt heap coals of fire upon his head, and the Lord shall reward thee."

What does this suggest to you? Why does Paul leave out the last phrase?

6. The miracles of Christ are described in Mark beginning with Chapter 1, verse 23. Do you think these miracles really happened? What are some miracles described in the Jewish Bible, especially in the stories of Elijah and Elisha? Ask your rabbi how he would interpret these miracles, and ask him to tell you whether or not miracles are important in Judaism.

7. Read through the Sermon on the Mount and try to find how many of the thoughts expressed are in the Jewish Bible. Ask your rabbi to help you.

8. One of President Lyndon B. Johnson's frequent quotations is from the second chapter of the Book of Isaiah. It begins: " 'Come now, and let us reason together,' saith the

Lord." Complete the quotation and discuss it in class. Why do you think this verse would have such appeal to President Johnson?

President John F. Kennedy's favorite passages from the Bible

It is of interest to note that of the six Bible passages which Bishop Philip M. Hannan of Washington, D.C. read at John F. Kennedy's funeral service on November 25, 1963, because they were the late President's favorite quotations from the Scriptures, five are from the so-called Old Testament:

JOEL 3:21. And it shall come to pass afterward, that I will pour out My spirit upon all flesh; and your sons and daughters shall prophesy, your old men shall dream dreams, your young men shall see visions.

PROVERBS 29:18. Where there is no vision, the people cast off restraint . . .

PSALM 127:1. Except the Lord build the house, they labor in vain that build it; except the Lord keep the city, the watchman waketh but in vain.

ISAIAH 40:31. But they that wait for the Lord shall renew their strength; they shall mount up with wings as eagles; they shall run, and not be weary; they shall walk and not faint.

LUKE 9:62. And Jesus said unto him, No man, having put his hand to the plow, and looking back, is fit for the kingdom of God.

ECCLESIASTES 3:1–8. To every thing there is a season, and a time to every purpose under the heaven:

A time to be born, and a time to die; a time to plant, and a time to pluck up that which is planted;

A time to kill and a time to heal; a time to break down, and a time to build up;

A time to weep, and a time to laugh; a time to mourn, and a time to dance;

A time to cast away stones, and a time to gather stones together; a time to embrace, and a time to refrain from embracing;

A time to seek, and a time to lose; a time to keep, and a time to cast away.

A time to rend, a time to sew; a time to keep silence, and a time to speak;

A time to love, and a time to hate; a time for war and a time for peace.

Why do you think John Kennedy liked these verses from the Bible? What do they mean to you?

SELECTED QUOTATIONS

The most democratic book in the world

The Bible has been the Magna Charta of the poor and of the oppressed. Down to modern times, no state has had a constitution in which the interests of the people are so largely taken into account; in which the duties, so much more than the privileges, of the rulers are insisted upon, as that drawn up for Israel in Deuteronomy and Leviticus. Nowhere is the fundamental truth, that the welfare of the state, in the long run, depends on the righteousness of the citizen, so strongly laid down. The Bible is the most democratic book in the world.

—THOMAS HUXLEY

The Bible

Unfortunately, the Bible is most often dressed in gloomy black. This misleads us into believing that the Bible is a sad, dismal book. Nothing could be further from the truth. On the contrary, its pages shine with the valiant and ofttimes thrilling deeds of daring men and brave women. It teaches wisdom for daily living. It sings of love and adventure. It records great sacrifices and noble faith. It is filled with beautiful and tender poetry. It is rich with stirring drama. It contains majestic and eloquent oratory. It describes battles and campaigns of swift-moving, shrewd military leaders. It recounts how the Jews conquered a land for themselves, built a glorious kingdom there, and played their role in the international world of that age. Across its pages march those inspired men—the Hebrew prophets—whose words still ring through the centuries, proclaiming that God wants men to live righteously and act Justly.

The Bible also exposes all the evil deeds men do that make life dark and sad with pain and sorrow. It does not hide the sins of the great. It does not excuse the mistakes of Israel. It records everything. The Bible is the story of a living exciting world, teeming with life and struggle, good and evil, defeat and triumph. This story the Bible tells with all its varied lights and shadows. Truly, it should be bound in the golden colors of the sun.

—MORTIMER J. COHEN,
Pathways Through the Bible

The books of the Bible

I am God's wonderful library.
I am always—and above all—the truth.
To the weary pilgrim I am a good strong
   staff.
To the one who sits in black gloom I am
   glorious light.
To those who stop beneath heavy
   burdens I am sweet rest.
To him who has lost his way
   I am a safe guide.
To those who have been hurt by sin
   I am healing balm.
To the discouraged I whisper
   a glad message of hope.
To those who are distressed by the storms
   of life I am an anchor, sure and steadfast.

To them who suffer in lonely solitude
   I am as a cool, soft hand
   resting on a fevered brow.
Oh, child of man, to best defend me,
   just use me.
I am the Bible.

—HAROLD D. HAHN

The meaning of Torah

The Jewish people survived because of Torah. We loved life and our sages knew that life needs directions, norms and discipline.

We denied ourselves that we might live. We had strength to chain the fury of passion, and the wisdom to escape quietism and negation. We placed ourselves under the yoke of Torah and rejoiced that we had mitzvot.

We survived because of Moses, who smashed the popular golden calf; because of Nathan, who pointed a finger at his king: "Thou are the guilty man"; because of Elijah who thundered at his king: "Hast thou killed and also taken possession?" There was Amos, who demanded: "Let justice well up as the waters and righteousness as a mighty stream."

—RABBI SOLOMON GOLDMAN

Understanding the Bible

The need to be ready to stand alone by pioneering convictions is the Reform concept of the Hebrew Bible. There are two possible points of view about the Bible. One is that it is the word of God. The other view maintains that it is the record of man's quest for the word of God. A world of difference divides the two opinions. When we insist that the Bible is the word of God, we are thrown into a heap of confusion within ourselves, toward our children, and toward the non-Jewish world in attempting to reconcile the irreconcilable magnificent portions of the Bible with myths and legends, the crudities and cruelties to be found in it. Whereas, if we see the Bible as the record of man's quest for the word of God, the perspective is clear, with man one moment reaching to heights of eternal visions, the next moment bogged down by his human frailties, limitations and passions.

—RABBI JOSEPH R. NAROT

The Sermon on the Mount

The Sermon on the Mount is not a repudiation of Judaism. It is much more nearly a culmination of its highest teachings in the field of morality. What Jesus said about peacefulness and forgiveness and loving one's enemies had already been suggested by great Pharisees like Hillel; and his warnings against love of possessions and outward show would have been agreed to by any good Jewish rabbi. The subject of the Sermon on the Mount is "righteousness," (Matt. 5:20) and at no point does it contain anything that would contradict the best in first-century Judaism.

—MARCHETTE CHUTE, *Jesus of Israel,* E. P. Dutton & Co., Inc.

Not to Destroy, But to Fulfill

Jesus once said, "Think not that I am come to destroy the law, or the prophets; I am not come to destroy, but to fulfill." (Matt. 5:17) He obeyed the Law in matters of ceremony and was faithful to its spirit, but in one sense at least he was not

a good Jew. He would not bow to accredited authority.

This had been true of all the great prophets of Israel. The only authority they would accept came direct from God, and from the point of view of the community nearly all of them had been troublemakers.

—*Ibid.*

The search for God

The Bible nowhere calls upon men to go out in search of peace of mind. It does call upon men to go out in search of God and the things of God. It challenges men to hunger and thirst after righteousness, to relieve the oppressed, to proclaim liberty to the captives, and to establish peace in the world.

—RABBI ABBA HILLEL SILVER

SELECTED READINGS

ALPER, MICHAEL, *Introduction to the Bible*

COHEN, MORTIMER, *Pathways Through the Bible*

GOODMAN, HANNAH GRAD, *The Story of Prophecy*

GWYNNE, J. HAROLD, *The Rainbow Book of Bible Stories,* pp. 229*ff.* (from the New Testament)

HEATON, E. W., *Everyday Life in Old Testament Times*

HEIDERSTADT, DOROTHY, *To All Nations: How the Bible Came to the People*

SCHWARTZMAN, SYLVAN D. and SPIRO, JACK D., *The Living Bible,* UAHC

SILVERMAN, WILLIAM B., *The Still Small Voice,* Chapters 3–7

SIMON, SOLOMON, and BIAL, MORRISON DAVID, *The Rabbis' Bible*

10

The Synagogue and the Catholic Church

The statue of the king

The Midrash tells of three enemies of a king who wanted to destroy the king's statue in a public place. They were very worried about the possibility of being discovered. To be discovered would mean death. So, they discussed how they could get away with it without being caught and punished. Finally one of the conspirators said: "We won't even touch the statue of the king. Instead we will dig around the foundation of the statue and so weaken it, that it will topple over and smash into pieces when we aren't even around." This they did. They so weakened the foundation that when people walked near the statue it toppled over and broke into many pieces.

The rabbis compared the foundation to the synagogue, and the statue of the king to God, the King of all kings. What does this Midrash teach us about the importance of the synagogue?

Moses and the broken Tablets of the Law

Another Midrash tells us that when Moses came into the camp and saw the children of Israel dancing and shouting as they worshiped the golden calf, he became so angry that the Tablets of the Law dropped to the ground and shattered into many pieces.

The rabbi asked, "Was it right for Moses to permit this to happen, no matter how angry he was?" After all, the Tablets of the Law were sacred.

They gave this explanation. When Moses saw the children of Israel breaking the Ten Commandments the letters of the commandments flew away, leaving only stones, so cold and so heavy that they dropped from Moses' hands. Without the words of God the tablets were only stone and were no longer sacred.

How would you interpret this to apply to a synagogue? What happens when the spirit of holiness leaves a synagogue, and the words and commandments of God are no longer obeyed? What really makes a synagogue a House of God?

The synagogue has been more than a building for the Jews. It has been a vital force in preserving the Jewish people and the Jewish faith.

WE SPEAK FOR JUDAISM

The word *synagogue* is taken from a Greek term which means "to assemble." Sometimes

Synagogues the world over reflect the architectural style of their time and place. This Sephardic Synagogue in Venice typifies Mediterranean architecture. It was built in 1584 and more elaborately ornamented in 1635.

a synagogue is also called a "temple." Whatever the name, it is our House of God and is very sacred to us.

There are other names for the synagogue. It is also called a *Bet ha-Keneset,* which means a House of Assembly, because Jews have always assembled in the synagogue not only for prayer, but for occasions of joy and sorrow, too. The Hebrew words for Sanctuary are *Bet ha-Mikdash.* It has another name, *Bet ha-Midrash,* "House of Study," because Jews have always used the synagogue as a school to study the Torah and the holy books. The sacred objects such as the Ark, the Menorah, the Eternal Light are called *K'lei Kodesh,* which means "holy utensils."

1. Imagine that you are part of a group called "We Speak for Judaism" and you are called upon to explain about the synagogue to Christian groups. How would you explain to a Christian group the meaning of:

a. The *Aron Kodesh* or Ark
b. The *Ner Tamid* or Eternal Light
c. The Menorahs or Candelabra
d. The Scrolls of the Torah

Where in the Bible are Jews commanded to keep a light burning perpetually on their altars? What does the *Ner Tamid* symbolize to us today?

When did the Jews first build the Holy Ark? How was it used in Biblical times? How is it used today? When and why did it become a part of the synagogue?

When was the Torah first put together in its present form?

What books of the Bible are in it?

What is the title of the person who writes the Torah?

When is the Torah read in the synagogue?

Where is it referred to in the Bible?

What did it symbolize in the past? What does it mean to us today?

2. Identify: *Parokhet, Yad, Keter, Ri-monim, Etz Hayim.*

3. Explain the meaning of the synagogue as a—

a. House of Prayer
b. House of Study
c. House of Assembly

4. Read in the *Universal Jewish Encyclopedia* how the synagogue came into being and its special importance after the Temple was destroyed, and then tell how you would explain this to a Christian group visiting your synagogue.

5. There are two kinds of Menorah, the seven-branched and the nine-branched. Why? Which is called a *Hanukkiyah* in Israel?

A CATHOLIC CHURCH SERVICE

Just as Christian groups visit synagogues and temples, so Jewish groups visit Catholic and Protestant churches. There are things we should know as we prepare to visit a Catholic church. Girls should wear hats or some kind of head covering. The boys will dress as they usually dress when we visit churches, with shirts, ties and jackets. Some money should be brought for the collection.

As for our conduct and behavior, we should just remember that we are in a House of God. We Jews respect all faiths and we show reverence in any House of God, whether it is our own or not.

This is what we will see when we enter a Catholic church.

The Roman Catholic Church

Some Catholic churches are built in the shape of a cross. Others are built in different shapes and in varying types of architecture. In the front, on the altar, there is a *tabernacle,* which looks like a box that is decorated. Inside the tabernacle there is a consecrated bread kept from other masses. This bread represents the body or the flesh of Jesus. Above the alter is a huge crucifix, depicting Jesus hung on the cross.

When the worshipers come into the church and see the altar in front of the sanctuary with the tabernacle and the altar table, they genuflect, that is they bend the knee to show their reverence for Jesus.

Usually there will be a censer with burning incense. Its use is taken from an ancient practice of the Jewish Temple when incense was thought to be pleasing to God.

The worshipers will make the sign of the cross with their right hand which is dipped in holy water to remind them of their baptism.

In most churches there are niches in the wall with statues of the saints. Larger and more beautiful than the other images will be a statue of the Virgin Mary. In front of the statues are burning candles which have been placed there by worshipers. People burn candles to the saints as a sign of respect and great reverence.

As we look around we will see containers of holy water blessed by the priest. This is thought to have the power of protecting the worshipers from evil.

During the mass, people look to the altar which is made of stone, and in some churches contains small pieces of bone, relics of the martyrs who have given their lives for the church. Two candles burn on the altar. We also see a cup called the *chalice.* The cup is of silver or gold and contains water with the wine that has been blessed. The wine represents the blood of Jesus. The service is conducted by a priest, who chants the ritual. He wears rich and colorful robes. He is usually assisted by altar boys. There is often a choir and organ as well.

When it is time for the worshiper to partake of the mass, the people come to the front and kneel at the altar rail. The priest partakes of both the bread wafer, called the *host,* and the holy wine. The worshiper receives only the wafer, which is placed on his tongue. This is known as "receiving Communion." Following communion, the priest washes his hands, reads from the Bible and offers prayers. Bells are rung from time to time as a signal for the worshipers to kneel on the special little benches built into the pews.

During the service, which once was entirely in Latin, but in which English is now more widely used, the worshipers are seated in a section called the *nave.* Most Catholic churches have side chapels, each with its own crucifix and altar. Sometimes the chapel is dedicated to a special saint. The chapels are used for smaller worship services and for private prayers.

QUESTIONS AND COMPARISONS

1. What is the difference between *tabernacle* as used in the Catholic Church and *tabernacle* as used in Judaism?

2. Compare the use of candles in a Catholic church with candles or lights used in Jewish worship.

3. What are the differences in the use of the chalice and the kiddush cup?

4. When is it customary to wash the hands in Jewish religious practice? According to Jewish tradition when are the hands washed during the Passover seder?

5. What is the Hebrew term for the "washing of hands"?

6. Why is it that synagogues do not have statues of great Jewish personalities?

7. Why is it that there are no "saints" in the Jewish tradition?

8. Compare genuflecting with the Jewish practice of bowing the head and bending the knee before the Holy Ark during the "Adoration."

9. The priest who officiates or celebrates the Mass drinks of the wine.

Are there customs in Judaism where only the rabbi or the cantor will drink of the wine during the service?

Catholics believe in saints. Saints are men and women who are supposed to have done great and heroic deeds for God and their faith and have gone to Heaven. They have been *canonized,* or officially regarded as saints. It sometimes takes a hundred or more years for the investigation by the Church to be completed, and they are beatified and canonized and declared to be saints. People burn candles to them and think about their sacrifices and their lives with the hope that they may follow their holy example. They also pray to the saints to plead for them to God. There are many saints who have special powers. People offer prayers to the particular saint they think may help them. Every Catholic chooses a patron saint, often the saint on whose day the worshiper was born. Also, various trades and professions have their patron saints, as do cities and towns. On the town's "saint day" there are great parades and gala festivities.

The Virgin Mary

The Catholic Church reveres Mary as the Mother of Jesus. Jesus is regarded as the only son of God. According to Catholic belief, Mary did not become pregnant as other women do. A miracle took place and she became with child through the Holy Ghost. The Holy Ghost means "the Holy Spirit," which is part of the Trinity. The Trinity is made up of God the Father, Jesus the Son, and the Holy Ghost. This means that God is one in three parts.

Catholics believe that the Holy Mother Mary is very close to God and that when they pray to her she carries their prayers to God. Mary dwells in Heaven in complete bodily form. Because she is the Mother of the Lord,

Jesus Christ, she is considered holy beyond words. Most Catholic women pray to her rather than to Jesus or God as they think that she understands the troubles of a woman better.

The priests

Priests are called "father." Sometimes a priest is honored by becoming a Monsignor.

The Church as a whole has what is known as a *hierarchy.* This means a chain of command not unlike that of an army. Each separate church has its priests, one of whom is in command. He is called the *pastor,* though all priests are addressed as "father."

In charge of a large group of churches is a bishop, appointed by the Pope, who is himself the bishop of Rome. Over the bishops there are archbishops. Some of the archbishops and bishops are also raised by the Pope to be cardinals. The College of Cardinals, as it is called, is the supreme legislative body of the Roman Catholic Church. Each priest when he is ordained takes a vow of obedience to his superiors and even the cardinal must obey the orders of the Pope.

When a Pope dies his successor is elected by the College of Cardinals.

All priests also take a vow of celibacy, which means that they will never marry. In recent years, some liberal priests have requested the Pope to remove this requirement from priests and allow them to marry as other men do. They point to the Greek Orthodox Church in which priests are allowed to be married. However, in the Greek Orthodox Church married priests can never rise to be bishops or archimandrites or metropolitans, the higher ranks within their hierarchy.

Monks and nuns

The Roman Catholic and Greek Orthodox Churches also have monks and nuns who

St. Patrick's Cathedral in New York City echoes the Gothic architecture of medieval Europe, with delicate towers pointing heavenward.

take holy vows. In both churches, neither nuns nor monks may marry. They also take vows of poverty and of obedience to their superiors. Some of them spend their lives at prayer; almost every waking moment is spent praying. Others are very useful to society, serving as teachers or nurses and doctors, or as missionaries in Africa or Asia. And there are some who keep themselves occupied as farmers or housekeepers and cooks, but do so for the monastery or convent they serve, and without any pay.

Nuns and monks have no priestly duties, and they cannot say the Mass or hear confession as priests do.

Some priests, too, belong to holy orders, such as the Jesuits, and do not take care of churches and congregations, but spend their lives as teachers or missionaries, or workers and managers within the Church's administration.

Confession

All priests hear confessions. In the church there are confession booths. The priest is not supposed to see or know the identity of the one who makes confession. First the Catholic who comes to confess must examine himself and think about his sins. He then makes confession to the priest who gives him a *penance,* which means that he has to make a contribution to the church or a charity, or say prayers or do something to atone for his sins. The priest then grants *absolution,* or forgiveness.

According to Judaism it is only God who can forgive sins, not priests or rabbis or ministers. Catholics, however, believe that priests can forgive sins. If a Catholic does not confess a sin, it remains as a stain on his soul. After he dies, he will have to bear punishment for any unforgiven sins.

When priests forgive sins, they act in behalf of the Church and Christ. Priests have been made holy through ordination and are

not like ordinary men. As for telling what they heard in confession, there is what is called "the seal of confession," and no priest would ever reveal what has been told to him. This would be a terrible sin.

Vestments

The priest wears around his neck something that looks like a *Tallit.* They call it a *stole.* The garments or the robes they wear are called *vestments,* and are very much like the garments worn in ancient Rome. Each vestment symbolizes an act of preparation for worship. Different colors are worn at different seasons. The same color will be shown on the altar and hung over the tabernacle. White is the most usual. Black is used on Good Friday when the Church mourns the crucifixion of Jesus. Certain colors are worn for special occasions. The *Missal,* the priest's book, gives all the directions as to what color vestment to wear on each occasion, as well as all the special prayers for each day of the year.

Baptism

In the Catholic Church there is always a baptismal font. Catholics believe that baptism is the first sacrament and that it is essential to be baptised to be saved and go to Heaven. When the infant is baptized he receives his Christian name. Adults, however, may be baptized too. Water is poured on the head of the individual in the name of the Father, the Son and the Holy Ghost. This symbolizes the resurrected life, and the washing away of the original sin in Adam. With baptism, the individual is united with the Church, which is the Body of Christ. He has now received the grace of God and is eligible to go to Heaven. Every sin removes him from the state of grace, but the priest's absolution after confession restores it.

Nineteenth-century nuns were distinguished by elaborate habits, typical of the time. Below, a modern nun, Sister Paul, also a doctor, enjoys a week end visit with friends at the convent.

QUESTIONS AND COMPARISONS

1. How do you think Catholics explain offering prayers to Mary and to saints when they say they, too, believe in one God? In Judaism, is it ever proper to pray to Moses or the prophets or great rabbis? Why not?

2. What is your reaction to the Catholic worship of Mary as the Mother of God? How would Judaism react to the Catholic belief that a miracle took place when Mary became pregnant with Jesus? How does Judaism react to the idea of someone being in Heaven in complete bodily form?

3. Compare vestments with the *Tallit*. Explain the religious significance of the *Tallit*.

4. There is confession in Judaism as well as in Catholicism. During the Day of Atonement service, this confession is called *viddui*. To whom does the Jew make confession? How is he forgiven for his sins? Why it is that rabbis do not have the power to forgive sins? When Jews tell rabbis their troubles and problems, is this regarded as confession?

How does it differ from confession in the Catholic Church?

5. How did the idea of baptism come from Judaism? How does immersion in a *mikveh* differ from Catholic baptism?

6. In Catholic baptism there is the washing away of the original sin of Adam. What is original sin according to Catholics? Read Genesis, Chapter 3, and describe what original sin was according to the Bible. Do Jews believe in original sin today?

7. What do you think the Catholics mean when they say that the Church is the Body of Christ? How would you compare this with the Jewish view of the synagogue?

CHRISTIANITY: THE DAUGHTER RELIGION

Sometimes we forget that Judaism is the mother religion and Christianity is the daughter religion. The idea of the church came from the synagogue, just as the idea of the priest from the rabbi, and many of the church observances are derived from Judaism.

We have to remember that the earliest Christians were once Jews and broke away from the mother religion. Paul, the apostle, a man of amazing energy and organizational ability, was as we have seen, originally a Jew. He helped found Christianity, but until he was converted at Damascus he is supposed to have been an observing and loyal Jew. Paul never knew Jesus. Jesus had died before Paul began his work, but he believed in Jesus and tried to convince the Jews that Jesus was the Messiah, the only begotten son of God.

When the Jews refused to accept Jesus, Paul and his friends separated from Judaism to create a new religion based on the belief in Jesus as the Messiah. Paul traveled widely and converted many of the pagans to the belief in Jesus. These people were known as *Gentiles,* or non-Jewish Christians, as compared with the early Jewish Christians.

In time, Christianity became a combination of Judaism and Greek practices and ancient beliefs. Many of these beliefs were taken from what is called "mystery" religions of the Greek culture. Christianity became a separate religion, even though Jesus was a Jew and all the original followers of Jesus were Jews, too.

The Jewish Christians separate from Judaism

To understand how Christianity became a separate religion we must also understand that when Paul tried to convert the pagan people to Judaism, he found it very difficult because the pagans believed in many gods, and it was almost impossible for them to believe in the one God of Israel, who could not be seen. What is more, the Jewish practices of circumcision and observance of the dietary laws discouraged other people from accepting Judaism.

We know that around the late 40's of the Common Era, Paul worked and taught in communities of the Mediterranean world. He organized small groups and taught them about Jesus as the Messiah.

Soon Paul's work met with ever-increasing success. More and more people from the Greek world joined his Christian groups and accepted the belief in the rebirth of Jesus, and that Jesus was more than a man, the true son of God.

The Jewish authorities in Jerusalem were at first irritated with Paul and then they became angry. Paul told the Gentile-Greek Christians that they didn't have to observe all the religious laws of the Torah. Moreover, he taught religious beliefs that were very different from the beliefs of Judaism.

He did not require his disciples and those who belonged to his "groups" to keep the *mitzvot,* the good deeds ordained by the Torah. When Paul taught that people could become saved from Hell by believing in Jesus, and that human beings who did not believe in Jesus were unclean and sinful and "lost" and "damned," the Jewish leaders in Jerusalem accused him of being a heretic. This did not stop Paul.

It soon became clear that Paul was teaching and advocating a new religion and that he no longer required "the laws of Moses," but only faith in Jesus Christ. Those who believed as he did soon withdrew from synagogue life. They insisted that their religion of the Messiah was the "new" revelation of God, and that Judaism was the "old." The "old" religion was simply to prepare the way for Jesus. Now there was no longer a need for Judaism.

Believing and doing

The Jews denied vigorously that this was so, insisting that faith, whether in Jesus, or in God, isn't enough. Man must show his love of God by "doing" and not just by "believing." Good deeds, *mitzvot,* are essential. What is more, the Jews felt that the worship of Jesus was a betrayal of the belief in the one true God. How can man be considered totally sinful and unclean as Paul said, they asked? Man is created in the image of God and is sacred. No, the Jews did not need Jesus. They had God to teach them His ways.

By this time, the advocates of each religion were arguing with each other, claiming that the others were wrong. Soon there was a division, and by the time that Jerusalem was destroyed by the Romans in the year 70 C.E., the separation of Christianity from Judaism had become definite.

Before long the Christians had their own Bible, their own beliefs, their own prayers, their own practices and observances and Sabbath and their own church where they worshiped their own way. There were two different religions. The daughter religion, Christianity, went its own way, and developed new practices and beliefs. The mother religion still kept the laws of Moses, the belief in one God, and the traditions that their fathers had respected for a thousand years.

Sometimes we ask ourselves: "Imagine what would have happened if instead of Christianity becoming the world religion, Judaism had become the world religion. What would have happened if Christianity had never come into being?"

These are fascinating questions and we could speculate about them for a long time, but right now we should think of Judaism and Christianity, each with its own ways, differing and yet sharing much in common.

We should know this background of the origins of Christianity so that we can understand better how the church came from the synagogue, and realize how much Christianity has borrowed from Judaism.

When the Christians separated from the Jews, they first organized the Catholic, or "universal," Church later formally split into Eastern and Western divisions. Then just as the Christians broke away from Judaism, a group of Christians broke away from the Catholics and called themselves "Protestants." As we know, this didn't happen until Martin Luther and the Reformation in Germany in the sixteenth century. That is another fascinating story that we will soon consider.

THINGS TO DO

1. Visit a Catholic church with your class and then compare the church with the synagogue.

2. Write an essay on the life and teachings of Paul.

3. Discuss in class the doctrine of "the infallibility of the Pope." The word *infallibility* means without error or fault. Catholics do not believe the Pope can do wrong, but Catholics

do believe that the Pope is preserved by God from leading the Church into error on religious matters. Catholics must listen to the Pope when he makes pronouncements on matters of faith or morals. Everything that the Church teaches as infallible doctrine, a Catholic must accept. How is this idea of infallibility regarded in Judaism? Do you favor having a Jewish pope with authority over Jews? Discuss the advantages and disadvantages of such a Jewish pope.

4. Identify and tell about the teachings of St. Augustine, Thomas Aquinas, and Ignatius of Loyola.

5. Read the article, "What is a Catholic?" in Leo Rosten's *Religions in America,* and summarize it in an essay.

6. Look up the meaning of *confirmation* in the Catholic Church. Compare Catholic confirmation with Jewish confirmation and Bar Mitzvah.

7. The word *church* comes from the Greek word *curios,* or *Kyrios,* which means "Lord." The word *synagogue* comes from the Greek *synago,* "to bring together." The word *temple* is from the Latin "templum." Discuss in class whether you think religious unity would be promoted if Christians and Jews all used the same name for their house of worship.

8. Look up the description of the building of the Temple of Solomon in I Kings, Chapters 5–7 and II Chronicles, Chapters 2–6, and write an essay describing the appearance of the Temple and what it contained.

9. One of the oldest synagogue inscriptions found in Palestine, written in Greek and dating from the years preceding the destruction of Jerusalem in the year 70 C.E., defines the purpose of the synagogue as a place of religious education and of welfare:

Theodotos, son of Bettenos . . . built the synagogue for the reading of the Torah and the teaching of the commandments,

furthermore, the hospice, chambers and water installation for lodging of needy strangers.

—DAVID JACKSON, trans.

Discuss in class whether this inscription indicates the purpose and the function of the synagogue.

10. Look up in the *Encyclopedia Britannica* the article on Mithros. Mithros was one of the gods of the Greek "mystery religions," and many of the holidays and much of the church service of the Christians were borrowed from this ancient pagan faith. Write an essay which lists these borrowings and how they were altered to fit the new religion.

QUESTIONS FOR DISCUSSION

1. A nineteenth-century pope, Pius IX, wrote: "It is to be held as of faith that none can be saved outside the Apostolic Roman Church . . . but, nevertheless, it is equally certain that those who are ignorant of the true religion, if that ignorance is invincible, will not be held guilty in the eyes of the Lord." Does this mean that Catholics believe that theirs is the only true religion and that a person has to be a Catholic to be "saved"?

2. An authority on the Catholic religion wrote: "Catholics believe that Satan [the leader of the fallen angels] and his cohorts are pure spirits with an intelligence of a very high order and a will which is . . . bent on evil. The Devil and the other fallen angels can tempt and torment men. . . ." What do you think of this statement? What do you think is the attitude of Judaism to the idea of a devil?

3. Catholic priests do not marry. Do you think rabbis could serve more adequately if they were not permitted to marry? Why do you think the Catholic Church does not permit priest or nuns to marry?

4. The Catholic Church does not approve of divorce. What is the attitude of Judaism toward divorce?

5. How do you think religion can help toward a stable home and lasting marriage?

SELECTED QUOTATIONS

The Pope

The spiritual head of Roman Catholicism is, of course, the Pope, and he presides over the "College of Cardinals," who are presently seventy-five in number.[1] Cardinals are principally bishops and archbishops, though there are some who are simply priests, and they are appointed by the Pope, largely for the tasks of Church administration in Rome. When a pope dies, it is the College of Cardinals which selects his successor.

—MILTON G. MILLER and
SYLVAN D. SCHWARTZMAN,
Our Religion and Our Neighbors

Four distinctive marks

The Catholic Church claims four distinctive marks: it is *one* (in doctrine, authority and worship), *holy* (perfect observance of its teachings leads inevitably to sanctity), *catholic* (it is unchanging in its essential teachings and preaches the same gospel and administers the same sacraments to men of all time in all places), and *apostolic,* (it traces its ancestry back to the Apostles and, like them, carries the message of Christ to all, regardless of race, nationality, station or class).

—LEO ROSTEN,
Religions in America

[1]This number was increased to 120 in 1967 by Pope Paul VI.

The Gloria

In many Masses, Catholics say the prayer called the Gloria. This prayer begins with the song of the angels on the first Christmas. The worshipers thank god for His great glory, to show their happiness that Christ has come and has made all Christians brothers and sisters.

Priest: Glory to God in the highest.
People: And on earth peace to men
    of good will.
    We praise you. We bless you.
    We worship you. We glorify you.
    We give you thanks for your great glory.
    Lord God, heavenly King,
    God the Father almighty.
    Lord Jesus Christ, the
    only-begotten Son.
    Lord God, Lamb of God,
    Son of the Father.
    You, who take away the sins of the
    world, have mercy on us.
    You, who take away the sins of the
    world, receive our prayer.
    You, who sit at the right hand of the
    Father, have mercy on us.
People: Holy, holy, holy Lord God
    of Hosts.
    Heaven and earth are filled
    with your glory.
    Hosanna in the highest.
    Blessed is he who comes in the name
    of the Lord.
    Hosanna in the highest.

At the end of the great prayer which consecrates the gifts, the priest raises the host and chalice together, showing that all are surrendering themselves to the Father with Christ. As proof that this is the desire of every member of the family, they all join in saying together the end of this great prayer.

Priest . . . per omnia saecula saeculorum.
   [forever and ever]
People: Amen.

—Catholic Mass

Our greatest citadel

For the Jew can continue to live only when he holds fast to his books, his ideals, his cultural heritage, his Synagogue. Whatever unity we maintain, whatever worth we possess, whatever hopes are ours are all dependent upon the extent of our devotion to our greatest citadel, the Synagogue.
                    —*The American Jewish Outlook*

Let them make me a sanctuary

When God said to Moses: "Let them make me a sanctuary that I may dwell among them (Ex. 25:8), Moses answered, "Who can do so? Is it not written that your presence fills heaven and earth; the heaven is Your throne and the earth is Your footstool." Then God said, "Ye are the children of the Lord Your God, and I am your Father (Deut: 14:1). Therefore make a house for the Father according to your capacity that He may dwell near His children."

Where is God to be found? He is there where he is asked to enter.

—The Midrash

SELECTED READINGS

FITCH, FLORENCE M., *One God*, section on Catholicism

FREEMAN, GRACE R., *Inside the Synagogue*, UAHC

GAER, JOSEPH, *How the Great Religions Began*

GILBERT, ARTHUR, *Your Neighbor Worships*

LEVIN, MEYER, and KURZBAND, TOBY K., *The History of the Synagogue*

MILLER, MILTON G., and SCHWARTZMAN, SYLVAN D., *Our Religion and Our Neighbors*

11

The Synagogue and the Protestant Church

THE WRESTLING MATCH

In the book of Genesis we read about Jacob wrestling with an angel (32:25–33). In Greek mythology we read about another wrestling contest. The story is told of Antaeus, the son of Mother Earth and the monarch of Lybia, who was a huge man, famed for his strength. Even the Greek gods were afraid of him, and so they called in Hercules to wrestle with him and destroy him. Hercules and Antaeus engaged in combat and wrestled to "the death." Every time it seemed that Antaeus was about to be defeated he managed to touch the soil, which was the source of his great strength, and he fought on with renewed power. Hercules noticed this and so he lifted Antaeus high above his head, above the soil, the source of his strength, and Antaeus' strength ebbed and thus Hercules was able to defeat him.

This is a mythical story told by the Greeks, and yet there is a lesson here that applies to the story of the synagogue in Jewish history. In every age, whenever the Jews deserted the synagogue or were forced away from the synagogue, they became weak. No matter how great the persecution, whenever the Jews turned to the synagogue, they found renewed strength to struggle and remain alive and steadfast in their faith.

How do you think the synagogue can give strength to modern Jews to fight against enemies such as injustice, prejudice, hatred, pessimism and despair?

Antaeus found new strength when he touched his mother, the earth. How can the synagogue help you to find new strength to be just, kind, merciful, truthful and honest?

What do you think would happen to Judaism, Jewish life and the Jewish people if we didn't have the synagogue today?

THE PROTESTANT CHURCHES

Just as the Catholic churches used the synagogue as a model, so we find that when the Protestant churches came into being they, too, followed many of the patterns of the synagogue. (Remember, Episcopalian churches are more like Catholic churches, even though their members are generally counted as Protestants.)

When the people enter most Protestant churches they do not genuflect, as do the Catholics in their churches, but walk directly to the pews. The Protestant church is usually simply constructed with no niches and no statues of saints. In the front there is an altar table with candles on either side. Above the altar there will be a large but simple cross Sometimes beautiful stained glass windows depict various events in the life of Jesus.

There are two lecterns, one to the right of the altar and one to the left. On one lectern there is a large Bible. The other lectern is where the minister gives the sermon.

With the organ prelude the choir comes down the aisle singing a hymn. The choir is followed by the minister, who takes his place before the altar. He wears a ministerial robe. Sometimes he wears a white or red or green stole. The stole looks like a small *Tallit*.

Twenty-nine bishops marched in this processional at the time of a Convention of the Protestant Episcopal Church.

The service continues with a hymn, then responsive reading from the psalms, praise to God, called the Doxology, and readings from both the Old and the New testaments. After the collection is taken there is another hymn and then the minister preaches his sermon. After the sermon there is a solo, another hymn, and the choir marches to the rear of the church with the minister. The minister gives the benediction and then the service is over.

Protestant churches have no confessionals as do Roman Catholic churches. Protestant ministers do counseling, and people often confess their sins and tell the ministers their troubles, but the ministers do not have the power or the authority to forgive sins.

Baptism

In Baptist churches there is a deep baptismal font behind the altar. The minister dresses in waterproof garments and baptizes the person by what is called total immersion. Baptists do not baptize infants, for they say that the person must be old enough to understand what is involved and make a serious commitment for himself. However, until the commitment is made and the person baptized, the child is tainted by original sin and cannot hope to enter Heaven. In rural areas, baptism will be in a lake or river or even a swimming pool.

Methodists baptize infants, though not exactly the same way as Catholics. They believe that Jesus said, "Suffer the little children to come unto me, and forbid them not, for of such is the Kingdom of God." That is why they feel that the baptism of little children is proper.

There are many different ways of baptizing. In some churches there is baptism by sprinkling. In others, by pouring water. In some, a wet wash cloth is passed over the baby's head very gently.

Communion

Protestants believe in communion but not always at every service. The "Supper of the Lord" is supposed to be the sign of the love which Christians ought to have for each other.

Different Protestant churches observe communion in different ways. In the Mass, Roman Catholics believe that the bread, when blessed, *is* the Body of Christ and the wine, when blessed, *is* the Blood of Christ. Lutherans believe that when the bread and wine reach the stomach they are transformed into the flesh and blood of Christ. Most Protestants believe that the bread and wine are symbols. Therefore, to them the body of Christ is taken only in "a heavenly and spiritual manner."

When liberal Protestants have communion service, ushers pass a tray of little cups of wine or more often grape juice and pieces of bread and each worshiper takes Communion for himself. In the Lutheran church the worshipers kneel at the altar rail and receive both the bread and the wine. The minister places the wafer on the tongue, and each one takes the small vial of wine for himself. Only those who have been confirmed may take communion. You see that Protestants observe the Lord's Supper or Communion in different ways.

The Protestant Reformation

We may wonder how the Protestants came into being. Once a group broke away from Judaism and became Christians. Then the Christians were divided into Roman Catholic, Greek Orthodox, and many smaller sects. Then the Protestants broke away from the Roman Catholics. How did this begin?

On October 31, 1517, a priest named Martin Luther nailed three sheets of parchment on the door of the castle church of Wittenberg. These three sheets contained ninety-five statements objecting to practices of the Catholic Church and calling for public debate. The old Church had come on evil days and there was much corruption and abuse of the people.

Luther was summoned to Rome to stand trial for heresy, but he refused to go. When the Pope learned of his great popularity in Germany, he tried to win Luther over to his side and persuade him that he should cease his protests. Notice the word *protest*. Others who were to join Martin Luther in making protests were called *protestants*. However, the word "Protestant" comes from the Latin and means to "profess," "to bear witness," "to proclaim."

Martin Luther persisted and denied the supremacy of the Pope. He denied the effectiveness of the confessional booth in atoning for sin. He said that saints and Mary have no special role in Heaven and cannot intercede for anyone. Mary was blessed in having a son born to her while she was still a virgin. However, her many other children were born in a completely natural way. He denounced the images of saints as a kind of paganism. He said that the service should not be in Latin but in the language the worshipers would understand. In addition, he insisted that the Bible had greater authority than the Catholic Church. In 1520 the Pope ordered Luther's writings burned and Luther was *excommunicated,* that is, denied all Catholic sacraments.

Luther sought refuge with a powerful friend and began writing books to spread his ideas. He also translated the Bible into German so that the people could read the Bible and understand that the Bible had greater authority than the Church. The Catholic Church utterly denied the right of the people to read the Bible, in any language, lest they get ideas of rebellion against the authority of the bishops and the Pope.

Luther found that many others shared his

This modest baptismal ceremony in Washington, D.C., is in keeping with the simplicity of Methodist church services. The minister, unattended, wears no stole.

beliefs and demanded a reformation of the Catholic Church. The Protestant Reformation spread through much of Europe. Groups broke with the Catholic Church and formed "protestant" religious organizations. Thus the Protestant movement was born. Wars, savage and destructive, were fought for a hundred years between Catholic and Protestant princes. There were dreadful massacres. Finally the two sides made a reluctant peace.

John Calvin and John Knox helped form the Presbyterian Church. *Presbyterian* is derived from a Greek word, meaning "elder." Calvin insisted upon having elders elected by the people govern the church. The Lutherans continued to have bishops, who appointed other bishops and priests.

In England there came into being the Anglican Church, called the Church of England. In Scotland and in the United States it is known as the "Episcopal" Church. It is much closer to the Catholics in many ways and was really a national breaking away from Rome. Many Episcopalian churches have confession and genuflection and their priests are called fathers.

A group that broke away from the Anglican Church became known as Congregationalists. They wanted a much simpler service and the rule of the church by all the members.

Another group that originated in England at a later time is the Methodists. John Wesley, its founder, remained a minister of the

Church of England, although he did not agree with its practices. In time the Methodists became a separate group placing great emphasis upon the inner faith and the application of religion to the social needs and problems of the times. The Methodists, like the Congregationalists, have a simple service and no elaborate vestments.

There are hundreds of other Protestant denominations in this country. One of the larger has a third Testament, the *Book of Mormon*. The group is known as the Church of the Latter Day Saints, or Mormons.

QUESTIONS FOR DISCUSSION

1. Almost all Protestants agree in affirming:

Faith in Jesus Christ as Lord and Savior.

The Bible as the primary source of what is true and right.

The loving concern of God for every human being.

Direct and constant fellowship between God and each believer.

God's forgiveness in response to each person's penitence and faith.

The Church as the community of followers of Christ.

The responsibility of every Christian for his faith and life (the "priesthood of all believers").

The duty to discover and do God's will in his daily work.

The obligation to seek to advance the Kingdom of God in the world.

Eternal life with God in the "communion of saints."

Examine each of these beliefs and tell which ones you accept and which ones you reject. Give your reasons.

2. There are more ritual requirements, obligations and duties to being a Catholic than to being a Protestant. Do you think these disciplines and requirements bring Catholics closer to their religion and help make them better Christians than Protestants? What are your reasons?

3. Do you think that the synagogues have been more of a factor in preserving Judaism than the churches have been in preserving Catholicism and Protestantism? Give your reasons.

4. Do you believe that the threefold function of the synagogue as a House of Prayer, Study and Assembly applies in the same way to the Catholic and Protestant churches? Explain.

5. Discuss the benefits and disadvantages of having "one church" where Jews, Catholics and Protestants may worship together.

6. What do you think Isaiah meant when he said: "My house shall be a house of prayer for all peoples"? (56:7)

7. What do you think is the real meaning of the verse from Exodus: "Let them build for me a Sanctuary that I may dwell among them."? (25:8) Why doesn't the verse end, "that I may dwell in it"?

HOW THE SYNAGOGUE BEGAN

When we study the history and practices of the Catholic and Protestant churches we realize how much they have borrowed from Judaism. We are ready now to consider how the synagogue itself came into being, when it started and when the Jews stopped going to the one Temple in Jerusalem and created the institution of the synagogue.

Let us begin by going back to the time of the Temple. Pilgrims flocked to Jerusalem three times a year to bring their sacrifices to the Temple. The priests and Levites offered the daily sacrifices and carried on the worship services, based mainly upon sacrifices.

When the Temple was destroyed by the Babylonians led by Nebuchadnezzar in 586 B.C.E., and the Jews were exiled to Babylonia, it appeared to be the end for the Jews and the Jewish religion. How could they worship their God without the Temple? How could they offer sacrifices now that the holy Temple had been reduced to ashes?

The letter that saved a religion

When all seemed lost, the Hebrew prophets taught that God could be worshiped anywhere, even in Babylonia, through prayer. Sacrifices at the Temple were not the only way to worship. The prophet Jeremiah sent an important letter to the Jews of Babylonia, telling them to build houses and live in them, to plant vineyards and eat of their fruit, to allow their sons and daughters to marry there. God had not deserted them. God is everywhere, he taught, and could be worshiped wherever people gathered together in reverence and holiness. So the exiled Jews began to meet in private homes to study the teachings of the Torah. They met at the time of the day when the sacrifices had been offered when the Temple stood on Mount Moriah. They read the prayers that accompanied the sacrifices and they read the Biblical injunctions to perform the sacrifices. But no sacrifices were performed. Sometimes the meetings would begin with prayers asking God to bring them back to their homeland. Sometimes the prayers would ask God to watch over them and help them be true to their religion.

The Jews meet together

Soon homes were not large enough for all the people to meet together, so they had to have a a larger meeting place. These meetings mark the beginning of the synagogue. The word *synagogue* is not Hebrew. It is Greek

and means: "meeting place." Through these meeting places the Jews continued to worship God even without sacrifices, and the synagogues saved Judaism.

In the year 539 B.C.E., Cyrus, who had conquered the Babylonians, allowed the exiled Jews to return to their homeland in Palestine. When the Jews returned they took with them the idea of the synagogue. Now instead of all the people making pilgrimages to one central place, they had their own meeting house in their own villages and cities. Even when the second Temple was built the people still continued to worship in their synagogues. Many synagogues were built all over Palestine and in other lands where Jews lived.

This was indeed fortunate because when the second Temple was destroyed by the Romans in the year 70 C.E., the synagogues were now recognized as part of Judaism and they took over the functions of the Temple. Because prayers were substituted for sacrifices, a collection of prayers came into being. Though the people still mourned for their destroyed Temple, the synagogue in many ways served the individual worshiper far better than the Temple ever could. Many centuries later Jewish scholars could look back and say that though the Roman destruction of the Temple was tragic in that the magnificent center of Jewish worship was razed and tens of thousands of Jews massacred and crucified by the pitiless legions of Rome, yet Judaism had actually outgrown the whole idea of sacrifice and of one center of worship for all of world Jewry.

Within a brief time the synagogue and the *yeshivah,* the academy for the study of the Torah, had supplied Judaism with a far more valuable substitute. Each Jew could attend the synagogue and *yeshivah* in his own community and thus feel his own role important at worship and in study. The priests' role became unimportant. Now any dedicated student, no matter what his lineage, could become a rabbi or a community leader. With the Temple's fall, Judaism was completely democratized.

The rabbis

The term *rabbi* means "my teacher," and the institution of the rabbinate did not really come into being until there were synagogues. The people listened to the teachings of the rabbis, who also were the judges in the courts of law. The rabbis took no pay for judging or teaching. They were craftsmen, blacksmiths, sandal makers or merchants. Thus those who studied and taught the "law," the *Torah,* had become the true leaders of the community even before the Temple fell. Now they completely supplanted the priests except in a few minor ceremonies, and Judaism was capable of not only existing but of becoming stronger and even more valuable for the average Jew.

Like a miracle

So we see that even when the Temple was again destroyed and many of the Jews were driven into exile by Rome, they still had their teachers, the rabbis, and most important of all, they could organize new synagogues and meet together to worship God.

It seems almost a miracle, but whenever something vital in Jerusalem is destroyed and it would seem that it must perish, something new is created to save Judaism. We believe that God had a purpose in revealing to the Jews how they could save themselves for a great and holy mission.

It is interesting to note that though Reform and Conservative Jews use the terms *synagogue* or *temple,* Orthodox Jews most often use the term *shul.* This means "school" in German or Yiddish, and shows what is usually considered the most important aspect of a Jewish house of worship. Orthodox Jews never use the word Temple, as they restrict it to the Temple that stood on Mount Moriah in Jerusalem.

The synagogue kept Judaism alive

No matter what name we call it, we can clearly see that the synagogue has kept Judaism alive. When the Jews were persecuted they turned to the synagogue, and through study and prayer they gained a new will to live and to go on to fulfill their covenant with God.

It was in the synagogue that the people made plans to protect themselves from the enemy, or ransom Jewish leaders who were taken captive. It was in the synagogue that the child first learned the holy *Torah,* and then the *Mishnah* and *Talmud* and other holy writings. It was the synagogue that brought Jews together for daily and Sabbath worship, and to observe the festivals and High Holy Days. The synagogue was their spiritual home: in joy and in sorrow, for weddings and for lamentations over their dead. It was the synagogue that enabled the Jew to find new strength and direction to make his contribution to the world by creating sacred literature and new laws that brought him closer to God, to holiness, to justice and lovingkindness.

Do you think that Judaism would survive today without the synagogue? Suppose there would be no synagogues or temples but we would have all our other organizations and institutions, do you think that Judaism would continue to live and flourish?

WHAT DO YOU THINK?

1. Give an imaginary description of modern Jewish life without our synagogues, our temples. Tell what you think would happen to Jewish education and to the Jews them-

Shavuot is the usual time for Jewish confirmation services, and the synagogue is decked with flowers. This young confirmand stands in the pulpit of the Stephen Wise Free Synagogue in New York City.

selves. Without the synagogue do you think Jews would continue to be Jews? Without the synagogue do you think that our Jewish Federations and Jewish Community Centers, our Jewish organizations such as B'nai B'rith, Hadassah, National Council of Jewish Women would continue to serve so magnificently? Give your reasons.

2. Without the synagogue, do you think the Catholic Church or the Protestant churches would have come into existence? If so, would they be any different?

3. Without the synagogue do you think that Christianity would have come into existence? What are your reasons?

4. Do you think that Jewish life would be strengthened or weakened if we had only one kind of synagogue today, instead of Orthodox, Conservative and Reform synagogues? Give your reasons.

The highest building in the community

The Talmud declares that ten Jews living in any community are duty bound to establish a synagogue. Until a new synagogue is completed, it is forbidden to tear down the older one.

So important was the synagogue for the survival of Judaism, that Jews were commanded to construct one as soon as possible. The rabbis taught that the synagogue must be the tallest building in the community.

This was to be a symbol to the Jews that the synagogue must ever represent the most sacred and highest values of life. Jews were commanded to look up to the synagogue and that which it represented and taught. That is why the synagogue is so sacred to us. It is a symbol of God's presence in our homes, in our cities and towns and in our hearts. More

than the Jew has supported the synagogue, it is the synagogue that has preserved the Jew.

THINGS TO DO

1. Visit a Catholic church and a Protestant church and draw a diagram listing the holy items that you find. List all the items that have been taken from the idea of the synagogue or from Jewish practice.

2. Write a brief character study of the life and teachings of Martin Luther, John Calvin, John Knox or John Wesley.

3. Using the *Jewish Encyclopedia,* write an essay on "The Origin and Development of the Synagogue." Explain how the syna-

Sunlight dapples the remains of this second-century synagogue in Capernaum, once a biblical village. Experts believe the synagogue was built on the foundations of a still older one in which Jesus preached.

gogue came into being; its threefold function, and what it means to us today.

4. Write an essay comparing the work and role of the rabbi, the priest and the minister. How do they differ? How are they the same?

5. The Debate in Class:

Is it possible to be a good Jew and never go to the synagogue?

If the Jewish home is a small sanctuary, why do we need the synagogue?

Can't we have all our Judaism at home?

If Judaism is a way of life and is concerned with action, can't we be moral, ethical and upright Jews without the inspiration of the synagogue?

SELECTED QUOTATIONS

A revolutionary establishment

The synagogue as an institution is perhaps the most revolutionary religious establishment that mankind has devised to date. Had it not existed, the Christian church might never have succeeded in conquering the Roman Empire and the great Mohammedan religion might never have had the mobility necessary to bring Moslem equality to the peoples of North Africa, Arabia, and Turkestan.

—RABBI SOLOMON B. FREEHOF

The particular creation of the Jews

The Synagogue was the particular creation of the Jews. It had no hierarchy. It had no Priesthood. . . . It was a spontaneous creation of Jewish men and women. It became a place of assembly, a place of study where youth was instructed, a place where the stranger was welcomed. It went with Israel into exile. It witnessed Israel's

joys and Israel's sorrows. It was the refuge of the persecuted and the haunted soul of our people. . . ."

—RABBI ABBA HILLEL SILVER

What is the Ark?

When the Temple was destroyed the Ark became the focal point of the Synagogues that replaced it. It housed the Torah, the law of the Lord that was perfect restoring the soul; the testimony of the Lord that was sure, making wise the simple; the precepts of the Lord that were right, rejoicing the heart; the judgments of the Lord that were true and righteous altogether. To the Ark every Jew turned in prayer and rose in reverence at the most exalted moment of the service.

—RABBI PHILIP S. BERNSTEIN

The Temple service in the heart

But how could God be worshiped in exile with the Temple destroyed? The answer to this was the synagogue. It proved that God could be worshiped not only by sacrifices and by incense, but also by song and by prayer, and by study of Scripture, by what was called later *Avoda Sheb'lev* or "The Temple Service in the Heart."

The synagogue was firmly established in the old homeland after the return from Babylon. At first is was an informal institution where people gathered to hear the readings from the Prophets, from the Torah, to sing psalms of prayer and to learn to express themselves in the words of devotion. Silent and spoken prayers, private and public prayers, readings and interpretations, all became part of this new place of worship. The synagogue was the world's first institution whose ritual was not conducted by an hereditary priesthood, but, instead, consisted entirely of the utterances of the heart of man. It was the first regular house of prayer.

Thus the peculiar situation which brought the synagogue into existence was produced by the fact that, though exiled physically, the Jews could not be exiled from the presence of their God.

—RABBI SOLOMON B. FREEHOF

The sanctuary of Israel

The synagogue is the sanctuary of Israel. It was born out of Israel's longing for the living God. It has been to Israel throughout his endless wanderings a visible token of the presence of God in the midst of the people. It has shed a beauty that is the beauty of holiness and has ever stood on the high places of the earth. It is Israel's sublime gift to the world. Its truths are true for all men; its love is a love for all men; its God is the God of all men, even as was prophesied of old: "My house shall be called a house of prayer for all peoples."

—*The Union Prayerbook*

I am the Synagogue

I am the Synagogue.

I am the heart of Jewry. I have shielded you for more than two thousand five hundred years. Through all these cruel ages, swept by wrath of fire and sword, I nursed you with the word of God, healed your wounds with the balm of faith, steadied your minds and fortified your hearts with the vision of the Eternal.

When your fathers wept by the waters of Babylon, I came into the world, summoned by their need; whenever they were in the valleys of many shadows under the heels of the pirates of all ages and all lands, I gave them loving asylum. In Babylon and in Persia, in Greece and in Rome, in the face of the howling crusaders and in the clutches of the black Inquisition, in the pogroms of Poland and in the concentration camps of the Nazis, I have been, and by my presence brought the living waters of the Eternal to the parched lips of your fathers.

When the world derided them, I restored them. When men cursed them, I blessed them.

I am old and I am young. I am older than the memories of the historians; and as young as the youngest child.

I bring you peace by teaching you duty. I sanctify your lives with holy seasons. I preserve your heritage. I make the faith of the fathers the faith of the children. Behold, a good doctrine do I give unto you; forsake it not.

—RABBI BERYL D. COHON

SELECTED READINGS

FREEHOF, SOLOMON, *The Small Sanctuary*

FREEMAN, GRACE, *Inside the Synagogue*, UAHC

LEVIN, MEYER, and KURZBAND, TOBY K., *The Story of the Synagogue*

MANWELL, REGINALD D., and FAHS, SOPHIA L., *The Church Across the Street*, Chapters 2–4, 6, 9–10

SILVERMAN, WILLIAM B., *The Still Small Voice Today*, Chapter 2

UNIVERSAL JEWISH ENCYCLOPEDIA, Volume 10, pp. 119–130

12

Festivals and Holy Days Compared

NO, YOU CAN'T HAVE A CHRISTMAS TREE!

Michelle darling,

No, you can't have a Christmas tree. Not this year, or any year. And somehow I think that this is no sign of fuddy-duddyism, intolerance or cruelty on our part.

Why? There are many reasons. Christmas is a Christian festival; we are Jews, and proud of it. It would be wrong and in bad taste to ape another religion's customs. Just imagine a Methodist family hiding the *afikoman* and singing *Chad Gadyah* on the eve of Passover! For Jews to celebrate Christmas is no less ridiculous. Disloyal as it is to our own faith, it is an insult to true Christians for whom this occasion is very holy indeed. . . . Besides, to be frank, Christmas is not even a Christian festival. Originally, long before Christianity was founded, such a feast existed in pagan societies: it was only later baptized and, somewhat uneasily, accepted as suitable for Christian culture. And in the last few decades Christmas has again ceased to be Christian. Nowadays—and Christian thinkers are first to admit and lament this! —it is but an excuse for vulgar commercialism and loud merry making. Christians venerate as one of their spiritual giants,

St. Francis of Sales. This winter event canonizes St. Sales, without the Francis. And St. Dollar, for good measure. So, my little sweetheart, whichever way we look at it, Christmas (viewed as Christian or pagan) is not for us.

Am I a spoil-sport? I don't really think so. Our festivals, and family celebrations, afford us plenty of chances to get and give presents, throw parties, delight to our heart's content.

And much the same goes as a reply to your sobbing objection, "What's wrong with taking part in the season of good will to all men?" Only this, honey: to us, every season, every day of the year, is a season of goodwill to all men. We do not have to set aside a few weeks for that purpose. With us it comes naturally, all the time.

Let me remind you of Chanukah. It has every bit as much joy, color, beauty, depth, meaning, as any other people's any other festival. The glow and glory of the candles, the lilt of *Maoz Tsur,* the dizzy spin of the dreidel, can and should, absorb so much of the Jew's soul that there is simply no spare feeling left over to entangle in alien webs. While wishing men and women and children of other religions most cordial greetings, we must insist that our own fulfillment is to be found in Judaism's treasury, wholly and always.

Well, girlie, that's that. Yes, you can go to Mary's Christmas party—it is nice of her to have asked you. No, you can't go to Rachel's: she has no business to give one any more than we do. And naturally, we shall be happy to have both Rachel and Mary and all your other friends at our own Chanukah party.

Till then, with love,

Your
Daddy*

WHAT DO YOU THINK?

1. Do you agree or disagree with Michelle's father? What are your reasons?

2. How do you think Christians react to Jews who observe Christmas?

3. It has been argued that Christmas is more of an American holiday than a Christian holiday. What is your opinion?

4. Does it make sense for a Jew to observe both Christmas and Ḥanukkah? Why or why not? Which holiday do you think would receive the greater attention?

*From *Bulletin* at Temple B'nai Abraham, Newark, N. J.

The ritual of lighting and blessing the candles on Sabbath eve ushers in a day of "solemn rest, a holy sabbath unto the Lord" (Exodus 16:23)—a sign between God and Israel.

5. What is your reaction to Michelle's father writing, "Yes, you can go to Mary's Christmas party . . . No, you can't go to Rachel's"?

6. Forgetting what happened in Judea at the time of the Maccabees, what modern ethical meaning does Ḥanukkah have for Jews today?

ADVENT

Jews and Christians share the idea and the celebration of the Sabbath. There are other major days in the religious year which are not common to both religions.

The Christian year is centered around two great feasts: Easter and Christmas. The season of *Advent,* which means "a coming," is a four-week preparation for the coming of Christ, beginning four Sundays before Christmas.

Throughout this season, the mood of the liturgy is one of longing and expectation. The coming of Christ is considered under three aspects: the historical coming —Jesus' birth about 6 B.C.E.—a memorial of an event; Christ's glorious coming—His second coming as judge of mankind at the end of the world—an expectation of an event; and Christ's coming on the Feast of Christmas to fill Christians with His light, grace and love—a spiritual event in the present.

The liturgy of Advent admonishes Christians to do penance for sins and to purify their hearts for the coming of Christ at Christmas. Underneath this theme there prevails a note of joy and hope. The Church wants her members to think of death and judgment day during Advent because remembrance of Christ's last coming helps them to prepare better for His coming into their hearts in the present.

During this season Christians are united to the Jewish people through prayer taken from the *Tenach* (the Jewish Bible) and through the reading of the Prophets who rallied their people with the hope in the Messiah's coming. In the liturgy of Advent Christians share the Prophets' expectations which, they believe, were fulfilled in Christ. In the Prayers of the seven days immediately preceding Christmas there occur seven antiphons which begin with biblical titles applied to the coming Messiah: O Wisdom, . . . O Lord, . . . O Root of Jesse . . .; O Key of David . . . ; O Oriens (*i.e.,* rising sun) . . . ; O King of Gentiles . . . ; O Emmanuel . . ."

—FATHER LAWRENCE GUILLOT,
from lecture material, quoted
by permission

ḤANUKKAH AND CHRISTMAS TODAY

The Jews naturally have no holiday which is like Christmas, since they do not celebrate the birth of any divine figure. Ḥanukkah occurs around the same time as Christmas, but it is not nearly as important a holiday in the Jewish year as Christmas is in the Christian.

Some people ask? "What sense does lighting candles on Ḥanukkah have for us Jews today? Just because a miracle was supposed to have happened over 2,100 years ago, and the Temple was rededicated after the Jews managed to defeat their persecutors, do we have to go through the routine of lighting candles every year?"

If Ḥanukkah is only a matter of lighting candles, wax or tallow and a wick, then it doesn't appear to be very meaningful. But if Ḥanukkah is our Feast of Lights, and every time we light the Ḥanukkah candles we rededicate ourselves to the light of freedom, the light of truth, the light of justice, the light of mercy, and the light of brotherhood and peace, then Ḥanukkah is very important, and just as meaningful today as it was 2,100 years ago.

Read the description of Ḥanukkah in *The Still Small Voice Today,* by William B. Silverman, Chapter 3, and give the modern meaning of the Festival of Lights.

Discuss in class why we need Ḥanukkah today. How could the world and our present society benefit from the lessons of Ḥanukkah?

THE JEWISH AND CHRISTIAN SABBATH

Jews and Christians each have their own sacred calendars, which mark off the Holy Days of the religious year from the ordinary regular days of the year. By observing the calendar and participating in the Holy Days, Jews and Christians rise above the work-a-day world. They become special when they observe special days. For this reason, the calendar is really a gift of God to man, for by means of the calendar man's life is given order, holiness and special meaning.

The highlight of the Jewish and Christian calendar is the Sabbath. You may think this is strange since the Sabbath comes every week and you aren't accustomed to thinking of it as a particularly special holiday. Yet, it is just because it comes every week that it is the most important holiday. At the end of every week there is a day of rest and of holiness.

You may ask why should man rest? Why shouldn't he do the same things for seven instead of six days a week? Certainly he could finish more work and make more money if he continued for seven days with his tasks. The Romans thought that the Jews were wasting one-seventh of life.

There are several reasons why man must rest. According to the Torah, God created the world in six days and on the seventh He rested. And so the seventh day became the day of rest to celebrate the completion of God's work. The Sabbath celebrates the creation of the world every week of the year. Because it commemorates the creation, the Sabbath is more important than any other

holiday. And since the world is constantly being recreated, the Sabbath cannot be celebrated only once a year but must be marked every week.

Thus, the Jew is supposed to rest because he remembers the Creation and the Exodus from Egypt. The observance of the Sabbath is also one of the Ten Commandments. At the same time, a day of rest is a great benefit for man for through the Sabbath man is freed from his toil. One day a week man leaves the machines, the books, the tools, and the noise, the useful and the useless. One day a week he stops worrying about business and about money. Instead he enjoys nature and he develops what is most human in man—his spirit. Through prayer, study, family joy, and nature, man lifts his soul and really partakes of life.

All of our Jewish Holy Days and festivals, the Sabbath and every day of the Jewish calendar begin at night, with sundown. This may appear strange to us. Why then do we begin the Sabbath on Friday evening?

The rabbis showed that the Bible puts evening first: "And it was evening, and it was morning, the first day; which means that a day is from evening to evening. Anyone can believe in the day when the sun is shining. But we Jews have such faith in the coming of the dawn and the light that we begin our day at night. This also means the coming of the great day of God's kingdom on earth.

Different religions have different days of rest. The Muslims regard Friday as their Sabbath. Jews have Saturday, and Christians have Sunday. In the State of Israel, where the Jews are a majority, Christians have a difficult time keeping Sunday as a Sabbath because all the stores and schools and offices are closed on Saturday and open on Sunday.

We observed Saturday as our Sabbath more than a thousand of years before there was such a religion as Christianity. The early Christians kept Saturday as the Sabbath until it was changed to Sunday in order to show a difference between Judaism and Christianity. There are Christian groups that still keep Saturday as the Sabbath right here in the United States. Those who belong to this group are called Seventh Day Adventists, or Seventh Day Baptists.

WHAT DO YOU THINK?

1. Do you think it would be better for all religions to have their Sabbath on the same day? Give your reasons.

2. Would it be better for Jews to keep Sunday as the Sabbath in America, and Friday as the Sabbath in Morocco? Would it be better for Muslims and Christians to keep Saturday as the Sabbath in the State of Israel? Explain what you mean.

3. A Christian minister made the suggestion that Catholics and Protestants should give up Sunday as the Sabbath and observe Saturday with the Jews for the sake of religious unity. He pointed out that Jesus held that Saturday was the Sabbath. What do you think?

THINGS TO DO

1. Write an essay imagining that you are a Christian boy or girl living in the State of Israel. Explain the problems you would have keeping the Christian Sabbath and the Christian Christmas. Tell about some of the things that a Christian boy or girl might be telling parents about how much they want to do things on Saturday and how much they want a Ḥanukkah Menorah in the home. What do you think the Christian parents might say in answer to their children?

2. Discuss in class the beliefs of the Seventh Day Adventists, who keep Saturday as their Sabbath. Look up these beliefs.

3. The fourth commandment begins: "Remember the sabbath day to keep it holy."

How is it possible for a boy or girl of your age to keep it holy?

4. Discuss in class the differences in the fourth commandment as given in Exodus, 20:8–11 and Deuteronomy 5:12–15.

5. Explain the meaning of the prayer called *V'shamru:*

> The children of Israel shall keep the Sabbath, to observe the Sabbath throughout their generations as a perpetual covenant. It is a sign between Me and the children of Israel forever.

What is the origin of this prayer?

Discuss the meaning of *covenant.* How is the Sabbath a sign between God and the children of Israel? A sign of what?

QUESTIONS FOR DISCUSSION

1. Tell what is meant by these words from the writings of the modern Jewish philosopher Ahad Ha-Am: "More than Israel has kept the Sabbath, the Sabbath has kept Israel." How do you think the Sabbath has kept Israel?

2. How can the observance of the Sabbath help us to be better human beings, better Jews and better Americans?

3. Why is it that Jewish tradition teaches that the Sabbath is second in holiness and in importance only to the Sabbath of Sabbaths, which is Yom Kippur?

4. What are the similarities and the differences between the Jewish Sabbath and the Christian Sabbath? How does the Christian Sabbath help Christians to be better Christians?

5. Read Genesis 2:2–3 and then discuss in class the Biblical reason for the holiness of the Sabbath. Which day do you think it was that God blessed and hallowed: Saturday or Sunday? How can we bless and hallow the seventh day?

EASTER AND PASSOVER OBSERVANCES

There are some similarities between Easter and Passover, but there are major differences. Easter is the Christian celebration of Christ's rising from the grave after three days. Then the world was supposedly reborn. Just before Easter, Christians observe *Lent* for forty days. This means that during this period they deprive themselves of things they like and make some sacrifices, just as they believe that Jesus sacrificed his life for them. *Lent* means "spring," and begins with Ash Wednesday, when Catholics have a spot of ashes placed on their foreheads. The ashes are from the burned palm fronds of the preceding years' Palm Sunday. According to Christian tradition Lent is to be observed for forty days corresponding to the time that Jesus was in the wilderness and was tempted by the Devil.

As Lent comes to a close, Christians observe "Good Friday," the day that Jesus was crucified. Then on Sunday they rejoice in that he was resurrected, which means he rose from the grave and came to life again briefly before going up to heaven. Palm Sunday is the Sunday before Easter and commemorates Jesus' entrance into Jerusalem, when he was met by a throng waving palm branches.

The following quotations tell us more about Passover and Easter.

A new look at Passover

Passover is our people's Festival of Freedom. In Israel, it is observed in the same spirit as is the Fourth of July in this country. In Judaism, however, it is celebrated

Christian youngsters gather on the White House Lawn for Easter morning egg rolling. (The egg, featured in Easter festivities, is a symbol of eternal life.)

not only as a reminder of our miraculous deliverance from bondage in Egypt and Egypts in many lands throughout the centuries, but also as a reminder of our sacred duty to deliver our own brothers in our own time in whatever lands they still languish in bondage.

Passover is a time for remembering other people as well as our own. It is a time when we are emphatically reminded to remember the strangers, because we were once strangers. For in many areas, in many lands, we are still strangers to complete liberty, equality and fraternity, not only under the dictatorship of Russia, but also the democracy of America. We must still cry aloud and speak out—until absolute freedom for our people is granted everywhere.

It is not enough, however, to think only of ourselves. We must ever keep in mind that we shall never be entirely free until all our fellowmen are free, everywhere, all over the earth. And that holds true particularly for our fellow Americans, the Negroes. They are now engaged in a struggle for their long-overdue rights. In the true spirit of Passover, let us redouble our efforts to help bring about their deliverance in our time.

Let us look upon the promise of Elijah's coming to our Passover *Seder* table as the harbinger of a new birth of freedom for all our people everywhere—for the Negro people everywhere—and for all mankind. Let freedom ring!

—Temple Sholom, Chicago, *Bulletin*

Passover and Easter

Easter celebrates the redemption and resurrection of a personality; Passover the redemption of a people. Both involved great personalities—Moses, who gave the law; Jesus, who in the Easter story, is ac-

counted as one who came to fulfill it. Both emphasize freedom—Easter the freedom of man from the world; Passover, the freeing of man in and for the world. Both deal with the miraculous. In Passover the miracle is the crossing of the *Red Sea*. Easter commemorates the miracle of resurrection. However, in Passover, the miracle of the crossing of the Sea is secondary to the idea of freedom. In Easter, it is of primary significance. In all commemorations and miracles, the danger is that people wait too often for a miracle to happen. In reality, miracles occur only when we stop waiting for them to occur.

Hopeful man, the resurrection of a spirit and a people, both come in the spring when the newness of life revivifies our spirit.

—UAHC Release

THINGS TO DO

1. Read and study about Passover and Easter, then make a list of the similarities and differences.

2. Easter reminds Christians of the supposed resurrection of Jesus. How does Passover remind Jews to identify themselves with the principle of freedom? Discuss in class.

3. Look up the meaning of the Christian observance of Lent. Compare with (a) the Ten Days of Penitence; (b) the period between Passover and Shavuot; (c) the Day of Atonement; (d) the three weeks until Tisha be-Av.

4. Christians believe that when Jesus was resurrected the world was reborn. How does this compare with Rosh Hashana when a person can begin a new life?

5. *Communion*

Jesus Christ instituted the Holy Eucharist at the end of a Jewish Passover meal with His disciples, the night before He died. He took bread, gave thanks and presenting it to His disciples, said: "Take and eat, this is my Body which shall be given for you." Then, taking wine and blessing it, he handed it to his disciples, saying: "Drink all of you of this, for this is my blood of the New Covenant, which is being shed for you and for many that sins may be forgiven. Do this in remembrance of me." (MATT. 26:26–29, LUKE 22:14–20).

Since Christians believe that Jesus Christ is Divine, they believe that He had full power over material elements such as bread and wine, and over His own Body, so that if He wished, He could change bread and wine into His Body and Blood. They believe further, that with the words, "Do this in remembrance of me," Jesus gave to the apostles and to their successors in the priesthood, the power to celebrate the Holy Eucharist, and thus to change bread and wine into Jesus' flesh and blood. For Christians, the Holy Eucharist is considered as spiritual food for life everlasting. Christ unites Himself most intimately with them, unites them with each other, and and gives them power to live as children of God.

—FATHER LAWRENCE GUILLOT,
from lecture material,
quoted by permission

Write out your reaction to Father Guillot's description of Catholic Communion.

QUESTIONS FOR DISCUSSION

1. When a Jew goes to church should he take communion as a courtesy to his Christian friends with whom he is worshiping?

2. Both Easter and Passover are fixed by the lunar calendar. What is the lunar calendar? Why do Christians use the lunar calendar only for Easter and not for their other holidays?

3. How does the Catholic Mass differ from the Protestant communion?

HOW RELIGIONS BORROW FROM EACH OTHER

Judaism has borrowed some customs and practices from Christianity, but there are many more traditions that Christianity has borrowed from Judaism. Can anyone think of any other Christian custom or tradition that we haven't already discussed that has been taken from Judaism?

There is a Feast of Tabernacles in Christianity, too, and the people walk around with sprigs of Palm on Palm Sunday.

"Ash Wednesday" seems to be taken from Tisha be-Av, the Jewish fast day when the Jews used to put on sackcloth and cover themselves with ashes, as they once did on Yom Kippur, too.

WHAT DO YOU THINK?

1. Do you think that Jewish students should go to church and hear about Jesus, Easter and communion? Do you think there is anything to be gained from discussing whether this religion borrowed from that one, or whether Christianity has a custom or a festival that is like a festival in Judaism? What difference does it make to us or to Christians?

2. Compare the story of Jesus' resurrection with that of many ancient mystery deities such as the Greek Adonis and the Babylonian Tammuz.

ASH WEDNESDAY

Ash Wednesday opens the penitential season of Lent; forty days of fast, prayer, and penance in preparation for Easter. Just as Jonah and the Ninevites acknowledged their sinfulness by dressing in sackcloth and sprinkling themselves with ashes, so on Ash Wednesday Christians receive ashes as a symbol of sorrow and penance for sin. This signifies their desire to change their lives by avoiding sin and practicing virtue.

The Ashes, made by burning the Palm or Olive branches used on Palm Sunday of the preceding year, are placed on each person's forehead in the form of a cross, while the priest says the following words from Genesis 3:19: "Remember man that thou art dust and unto dust thou shalt return." This thought that man is totally dependent upon God, and that he must some day die must be kept in mind all during Lent, and for the rest of one's life.

—FATHER LAWRENCE GUILLOT,
from lecture material,
quoted by permission

Give your reaction to Father Guillot's description of Ash Wednesday. Where do you think this practice of using ashes may be found in Jewish tradition? Do you think we should bring back the Jewish custom of putting ashes on ourselves during Jewish fast days and days of sorrow?

THINGS TO DO

1. Write a brief essay on the meaning of the Feast of Tabernacles in Christianity.

2. Look up the significance of Ash Wednesday and write a paragraph comparing the observance of Ash Wednesday with the observance of Tisha be-Av.

3. Discuss in class the meaning of Shavuot. Is there anything in Christian observance that compares with it?

4. Write an essay on the ethical meanings of Sukkot, and compare with the ethical meanings of the Christian Feast of Tabernacles.

5. Shavuot commemorates the season of the giving of the law, the *Zeman Matan Torahtenu*. Jewish tradition tells that the law was given on Mount Sinai, in no man's land, that it was given in seventy voices, corresponding to the seventy languages of the time, and that the law is meant for all peoples. Is there any festival or observance in Christianity that teaches the Fatherhood of God and the universal brotherhood of man—and that the ethical teachings of Christianity are meant for all peoples?

6. How does the belief in resurrection differ in Orthodox, Conservative and Reform Judaism? How does the Christian idea of resurrection differ from the Jewish ideas of resurrection?

7. What are some of the Christian customs and practices that Jews have borrowed?

8. What do we mean when we say that learning about each other's religion means a great deal to the future of our world?

FEAST OF TABERNACLES

There is no one feast in the Catholic Church which corresponds exactly to the Jewish Feast of Tabernacles. However, the two main ideas which highlight *Sukkot* are to be found incorporated in the Christian liturgical period of Lent and the Feast of Easter. These are: (1) thanksgiving to God for the fruits of the earth, for all his favors to the Hebrew people during the Exodus out of Egypt; and (2) man's complete dependence upon God, symbolized by dwelling in frail *sukkot* or tents, which also symbolizes man's temporary sojourn on this earth as he journeys toward the Promised Land of eternity.

In Canada and the United States, the "harvest festival" aspect of the Feast of Tabernacles finds a parallel in the national Thanksgiving Holiday occurring in the fall of the year, when we thank God for all His great favors and for all the fruits of the harvest.

There is, further, in the Catholic Church,

At Westminster Cathedral, a Cardinal blesses the Palms on the morning of Palm Sunday. This day opens Holy Week, culminating in Easter.

an observance of "Ember Days," three days of fast, prayer and penance at the beginning of each season, to ask God's blessing on that season. The autumn Ember Days usually occur in September.

—FATHER LAWRENCE GUILLOT,
from lecture material,
quoted by permission

PALM SUNDAY

Six days before the Passover, Jesus entered the city of Jerusalem in a triumphal procession, riding on a donkey (John 12:1, 12–16). Christians see in this the fulfillment of a prophecy of Zechariah 9:9: ". . . See your king shall come to you; a just savior is he, meek, and riding on an ass, on a colt, the foal of an ass."

Today Christians have a procession on Palm Sunday, the Sunday before Easter Sunday, holding blessed palm or olive tree branches, singing appropriate Psalm verses, and repeating the Joyous words of the first Palm Sunday, as recorded in the Gospels: "Hosanna to the Son of David! Blessed is He who comes in the name of the Lord: Hosanna in the highest!" Thus Christians show their faith in Christ their King. The blessed palms are then kept in the home as a symbol of Christ's victory over sin and death in His death and resurrection.

—SISTER MARY DAVID

This gathering of Jews is seen assembled for Sukkot service at the historic Western Wall in Jerusalem.

Write an essay comparing Palm Sunday with Sukkot.

10. What are the differences between the Orthodox, Conservative and Reform ways of observing Rosh Hashanah, Sukkot and Passover?

SELECTED QUOTATIONS

Christmas: A Holy Day for Christians

Unless Christmas be truly Christ's mass with all the timeless and timely meaning of that term, then it should not bear that name in vain. . . .

As a rabbi I maintain that Christmas is, or most assuredly should be, a holy day for Christians only—and not for Jews.

—RABBI MAURICE N. EISENDRATH

The Christmas tree as a symbol

So tell the children, give your Christian friend a present and thank him very much for his present to you, but we respect his religion by not having a Christmas tree in our home. The Christmas tree is the symbol of the birth of his Savior and we are Jews. . . . They have the beautiful Christmas tree and we have the knowledge that we have been the living "witnesses" to the entire human story!

—HARRY GOLDEN

A spiritual remembrance

At Notre Dame de Sion Convent, Kansas City, Missouri, the boarders keep the old tradition of lighting the Advent Wreath each evening of the Advent season as a preparation for Christmas. This year, while the Jews celebrated Chanukah, they decided to join their prayers by introducing a Jewish Menorah in the Advent Wreath display. This spiritual remembrance seemed in the right place before the statue of Mary, who most likely as a Jewish maiden had lighted the Jewish Chanukah Menorah in her Nazareth home.

—*At the Crossroads,* Ratisbonne Center

The miracle of Ḥanukkah

If the visions and beliefs which Chanukah . . . celebrates had gone down in defeat, why, there would now be neither Chanukah nor Christmas and what light there is in the world, there would be less of it. That is the "miracle" of Chanukah.

—ISRAEL KNOX

The Last Supper

On the evening before his crucifixion, Jesus met with his disciples in an upstairs room in Jerusalem to partake of the Last Supper. According to the first three gospels, this was the Passover supper, the highly ceremonial meal that took place at sundown as the Passover began. . . .

The Passover supper marked the opening of the seven days of Passover, symbolizing the departure of the children of Israel from Egypt, and the ritual of the meal was ancient and undeviating. If the Last Supper was the Passover supper, the meat the disciples ate was the sacrificial lamb that Moses had commanded, the lamb "without blemish." (Ex. 12:5) The bread that Jesus broke was unleavened bread, "the bread of affliction," (Deut. 16:3) and the hymn they all sang at the end was the "hallel," the selection from the Book of Psalms that always closed the meal. Jesus extended the symbolism of the occasion by saying that the bread they ate was his body and the wine they drank was his blood. Then he went out to the Mount of Olives, and there he was arrested, to be crucified. Since the Jewish day began at sundown, it

was therefore still the first day of Passover when Jesus was tried, executed and buried.

—MARCHETTE CHUTE, *Jesus of Israel,*
E. P. Dutton & Co., Inc.

Passover and Easter

Passover . . . commemorates an idea and an event. The exodus from Egypt of the Children of Israel who were then able to proceed to Mt. Sinai and the Promised Land is the event. The idea is the tribute to nature that men have always paid to the springtime of the year. . . .

Easter, on the other hand, is not the story of a people, but of an individual. It tells of Christian faith concerning the death and miraculous resurrection of Jesus. Originally, Easter was dependent on Passover Week. The early Christians who wanted to remain Jews but only add to their creed the idea that Jesus was the true Messiah looked upon Jesus as the "paschal lamb"; no doubt too, that the "last supper" was the Passover Seder. . . .

Easter and Passover could exist side by side as spring-time festivals, giving the adherents of both religions hope for the time to come. . . . Understanding between Christians and Jews will finally be built not on bridges of bigotry but on avenues of cooperation.

—JOSEPH R. NAROT

The hope for brotherhood

When the Shofar is sounded the Jew lifts his voice to God and prays: "Oh, hasten the blessed time when all dwellers on earth shall hearken unto the sound of the shofar and shall worship as one brotherhood at Thy holy mountain."

On the Day of Atonement the Jew cries out: "Father of mercies, we do not pray for ourselves alone but for all Thy children." The prayer continues: "Unite us in brotherhood of service to Thee and to our fellow men."

Mitzvah

Mitzvah means "command"—God's command, that is.

When a Jew fulfills *mitzvot,* he affirms that God exists, that life is holy, and that man's obligation is to hallow all life. By his deeds such a Jew says with the Psalmist, "This be the cry of my whole being. There is none like Thee, O Lord" (Ps. 35:10).

Our tradition counts 613 commands: 248 positive commands, things to be done, to correspond to the number of bones in the body; and 365 negative commands, to correspond to the 365 days in the year. . . .

Mitzvot are often divided into moral and ceremonial. Moral laws such as worship of God, refraining from blasphemy, reverence for life, restraint in sex, the practice of justice, obedience to public order with all the nuances which these general principles imply are, according to Jewish tradition, obligatory upon all mankind, Jew and Gentile alike. Ceremonial

laws, religious acts are binding for Jews only. . . .

. . . Many of us . . . would now agree with Leon Roth that "Ceremony is the device by which the feeling of the Presence of God is brought into everyday life. . . ."

Mitzvot—moral and ceremonial alike —impose themselves on the flesh of our bodies, the food we consume, the means of our livelihood, and the rhythm of our years.

As a people we have been sustained by *Mitzvot*—by the 613 commands—the performance of which has ever been our mark of distinction.

—WILLIAM G. BRAUDE

SELECTED READINGS

ANSLEY, DELIGHT, *The Good Ways,* Chapters 3 and 9

BIAL, MORRISON DAVID, *Liberal Judaism at Home,* pp. 89–140, Temple Sinai, 208 Summit Avenue, Summit, N.J. 07901

ELWELL, CLARENCE E., *The Vine and the Branches,* The Holy Faith Series

13

Christian Missionaries and the Mission of Israel

How would you answer?

A Baptist family lives next door to a Jewish family. One of the daughters, Martha, talks to her Jewish neighbor, Deborah, about religion. Martha says that when she grows up she is going to become a missionary. Deborah is puzzled because Martha keeps on saying that Deborah should accept Jesus as her savior, and that the Jews will not be saved until they see the light and believe the way she believes. Martha not only quotes from her Bible, The New Testament, but from the Hebrew Scriptures which she calls "your Old Testament." When Martha repeats the familiar lines they seem to have a very different meaning from any Deborah learned before.

1. What does Martha mean about "being saved"?
2. Is there a Jewish idea of "being saved"?
3. Why don't Jews have missionaries?
4. How can Biblical passages have such different interpretations?

CHRISTIAN MISSIONARIES

The Christian idea of salvation is a very important one and we will study it later. Right now, let's understand what the Christians mean by *missionaries,* and why they have missionaries.

A Christian missionary is a man or woman who is devoted to converting non-Christians to Christianity. There are different types of missionaries. Some go to foreign countries as teachers to bring education to backward peoples. Others establish orphanages to care for children without homes. There are medical missionaries who heal the sick and teach proper hygiene and sanitation. They establish hospitals and dispensaries and devote themselves to the poor and ignorant, saving many lives. These medical missionaries do a great deal of good and help many people.

No matter what they do, however, whether teaching or healing or serving, they have another purpose in mind, and that is to demonstrate the best that is in Christianity by providing an example, with the hope that

Nuns operate a hospital and school near Durados, Brazil. Most Brazilians are at least nominally Catholic. Need for health and education services in some parts of Brazil is severe.

others will become Christians, too. They believe that Christianity is good for them and good for others, and so they devote their lives to being missionaries, teaching and preaching and living by the Gospel of Jesus.

There is another type of missionary who may not travel to another country, but tries to convert people, in his own community or abroad, to Christianity. He does this by lectures, by personal meetings, visits and conversations. He may give out books and pamphlets. He may stand at a street corner and harangue anyone who passes. His purpose is to convince others to convert to the truth as he sees it, that without the Christian faith, mankind is doomed to hell. This is called "winning souls" or "saving souls for Christ."

WHAT DO YOU THINK?

1. What do you answer those who try to convert you to another religion?

2. What is your opinion of Christian missionaries? Even though many of them render great service as teachers or physicians, do you think they should try to convert others to their religion?

3. Why do they believe that theirs is the true religion for others as well as for themselves? Do they believe that they have a duty to the non-Christian? If so, why?

4. Do you think that Judaism should have missionaries to teach about our faith and convert non-Jews to Judaism? Give your reasons.

5. Try to get some of the missionary pamphlets meant for Jews from a local church. If you live in a big city, there will be at least one permanent mission to the Jews which distributes special editions of the Christian gospels and pamphlets that are written just for you and your fellow Jews. Read one of the pamphlets and look up the translation of the Bible passages they quote

in the Jewish Holy Scriptures. Consult with your teacher or rabbis as to the Jewish meaning of the verses quoted and why and how they have been torn from context and misused.

IS THERE A ONE, TRUE FAITH?

A pamphlet on Catholicism states, "We know that the Catholic Church is the one true Church established by Christ, because it alone has the marks (one, holy, universal, apostolic) of the true church."

John Cogley, editor of a magazine called *The Commonweal*, asks,

"Do Catholics believe theirs is the only true religion?" He answers:

Yes.

The fact that there are many religions, all holding different—often contradictory —doctrines about God and man strikes the Catholic as tragic. The idea that they are all equally true (those that hold Christ was divine and those that hold He was merely human, for instance) seems absurdly illogical. . . . Catholics believe that Christ, the Son of God, founded the Church and promised to remain with it, "even unto the consummation of the world." But when they say theirs is the only true religion, Catholics do not mean that they alone are the children of God or that only Catholics are righteous and God-fearing."

Now let us consider the Protestant view. Not all Protestants claim to have the only true faith, but they all do insist that Christ is the only true way to salvation.

In just a little while we will discuss the Christian idea of salvation and compare it with the Jewish idea of salvation, but right now let us consider what some other Protestant groups tell us about their idea of the one true faith.

G. Elson Ruff, editor of *The Lutheran* magazine asks, "Do Lutherans believe theirs is the only true religion?" He answers:

Yes, but they don't believe they are the only ones who have it. There are true Christian believers in a vast majority of the churches, perhaps in all.

Presbyterians believe that every man has the right to choose and practice the faith that he personally accepts. Baptists believe in full, complete religious freedom and demand it for other religions just as vigorously as they demand understanding toward all other religious bodies.

When we speak of Protestants, we have to understand that we are talking about various "denominations"—with different beliefs. There are at least 258 different Protestant groups in this country. Most of them send missionaries to other, backward, non-Christian countries, but only the extreme groups, called "fundamentalists," are active in trying to convert non-Christians in the United States to Christianity.

MISSIONARY VIEWS

There is an excellent book that tells about the various religious denominations and what they believe about missionary work and converting others. It is now called *Religions in America,* a revised edition, edited by Leo Rosten.

Beginning on page 178 there is a chapter that compares religious beliefs of fifteen American denominations. On page 190 the missionary views of the various churches are given. For example:

Baptists. The historic Baptist view holds that every church member and every professing Christian is an evangelist. Throughout their history, Baptists have engaged in very active missionary effort at home and abroad.

Catholics. The Catholic Church from its very beginning has sent out missionaries to all nations to make known to all men the Gospel of Christ and incorporate them into His Church. Catholicism is a world-wide religion meant for all men of all races at all times.

Episcopalians. The Church has been active in propagation of the faith, carrying missionary work throughout the world.

Lutherans. Lutherans believe that Christians are under compulsion to seek to convert all people to the Christian faith.

DO JEWS SEEK CONVERTS?

In Leo Rosten's book, under "Jews," we find this statement: "Modern Judaism is not a proselytizing creed." *Proselytizing* means seeking converts. Notice that it says "modern Judaism." A long time ago the Jews did seek converts.

During the pre-Christian period of history the Jews did attempt to attract people to Judaism. The history of the Jews was explained to the Greeks and Romans. Judaism had an appeal to some of the Romans, who were tired of their pagan religion, and some became converts to Judaism. Many Romans liked the ethical ideas of Judaism, but they didn't like the dietary laws and the other restrictive laws for all Jews, which were what we would call Orthodox today.

For a while Jewish missionaries traveled from country to country teaching about Judaism. The New Testament (Matt. 23:15) states that they would "compass sea and land to make one convert." Apparently they were successful because they antagonized the Roman leaders, who regarded the worship of Jupiter and Mars or of Mithras as an important way of preserving the Roman glorification of power and armed might.

With the beginning of the first century of the Common Era, Jewish missionary efforts increased. Many in the Roman world were ready for a new religion. The teachings of Judaism against idol worship and false gods were talked about and admired. What would happen? Would Judaism become the religion of the Roman world?

As we know, this did not happen. Instead of Judaism, Christianity became the religion of the Roman world, and Jewish missionary activity came to an end. Many scholars today believe that Paul did away with Jewish law in Christianity mainly to make the new religion easier for the pagans to adopt.

Why Jews stopped converting others

Christianity taught that the only salvation was through the belief in Jesus as the Christ and tried to make converts, insisting that there was only one true religion, and that the only way of going to heaven was to become a Christian.

From the first, Judaism felt that it had a clear and logical relationship with God. He had given the Jews the Torah after establishing them as a people by freeing them from Egypt. By observing the *mitzvot,* God's commandments, they earned God's love and His grace. If they sinned because of their mortal weakness, God forgave them if they freely atoned on the day He had given them for repentance.

That is why almost all the Jews refused to follow Jesus or Paul. They felt they needed no special redemption from an original sin they did not believe in. And they considered insulting the idea that God would throw anyone into hell because he didn't consider Jesus the only begotten son of God. They thought it insulting to their concept of God, and even more insulting to God Himself. To them it was blasphemy.

Moreover, the idea of only one way to

A number of Protestant churches establish agricultural missions in foreign lands. This agricultural missionary, a Methodist, is chatting with farmers near Angol, Chile.

God, of one true faith, was not acceptable to the Jews. They taught that "the righteous among all the peoples have a portion in the world to come." This means that one need not become converted to Judaism to achieve salvation. For the Jew, Judaism is the true faith, but we don't believe that Judaism is the only way that man can earn God's approbation.

Our sages taught that when the Torah was given at Mount Sinai it was given in seventy voices corresponding to the seventy languages of the time — and that the moral laws belong to all peoples and all religions. If people will observe the moral laws, even though they are not Jews they will have come close to God.

Moreover, since we believe in the one, universal God of mankind, and that there is but one God for all peoples and all nations, we worship the same God in different ways. God is the Father of all, and all people are His children.

Rabbi Emil Fackenheim wrote as follows in his book, *Paths to Jewish Belief:*

We must remember two things in order to understand the Jewish position toward

Christianity. First, Judaism is not a missionary religion. Jews have rarely tried to convert non-Jews to Judaism, though if a non-Jew sincerely wants to become Jewish he is accepted. While Judaism considers itself a true religion, it does not consider itself the only true religion. According to tradition, God gave 613 laws to Israel, and, through Noah, He gave seven laws to all mankind. Jews believe that a gentile who observes these seven laws — the basic laws of morality — is just as beloved of God as a Jew who observes all 613.

MANY PATHS TO GOD

Think of the house of the Lord. There are different paths leading to the house. Look at the drawing of roads leading to the house of the Lord.

There is the Jewish path to the house of the Lord. There is the Christian path, and there is the Muslim path, or the path of Islam. The other lines represent other religions. This was the idea of the great medieval Jewish philosopher Maimonides, and it is ours today.

Now, if we all direct our deeds and our thoughts upward, we all meet at the house, with God. It is true that Maimonides called Judaism the "royal road," but he did not deny that all the other paths also ended at God's house.

Many of the teachings of Judaism are meant for all peoples. For example, the Ten Commandments are meant for all peoples. The Book of Leviticus teaches: "Love thy neighbor as thyself." It doesn't say anything about the faith or religion of the neighbor or the color of his skin. When the prophet Micah teaches: "It hath been told thee, O man, what is good and what the Lord doth require of thee, but to do justly, to love mercy and to walk humbly with thy God," notice

that he says: "O man," not O white or black or yellow or brown: not O Jew, or O Christian, or O Muslim, but O man, universal man.

The prophet Isaiah taught: "My house shall be called a house of prayer for all peoples" (56.7).

The prophet Malachi asked: "Have we not all one Father? Hath not one God created us? Why do we deal treacherously every man against his brother . . . ?" (Mal. 2:10)

These verses tell us a great deal about the Jewish belief that everyone is a child of God, and that all religions are true when they teach justice, mercy, love for one's fellow man, holiness and peace.

SHOULD WE HAVE JEWISH MISSIONARIES?

Some Jews ask, "If Judaism is a universal religion, meant for all peoples, then why is it that we don't have Jewish missionaries to tell them about our faith and convince them to be Jewish?"

In the fourth century, when Christianity became the State religion, the Roman emperor Constantine made laws prohibiting any Christian from converting to Judaism. Both the proselyte and the person who converted him faced death.

Later, in the Middle Ages, it was very dangerous for the Jews when a Christian became a convert to Judaism. The Christian religious authorities became angry when a Christian left Christianity to become Jewish. They used this as an excuse to persecute and even murder the Jews. Every time a Christian became Jewish it meant trouble and tragedy for the Jewish community, so you can understand why the Jews were worried when a Christian thought of converting.

Today some Jewish leaders are giving more thought to providing information about the Jewish religion. In some of the larger cities there are Jewish Information Centers where those who have no religion, or those who want to inquire about Judaism may come and study.

Today there are many Christians who express an interest in becoming Jewish. Sometimes it is because they plan to marry someone of the Jewish faith. Sometimes it is because they can't accept the beliefs of Christianity. But in many temples and synagogues today there are conversion classes where Christians are studying Judaism.

Rabbi Milton Steinberg gives a clear description of the Jewish point of view:

> Anyone may become a Jew; but no one has to do so in order to be saved, whether in this world or the next.
>
> The tradition rules explicitly: "The righteous of all peoples have their share in the world to come."
>
> On which very consequential point Judaism stands in sharp constrast to historic Christianity.
>
> The universalism of the Christian religion has been frequently commented on, the fact that in its eyes and according to the teaching of Paul: "There is neither Jew nor Greek, there is neither bond nor free, there is neither male nor female: for ye are all one in Christ Jesus. And if ye be Christs, then are ye Abraham's seed, and heirs according to the promise." (GAL. 3:28–29)
>
> But what is often overlooked in Paul's preachments is the explicit condition he imposes, namely, *"If ye be Christ's."* Paul's universalism applies to professing Christians only. All other men, no matter how truth-loving, devout, and good are irretrievably damned.

—MILTON STEINBERG, *Basic Judaism,*
quoted by permission of
Harcourt, Brace & World, Inc.

Paul isn't the only one who limits salvation to Christians who subscribe to some special act or articles of faith. To put the thesis in the words of John 3:18, "He that believeth not is condemned."

Such was the position of Roman Catholicism: *extra ecclesiam nulla salus,* "outside the church there is no salvation." In recent years this strict interpretation has been softened among both Catholics and Protestants.

Judaism rejects such exclusiveness, and teaches that any righteous person may expect whatever rewards may come to the righteous in this world or the next.

It maintains the conviction that any good person, Jew or non-Jew, is acceptable before the Lord. Judaism . . . does not assume that it alone can save from eternal damnation.

There are no Jewish missionary movements because Judaism does not seek to attract anyone away from his own faith. Judaism does not believe that a man or woman must embrace Judaism to be saved. Judaism claims that the righteous of all peoples, each clinging to the highest ethical ideals of his faith, are equal before God!

This is what Moses Maimonides meant in the twelfth century when he wrote to Obadia, a convert to Judaism, who seemed troubled by the fact of being Jewish by choice rather than birth:

> You ask me if you, too, are allowed to say in the blessings and prayers you offer alone or in the congregation: *"Our* God and God of *our* fathers," "You who have sanctified *us* through Your commandments," "You who have separated *us,"* "You who have chosen *us,"* . . . 'You who have brought *us* out of the land of Egypt," and more of this kind.
>
> Yes, you may say all this in the prescribed order and not change it in the least. In the same way as every Jew by birth says his blessings and prayers, you, too, shall bless and pray alike, whether you are

alone or pray in the congregation. The reason for this is that Abraham, our father, taught the people, opened their minds, and revealed to them the true faith and the unity of God, he rejected the idols and abolished their adoration; he brought many children under the wings of the Divine Presence; he gave them counsel and advice, and ordered his sons and the members of his household after him to keep the ways of the Lord forever, as it is written, "For I have known him to the end that he may command his children and his household after him, that they may keep the way of the Lord, to do righteousness and justice" (Gen. 18:19). Ever since then whoever adopts Judaism and confesses the unity of the Divine Name, as it is prescribed in the Torah, is counted among the disciples of Abraham, our father, peace be with him. These men are Abraham's household, and he it is who converted them to righteousness.

In the same way as he converted his contemporaries through his words and teaching, he converts future generations through the testament he left to his children and household after him. Thus Abraham, our father, peace be with him, is the father of his pious posterity who keep his ways, and the father of his disciples and of all proselytes who adopt Judaism.

WHAT DO YOU THINK?

1. Do you think that a Christian who converts to Judaism is really Jewish? Explain what you mean.

Israel welcomes foreign students like this Burmese, who has come to study settlement methods. And Israeli technicians go abroad to help and teach. But no effort is made to convert others to Judaism.

2. Does a Jew have a right to give up his Judaism and become a convert to Christianity? Does he really become Christian?

3. A young Japanese man, Hiroshi Okamoto, came to the United States to become a convert to Judaism. He studied at the Hebrew Union College–Jewish Institute of Religion in Cincinnati, Ohio, and was ordained a rabbi in June, 1963. Returning to Japan, he has formed an organization to convert interested Japanese people to Judaism. Why do you think Hiroshi Okamoto became a convert to Judaism? Why do you think a number of Japanese people have become converted to Judaism instead of to Christianity?

4. On the basis of what you have studied about Christianity and Judaism, which religion do you think will have the greater appeal to college-educated people in the future? Give your reasons.

ARE THE JEWS THE CHOSEN PEOPLE?

Our Bible teaches us that God chose the Jews to be His people, to follow His ways and to teach the eternal truths of the Torah to all the nations and peoples of the earth.

The blessing we recite before the reading of the Torah says that we are the Chosen People. "Blessed art Thou, O Lord our God, Who has chosen us from among all peoples, and given us His Torah. Blessed art Thou, O Lord, Who gives the Torah."

According to the Book of Genesis, God told Abram, "in thee shall all the families of the earth be blessed" (12:3).

In the Book of Exodus, God says to the children of Israel: "I will take you to Me for a people, and I will be to you a God." In Exodus 19; 5–6 we read: "Now, therefore, if ye will hearken unto My voice, indeed, and keep My covenant, then ye shall be Mine own treasure from among all peoples, for the earth is Mine; and ye shall be unto Me a kingdom of priests and a holy people."

God says to the Egyptians: "Let My people go." In addition we read other verses in Exodus. Moses says to God: "Is it not in that Thou goest with us, so that we are distinguished, I and Thy people, from all the people that are upon the face of the earth?" In the Book of Deuteronomy, Moses tells the children of Israel: "And because He loved thy fathers and chose their seed after them, and brought thee out with His presence...." Later in Deuteronomy we read: "And the Lord hath avouched thee this day to be His own treasure, as He hath promised thee ... that thou mayest be a holy people unto the Lord thy God." There are many additional passages in the Torah, the prophets and writings showing that Israel is God's people, a kingdom of Priests and a holy people. Isaiah declared in the name of God: "Yet now hear, O Jacob, My servant, and Israel, whom I have chosen."

Furthermore, the prophet Hosea thought of God and Israel as being united in a special love, saying: "I will betroth thee unto me forever." The Song of Songs tells of the great love that God has for Israel and Israel for God in the words, "I am my beloved's and my beloved is mine" (6:3).

In rabbinic teachings of the Talmud and Midrash there are many stories to show that there is a special relationship between God and Israel and that God chose Israel for a great and holy purpose.

Are we better than others?

If we believe that God has chosen us, it doesn't mean that we are better than anyone else. It means we should try to act better than others. Once in the days of the prophet Amos, the children of Israel thought that they were better than anyone else, and that is when the prophet warned them in the following verses against the idea that God loves Israel alone:

Are ye not as the children of the Ethiopians
   unto Me,
O children of Israel? saith the Lord.
Have not I brought up Israel out of the
   land of Egypt,
And the Philistines from Caphtor,
And Aram from Kir?"

—AMOS 9:7

Amos taught that God loves all His children. He loved the dark-skinned Ethiopians just as He loved the children of Israel. And just as He brought the children of Israel out of the bondage of Egypt, so He brought the Philistines from the bondage of Caphtor, and the Arameans from the bondage of Kir.

There is another book of the Bible that rejects the idea that God loves the children of Israel alone. It is the story of the prophet Jonah, who refused to obey God's command to warn the people of Nineveh to repent and took a ship in the opposite direction. The book of Jonah was written to teach the children of Israel that God's love and mercy reaches out to all His children.

This may confuse us. First the Torah says that we are God's Chosen People, and then the Torah says that God loves all His children and that we aren't God's favorite people.

While we believe that God loves all His children, we also believe that God has a special relationship to Israel. The people of Israel were chosen not for reasons of favoritism or privilege. They were chosen to do God's work, to be God"s servants, and to fulfill God's holy purposes on earth.

THE CHOOSING PEOPLE

Actually, instead of calling ourselves the Chosen People, perhaps we should think of ourselves as Israel Zangwill said, as the choosing people. Not only did God choose Israel. Israel chose God and the ways of God, too.

The Midrash explains it in this way. When

God was about to give the Torah to man, He offered the Torah to the Amalekites who asked, "What is in it?" God said: "Thou shalt not kill." The Amalekites refused it. God offered it to the Ishmaelites who said, "What is in it?" God said: "Thou shalt not steal." They refused to accept it. God offered the Torah to the Moabites, who asked, "What is in it?" God said: "Thou shalt not commit adultery." They refused to accept it.

Then God offered the Torah to the children of Israel. They didn't ask what was in it. They said, *Na-aseh v'nishma.* "We will do and we will obey." God gave the Torah to the children of Israel because they were willing to accept it and live by it. In that sense, they were the choosing people—choosing God and the holy Torah. When they chose the Torah, then God chose them.

The holy mission

But to be a choosing people or a Chosen People means to accept a holy mission. Here is where we made a distinction between missionaries and mission. We are a people with a mission but without missionaries. Let me explain.

Following the destruction of the Temple in 586 B.C.E., when the majority of the Jews were taken as exiles into Babylonia, the second Isaiah, the prophet of the exile, taught that God had a great purpose for the Jews. They were to be scattered abroad to be a light unto the nations. The sacred destiny of the Jew was to bring God's word and God's eternal teachings to those who walked in darkness.

It is true, taught Isaiah, that Israel is now to be the suffering servant of God.

In Chapter 42 Isaiah declared in the name of God:

Behold, My servant, whom I uphold;
Mine elect, in whom My soul delighteth;

I have put My spirit upon him,
He shall make the right to go forth to the
nations.

The people of Israel were so to live and to act as to be witnesses of the truth of the eternal God. "Ye are my witnesses," saith the Lord.

Isaiah told the people that now they had a great mission, and that God had chosen Israel to bring justice and peace to the world:

I the Lord have called thee in
righteousness,
And have taken hold of thy hand,
And kept thee, and set thee for a
covenant of the people,
For a light of the nations;
To open the blind eyes,
To bring out the prisoners from the
dungeon,
And them that sit in darkness
out of the prison-house.

—ISAIAH 42:6–7

The Holy Land

Isaiah also taught that someday Palestine, the land of Israel, would be the center for the teaching of Torah, and an example of holiness and justice for all the nations and peoples of the world. He summed this up by saying, "From Zion shall go forth the Torah, and the word of the Lord from Jerusalem" (Isa. 2:3).

Throughout history, Jews always had a special love for the land of Israel. Rabbi Milton Steinberg has written about what was Palestine and is now the State of Israel:

Judaism looks upon Palestine . . . as sacred.

It was in the Holy Land . . . that revelation came to the prophets and was imparted by them to Israel and mankind. Palestine was the site of many of the su-

premely memorable incidents in Jewish history, and Hebrew was the medium for most of the precious utterances of the Jewish soul. . . .

. . . Similarly, the consciousness of Palestine pervades every phase of his religious life. The Scripture he reads, the prayers he recites, the rabbinic literature he studies are full of allusions to it.

—MILTON STEINBERG, *Basic Judaism,*
pp. 86–97, Quoted by permission of
Harcourt, Brace & World, Inc.

In 586 B.C.E., when the Jews were forced to leave their home in Palestine and were exiled to Babylonia, they wept when they remembered Zion. They yearned for the time when they would return home and rebuild their Temple. In 539 B.C.E., under Cyrus, they were permitted to return. The Temple was rebuilt and then destroyed again. As the years went by, the Jews were exiled, and dispersed throughout the world. The end of the Jewish state came in 70 C.E. and the Romans forced the Jews into exile. The Jewish State was not to come into existence again until 1948, when Israel became a sovereign and independent nation.

Ancient Palestine was not only sacred to the Jews, but it was the birthplace of two other religions: Islam and Christianity. It was the land where, according to the Gospels, Jesus and his early followers were born. It was there Christianity and the Moslem religion evolved. Mohammed taught the principles of the new religion of Islam. There the teachers of Christianity developed their new religion. Rome became the most important city of the Catholic Church. For the Jew, Jerusalem continued to be the holy city. It was more than an ancient capital city. It was a symbol of Jewish aspiration and hope. In prayer, the Jew turns in the direction of Jerusalem. When he reads from the Hagaddah on Passover he expresses the yearning, "Next year in Jerusalem." This does not mean that all Jews will return to Jerusalem and live there. It has always expressed the fervent hope that Jerusalem would be returned to the Jewish people.

During the holocaust thousands of Jews found refuge in Palestine. A million more emigrated after the Nazi terror was over and Hitler and his followers were defeated. With the establishment of the State of Israel in 1948, Jews throughout the world rejoiced not only in the nationhood of Israel, but in the new dignity that came to Jews everywhere.

In 1967, as a result of the Six Day War, the soldiers of Israel captured Jerusalem from the Arabs, and the old city of Jerusalem and the new city of Jerusalem were reunited. With this many of the sacred shrines and holy places were returned to Israel again. When the old city of Jerusalem was held by the Arabs, Jews were prohibited from visiting the Wailing Wall and other sacred shrines and places. Today, the State of Israel permits Christians and Arabs to visit and pray at their sacred shrines. In Israel, Jews learned to defend themselves against oppressors, and with pride and dignity resolve to destroy the idea of the helpless Jew, totally dependent upon others for protection and survival. Millions of Jews in Israel have built a new society where they have irrigated the desert, constructed housing, medical centers, schools and universities to provide a home for Jews everywhere who need a home, and to assure the survival of Judaism and the Jewish people.

A KINGDOM OF PRIESTS AND A HOLY PEOPLE

Judaism has no missionaries, but we have a mission, a purpose, a destiny and a cause. That is why we must continue to be "a kingdom of priests and a holy people."

This land in Ein Gedi, in the Judean desert, near the Dead Sea, lay desolate until transformed by modern reclamation efforts.

This same land in Ein Gedi now supports a tomato field—one more testimony to the kibbutzims' determination to make Israel a land of hope and fulfillment, part of a better world here and now.

This means that God kept the people of Israel alive through all these thousands of years for a reason: to teach other peoples to worship the one God, to keep his teachings of righteousness, mercy and holiness. Jews are commanded to work for justice, truth and goodness in every land and in every age.

That is the mission of Israel, which places special obligations upon us. This means that every Jew is to regard himself as doing God's holy work. We are not just an ordinary people; we are to be a *holy* people.

Jews often forget that they belong to one of the most ancient and distinguished of all peoples, and that our spiritual ancestry goes back to the time of Abraham and Moses.

The rabbi and the daughters of the American Revolution

Years ago there was a famous American rabbi. His name was Stephen S. Wise. He was a tall and imposing man, a man of great eloquence and spiritual strength.

Once Rabbi Wise was asked to speak to an organization called the Daughters of the American Revolution. After his talk, one of the ladies came up to him and said, "Rabbi Wise, do you know that my ancestors were present at the signing of the Declaration of Independence!"

Rabbi Wise stood up to his full height and said, "That's fine, Madam, but do you know that my ancestors were present at the signing of the Ten Commandments!"

The lady was bragging. She was proud of the fact that she could trace her ancestry back to the American revolution, which took place only about two hundred years ago.

The rabbi was saying that we Jews can trace our ancestors back almost four thousand years, and that we are one of the oldest of all peoples.

Each of us has two sets of spiritual ancestors. As Americans, our spiritual ancestors are Washington, Adams, Thomas Paine, Jefferson and Lincoln. But we have another set of ancestors.

As Jews our spiritual ancestors are Abraham, who left his home in Mesopotamia to help found a new religion; Moses, who stood at Sinai's height to receive the Ten Commandments; Amos, who spoke the word of God at Beth El; Isaiah, Jeremiah, Hosea, Ezekiel and other prophets.

Our ancestors were Saul, Solomon, David, and the psalmists; great rabbis, Hillel, Akiba, Johanan ben Zakkai, Judah Ha-Nasi; great philosophers like Judah Ha-Levi, Saadiah and Maimonides.

But it isn't enough to take pride in our spiritual ancestors. The real meaning of the mission of Israel is a feeling of obligation to carry on their work, to live up to their ideals and obey their teachings to help build a better world.

Will Jews be able to build a better tomorrow all alone, or will they need partners to join with them to make a dream come true?

Are we as Jews the only ones chosen to build God's Kingdom on earth?

THE CHRISTIAN BELIEF IN THE CHOSEN PEOPLE

The early Christians believed that the Jews were God's Chosen People—chosen to give Jesus to the world, not chosen to be God's servants. Once the Jews gave Jesus to the world, then their chosenness came to an end, and the Christians became God's Chosen People. Just as the Old Testament was fulfilled and then replaced by the New Testament, so many Christians believe that Judaism was only a preparation for the development of Christianity.

Some Christians believe that the Jews still are the Chosen People of God and that someday they will see the light and accept Jesus as their savior, and then the age of the Messiah will come and there will be a perfect world.

This brings us to the important subject of the Jewish and Christian idea of Salvation, Heaven and Hell, and the world to come.

WHAT DO YOU THINK?

1. Which do you think we are: a Chosen People, a choosing people, or both? Give your reasons.

2. Do you think there is any special significance in the passage from Isaiah where God calls Israel "Mine elect"? What is the difference between election and selection?

3. How is it possible for a Jew to be a servant of God today?

4. What did Isaiah mean when he called upon Israel to be a light of the nations; to open the blind eyes, to bring out the prisoners from the dungeon?

5. We are called "a kingdom of priests and a holy people." What do we have to do to be priests today? How do we become "holy"?

6. Rabbi Nathan Perilman in a sermon, "Why Not Jewish Missionaries," said:

Judaism has a mission and a message to give to the whole world, but first it will have to bring it to the descendants of Abraham. Before we attempt to convert others, we shall have to reconvert our own. . . .

For a long time we have known that Christian and Moslem missionaries would do well to work first in their own house before they offer their way of life to those who do not know the way. The same good counsel applies to us. The duty is ours, we are committed to the mission, but long before we can go out among others, we must first win over our own.

What is your opinion?

7. A great American rabbi, Dr. Mordecai Kaplan, thinks that the Jews have earned the enmity of the Gentiles because of the term Chosen People. In the Reconstructionist prayer book of his movement, the Torah blessing is "who has drawn us nigh to His service," rather than "chosen us." Do you like Dr. Kaplan's interpretation?

THINGS TO DO

1. Write to the Jewish Information Society, 127 N. Dearborn Street, Chicago, Illinois 60602, and ask for information about this organization. Request some of the pamphlets and tracts.

2. Write an essay on your idea of whether we should have Jewish missionaries to convert the nonaffiliated to Judaism.

3. Discuss in class the meaning of the Talmudic saying: "Just as it is not possible for the world to exist without the winds, so is it not possible for the world to exist without Israel."

4. Write to the Anti-Defamation League of B'nai B'rith, 515 Madison Avenue, New York, New York 10022, and order the film, "The Chosen People."

5. Interview a Christian minister and ask his views of the work of Christian missionaries, the efforts to convert Jews to Christianity, and the belief that the Jews are the Chosen People.

SELECTED QUOTATIONS

The village that became Jewish

In the 1930's about seventy families in the remote Italian village of San Nicandro voluntarily adopted Judaism, without ever having met a Jew. They were influenced by one of their own number, a half literate peasant named Manduzio . . . who had devoted himself to the study of religion. The Bible (distributed by Protestant missionaries, oddly) was the power which led him from Catholicism to Judaism. His enthusiasm was passed on to others. During the Fascist persecution, they openly maintained their Jewish faith and in 1946 they were formally accepted into the Jewish community. . . .

The entire Jewish community of San Nicandro has been transplanted to Israel, where their experience in farming is being put to excellent use.

—RABBI BERNARD J. BAMBERGER

You ver' strange priest

Shu Shung-Ho was the South Korean houseboy who took care of our tent which, besides myself, was occupied by two Protestant and two Catholic chaplains. Shung-Ho was an intelligent, industrious and artistic lad of seventeen, very adept at painting, a voracious reader in both Korean and English and a superb listener. One rainy afternoon we found ourselves alone in the tent, he said [to the Jewish chaplain]:

"You ver' strange Priest."

"Why," I asked, taken aback.

"You no try make me Christian."

"I'm not a Christian. I'm a Jew."

"Why you no try to make me Jew, then?"

"Why, Shung-Ho," I said, "I like you just the way you are."

The boy reflected for several moments, then said: "You know, Father, you first priest say that to me. You first man no try change me. I ver' happy. I like ver' much."

—*Congress Weekly*

We must evangelize

We must evangelize. We must spread the gospel in both a personal and corporate way. If religion, as we understand it, means anything to us at all, we ought to tell other people about it. We ought to make a real attempt to interest them and to win them for Christ and his church. This is personal evangelism and every Protestant Christian ought constantly to be at work in this way.

—*A Protestant Primer*

The religion of all mankind

If there be but one God, there can be only one religion; and the idea of unity in religion carries with it the idea of universality. Now, indeed, Israel alone knows and worships this God, but in His larger purpose it must one day be the religion of all mankind. Israel is His instrument for the accomplishment of this end; it is His prophet among the nations.

—Congregationalist minister and Harvard professor, GEORGE FOOT MOORE in his book, *Judaism*

Jewish missionaries

First, we should acknowledge that the crucial step is to win the heart of the Jew to Judaism. Unless we convince ourselves of our own worth and the validity of the Jewish message, unless we master our spiritual legacy, we are not in a position to share it with the entire world. Too many Jews today are lukewarm and negative. We must begin by being missionaries to our own people, heartening the indifferent and firing with zeal those whose spirits have turned away.

Second, we must pursue a policy of informing outsiders that they are welcome to our fellowship. This can be part of a program to publicize in a dignified way the beauty of Judaism. . . .

—RABBI ABRAM VOSSEN GOODMAN

Each in his own way

Jews do not believe that they must convert others and bring them into the Jewish peoplehood in order to achieve the redemption of humankind. Let each nation, each people, all religions, come to God, each in their own way. (Mic. 4:5) If only they will be faithful to that which is True in their revelation, then we can hope that despite differences, men will live together in love and work together for justice.

—RABBI ARTHUR GILBERT

SELECTED READINGS

BROWNE, LEWIS, *How Odd of God*

COHON, BERYL D., *Introduction to Judaism,* pp. 100–102

FACKENHEIM, EMIL L., *Paths to Jewish Belief* Chapter 10

LEVINGER, LEE J., LEVINGER, ELMA E., and GERSH, HARRY, *The Story of the Jew,* pp. 37, 40, 43–44, 78, 204, 284

TARSHISH, ALLAN, *Not by Power*

UNIVERSAL JEWISH ENCYCLOPEDIA, Volume 3, Chosen People, pp. 164–169

14

The World to Come

Are you saved?

My Friend:

I am asking you the most important question of life. Your joy or your sorrow for all eternity depends upon it. The question is: Are you saved?

It is not if you are a member of some church, but ARE YOU SAVED?

It is not how good you are, but ARE YOU SAVED?

No one can enjoy the blessings of God or go to heaven without being saved.

There is no chance to be saved unless you come to realize you are a sinner.

Because you are a sinner, you are condemned to die.

This means separation from God, in HELL, FOREVER.

　　　　—Berean Gospel Distributors, Inc.
　　　　　　　Indianapolis, Indiana

This is a pamphlet distributed by those who think that unless we believe a certain way we will go to hell and suffer forever. They teach about hell, damnation and punishment after we die.

We must remember that this is not typical of all Christian denominations. Most Christian ministers in this country do not teach this today, and it would be unfair to consider this as part of the belief of all Christians. Until recently people believed that sinners were punished in a fiery hell, and only those who accepted Jesus as their savior would go to heaven and be saved.

WHAT DO YOU THINK?

1. What does Judaism believe about hell, damnation and suffering in the next life?

2. What does Christianity think happens to people when they die?

3. If you were going to write a list of questions to ask a rabbi about the Jewish belief in the next life, what would you ask?

4. If you were to write a list of questions to ask a Christian minister about the Christian belief in the next life, what would you ask?

THE CATHOLIC BELIEF ABOUT SALVATION

Catholics believe that salvation is being "saved" from sin so that the soul may achieve a hereafter in Heaven. They further believe that salvation was won for all men of all time by the life, death and resurrection of Jesus Christ. Thus through a good life and through

This Van Eyck painting, "The Last Judgment" was made in the fifteenth century. Fewer Christians now hold to such grim ideas.

Christ's saving grace a person enters eternity to be judged. If he has lived a good life through the Church, then he is regarded as having found salvation through God's personal love.

Catholic doctrine teaches that there is a Heaven and a Hell for the souls of the dead. There is a Purgatory for the removal of sins that have not been forgiven. But actually they don't know the exact nature of Heaven and Hell. Some interpret Heaven as the state of eternal happiness and bliss, seeing and knowing God. Hell is the state of being cut off from knowing God in His Goodness and Love.

To Catholics there are two judgments — first, the personal judgment which takes place at the separation of soul and body at what is called death. Then the soul goes to Heaven, Hell or Purgatory. Then there is the General Judgment on the last day when Christ in Glory will come and judge all mankind. The Church does not define the "how, when or where" of the General Judgment.

They also believe that the souls of non-Catholics who were good people yet who were "invincibly ignorant" about Catholicism will go to a fourth place called limbo. This is a gray place without pain, yet also without joy.

Most Catholics try to follow the teachings and the practices of the Catholic Church and live the best kind of life that they can, trusting in Jesus' redeeming power to determine what will happen to them in the next life. By means of masses they believe they can help speed a dead relative's time in Purgatory and send his soul on to Heaven. This is why Catholics often leave money to the Church for masses for their own souls.

THE PROTESTANT BELIEF ABOUT SALVATION

Protestants believe that *salvation* means that they are "saved" from damnation and the wages of sin, and brought to God's grace. Through Jesus, God gave the world a chance to come closer to Him. To be saved is to so respond to God in faith that life is made full and complete in God through Christ.

Some Protestants believe in life after death because death is part of life's experience. The body is the temporary dwelling place of the person. They do not think that the next world is a place of "pearly gates or streets of gold"—but many believe that God gives a new body to those who die.

To many Protestants Hell is to exist but not really live, to be in the presence of the beautiful and have no awareness or appreciation of it. Heaven is the closeness to and fellowship with the God they love and worship.

Protestantism's main preachment used to be about the punishment of a God of wrath. Today more and more Christians are recognizing that God does not deal with them that way. If God were to really punish them for their sins, who would be able to stand before Him? Through "grace," God gives of His love.

Protestants believe that life is God's gift and goes through transformations. They teach the words of Jesus: "In the dwelling place of my Heavenly Father there is room for you. I go to prepare for your coming and will come again to meet you, that where I am, there you may be also." (See John 14:2–3.) The real return to God in the next world isn't so much physical as spiritual. They believe that the next life will be a new and wonderful fellowship with God in a wonderful Eternity of Beauty, goodness and love forever.

We are soon going to discuss the action of religion in building a better world. However, before we can do that, we must know a little about how Judaism and Christianity understand this world. Does this sound strange to you? After all, you might think,

the world is here and what is there to understand? Actually it isn't that simple. Whether you realize it or not, each of us has to decide what he will do in this world and how he will live his life. Such a decision depends on many things. If I believe the world to be worthless, I certainly won't work to improve it. Or, if I believe the world is in fine shape the way it is, I will not try to change things in it. Thus, it is clear that each man makes a decision on the value of the world and then on what he will do to decrease or increase its value.

Before we can discuss the role of religion in the world, we turn to the Jewish concept of salvation.

THE JEWISH BELIEF ABOUT SALVATION

Let us first consider what we *don't* believe. Judaism doesn't believe in an everlasting Hell, a place of eternal, terrible punishment in the next world. Judaism cannot believe that if a person doesn't accept a certain religion or follow a certain religious belief he will be punished through all eternity by God in the next world. By salvation we do not usually refer to what happens after death. The afterlife is a mystery which man cannot hope to understand. Though many traditional Jews feel sure of not only a Heaven but a place of punishment, it is more a place of purging from sin than of punishment, and no soul remains there for more than one year. For Judaism does not feel that a loving God could ever punish anyone with Hell fire eternally. As the late Rabbi Leo Baeck wrote, "A God who would doom his children to burn in fire forever would not be a God but a monster."

According to Jewish belief we think of salvation in terms of a society—a society whose citizens live up to God's moral laws and put them into practice, a society of justice, brotherhood and peace. If there is a

"The spirit of man is the lamp of the Lord." Proverbs 20:27 provides the inscription for this modern Yahrzeit lamp.

good society, then all citizens have a better chance of receiving the benefits and advantages of the "good life" and achieving spiritual attainment.

It is difficult for us Jews to think of an individual being "saved," nice and cozy and secure, while others who are God's children are hungry, unjustly treated, without jobs or sufficient clothing or medical care.

To us, God is our Father and a Father represents love. Would our own fathers want us to suffer now or in the next world?

Maybe you are thinking: "But what if we are bad? Shouldn't we be punished? And if we are good, shouldn't we be rewarded? If not, what's the whole point of being good?

If all good people and bad people are treated the same way, why be good?"

For goodness' sake

Judaism teaches that we should be good —for nothing. That is, be good for goodness' sake. Be good without the thought of receiving a reward for being good.

We are supposed to live lives of worth because we are children of God, and because God wants us to be good. What's more, being good brings us more joy and happiness than being bad. But that's not the point. Even if it were to bring us unhappiness, we are to be good because we should obey God's teachings—without thought of reward or punishment. A little child is good for the sake of a reward. A mature person is good for goodness' sake, without reward.

We want to be good because God is good and because we are created in the divine image; not because He will punish us if we are not good or reward us when we are good. Evil removes us from God. Goodness brings us closer to God. That is our real punishment and reward.

We believe in *retribution,* which means that we get paid back for what we do here in this world. If we do evil, then there are evil consequences for us and for others. Even if no one sees us, God sees us. Even if no one else knows what we did, we know what we did—and this has an effect on our character. Each time we do an evil deed, it weakens us so that we do more evil deeds. Each time we do an act of goodness, it strengthens us to do good again.

Liberal Jews do not believe that we will have bodies in the next world. Many years ago some of the rabbis believed that when people died they still had bodies even though they taught that "in the next world, there will be no eating or drinking or having children."

In the *Union Prayerbook* we read:

The soul which Thou, O God, hast given unto me came pure from Thee. Thou hast created it, Thou hast formed it, Thou hast breathed it into me, Thou hast preserved it in this body and, at the appointed time, Thou wilt take it from this earth that it may enter upon life everlasting. While the breath of life is within me, I will worship Thee, Sovereign of the world and Lord of all souls. Praised be Thou, O God, in whose hands are the souls of all the living and the spirits of all flesh."

—*The Union Prayerbook*, p. 101

This sums up in one prayer the Jewish belief that the soul returns to God. There are other prayers, such as:

Death is not the end; the earthly body vanishes, the immortal spirit lives on with God. In our hearts, also, our loved ones never die. Their love and memory abide as a lasting inspiration, moving us to noble deeds and blessing us ever more."

—*Ibid.*, p. 275

JUDAISM IS A THIS-WORLDLY RELIGION

We can't answer the question of what happens to the soul in the next world. That's a mystery too great for us to understand. Actually, we don't know what happens to the soul but we believe that the soul is with God. Since God is eternal love, could there be a greater good than to be one with God?

This is what the prayer, Adon Olam, means when it says:

Slums like this one on the West side of Chicago remind us that religion in action has far to go in building a better world "to come" here for its children.

How could better use of nature's God-given abundance provide a better world "here and now"? What causes Americans to crowd together in overgrown cities when they still have great stretches of unbroken countryside?

*Into Thy hand I commit my soul
Both when I sleep and when I wake;
And with my soul my body too,
The Lord is with me,
I shall not fear.*

A Jew doesn't fear God or an afterlife with God because God is "The Merciful One" and loves us as a Father loves his children.

This is why we concern ourselves not so much with the next world as much as this world, God's Kingdom of justice and righteousness on earth. We have work to do—God's work, to build a society where all mankind will have enough to eat, decent houses in which to live, a worthwhile and dignified way of earning his daily bread. We must join in building a society where all men are free, both in body and in mind, and where they can strive spiritually as well as physically.

Why should we think so much about the next world until we have brought justice to those who are oppressed in this world? Why should we think so much of Hell when people hate other people because of the color of their skin, or because of what they believe or the way they worship? No. Judaism insists that we must do all we can to bring justice, righteousness, brotherhood and peace to all people in this world.

IS THERE A DEVIL?

We know that we don't believe in Hell or punishment by fire or eternal damnation, but does Judaism believe in a devil? What about the book of Job, that tells about Satan walk-in to and fro on the earth? What about angels and demons, do we believe in them?

It is true that there are references to Satan in Jewish literature—and we even read about *sheol,* a shadowy place for spirits. Then, too, there is mention made of angels. The reference to Satan is only a literary means to tell a story. Even in the book of Job, Satan is a servant of God and is controlled by God, but actually we don't believe in Satan or the devil. How could we, and still say the *Shema Yisrael?*

When we say: "Hear, O Israel, the Lord our God, the Lord is one," we declare that there can't be any other god—not even a god of evil.

During the Persian influence, some of the teachings of Zoroaster crept into Judaism, the belief in a God of goodness and light who rules over Heaven, and a god of evil and darkness who rules over Hell. The Persian belief in angels and demons also found its way into some Jewish literature, but we to-day do not believe in angels or demons or Satan or the devil.

How can we talk of a God of love and believe that there is a devil, who can compete with God and bring about evil?

WHAT DO YOU THINK?

1. *A Protestant Primer* refers to "Justification by Faith." This is a distinctive religious belief of the Protestant churches. It means that "salvation is a gift made possible by Jesus Christ. Such Protestants believe that we can never earn salvation or even come to the point where we feel that we deserve it because of the many good works which we have done. We can only receive the loving forgiveness of God and the salvation which He offers to us as a result of all that Christ did for mankind. What do you think? What do you think Judaism would say about this?

2. An Associated Press report from London states that the Church of England, revising its prayer book, had planned to remove all mention of the devil. Because of protests, this will not be done. A Church commission has suggested this wording: "Renounce the devil and fight against evil." What do you think? What is the attitude of Judaism toward the concept of the devil?

3. Judaism has been called "a this-worldly religion." Explain what this means.

Do you think that most Jews today believe in the immortality of the body? What are your reasons? Interview an Orthodox, Conservative and Reform rabbi and find out what modern day Judaism believes about the resurrection of the body and the continuation of the body after death.

4. Rabbi Fackenheim in *Paths To Jewish Belief* writes:

> Many Jewish thinkers have believed that the body as well as the soul is immortal. Other Jewish thinkers have held that the soul alone survives.
>
> But no matter how strongly we hold either belief, we can never *prove* that even the soul continues to exist . . . How can a disembodied soul think, feel, act, will?

Yet is it not much more credible to believe that a person who has lived once will live again, than that a person who has never lived will live? However, we witness births all about us and we are not surprised. Why can not the mind and spirit of a person once alive continue to persist? These are unanswerable questions. The wisest Jewish thinkers tell us to believe in an afterlife, but to refrain from speculating about what it is like.

What do you think?

5. The St. Paul's Episcopal Church of Kansas City, Missouri, had the following statement in its church bulletin:

So man's soul, we believe, needs a body for its completion and fulfillment. We were not intended by God to be disincarnate and disembodied ghosts. God, in His goodness, proposes that we shall have a body, even after the powers of physical death have caused the decay and dissolution of this particular bundle of matter with which we go into the grave.

This is what we assert today when we rejoice in the fact of the Resurrection. Jesus, by His rising to life again, guarantees to us a complete body and soul existence again. Let us give thanks.

What do you think?

THINGS TO DO

1. Make a chart and list the Jewish, Catholic and Protestant beliefs in salvation, retribution (reward and punishment), the immortality of the soul, and the life after death.

2. Act out a socio-drama where a missionary approaches a Jew and tells him that unless he accepts Jesus he will go to Hell. Make a list of all the arguments the missionary will use, and a list of how the Jew will answer the arguments.

3. Three members of the class should be selected with the assignment of one interviewing a priest, another interviewing a minster, and the third one interviewing a rabbi on their beliefs about: (a) the devil; (b) the second coming of Jesus; (c) reward and punishment in this world; (d) reward and punishment in the next world; (e) do all souls, even the souls of evil men and women, go to God after death? Report back to class and discuss the reports.

4. Discuss in class: "What arguments can be given by the fundamentalist who passes out tracts about sinners burning in Hell to show that bodies continue after death?"

5. Discuss in class why Jews usually have no fear of Hell or damnation after death.

6. Debate in class the importance of "Faith versus Good Works." What is the attitude of Judaism to faith without good works?

7. After doing research, write an essay comparing the Catholic and Protestant, and the Orthodox, Conservative and Reform Jewish belief about the resurrection of the dead.

8. Sister Mary David writes:

The word "resurrection" means the return of a dead man to life.

The RESURRECTION refers to the great event celebrated by Christians on Easter Sunday: on the third day after His death, Jesus united his soul again with his body and rose gloriously from the dead. [Cf. the Gospel according to St. Luke, Chapter 24]. According to Christian belief, the Resurrection of Jesus was unlike any of the events recorded in the Bible, when men were apparently brought back to life. Jesus' Resurrection was a result of a victory over death, and therefore accompanied by the spiritualization of the body which is perfectly reunited with the soul, completely united to God.

For Christians, the Resurrection is the foundation of their faith and the greatest proof of the Divinity of Jesus Christ. As St. Paul says, ". . . if Christ has not risen, . . . vain is your faith." [1 Cor. 15:14.]

On the Feast of the Resurrection Christians are reminded of their Baptism by which they arose from sin to a share in the Divine life, and also they look forward to the resurrection of their own bodies at the end of the world, unto life eternal.

Write an essay comparing her Catholic belief with the teachings of Orthodox Judaism about resurrection.

9. Read the following statement by Rabbi Fackenheim and compare with Sister David's belief.

Some people, Jew as well as Christians, believe that at the Day of Last Judgment every human body will be restored to life and reunited to its soul. Sometimes they base this belief on the 37th Chapter of Ezekiel. But if the matter of a human body has turned into other matter, how can it be restored to its original shape?

Jewish believers in bodily immortality were so deeply convinced that the body, being a gift of God, is good, that they were prepared to accept the difficult belief in

To "redeem the world from evil" man must banish the threat of hunger. At experiment stations in India and other lands, men try new ways of rice planting. UNESCO agencies help fight hunger around the world.

the resurrection of the body. To make this belief acceptable, they said that resurrection could occur by divine miracle. Since God created the whole universe and all the life in it, surely it would be possible for Him miraculously to resurrect life.

SELECTED QUOTATIONS

Personal salvation is here and now

Personal salvation is attained here and now and its reward is enjoyed here and now. In Judaism, there is no stress on the rewards of Heaven or the threat of Hell. "Better one hour of repentance and good deeds in this world," say the sages, "than all the life of the world-to-come." Judaism is not a religion of prizes and penalties. The religious Jew is good and does good because he believes that this is what God wants him to do and because he believes that this is the only proper way to live. The only reward he expects for doing good is the inner satisfaction that comes with and from the doing.

—RABBI DAVID MAX EICHHORN

To do justly

Salvation for the individual and for the human race lies in the process of seeking to make secure, in ever increasing measure, the lives and the fortunes of every human being. Just where this will lead, no one knows and none can foretell. In all probability, we are not the first nor the last group of sentient beings who have populated or who will populate this planet. If we end by blowing ourselves to bits, another human race may someday succeed where we have failed. But, while life and hope remain, Judaism will continue to teach contemporary mankind that it must turn from its evil ways and follow

Him Who has ordained that all are brothers and equals and Who has willed that the Jew may not rest content until every person on earth has learned to obey His prophet's words:

DO JUSTLY:

LOVE MERCY:

WALK HUMBLY

BEFORE GOD.

—RABBI DAVID MAX EICHHORN

"Every day is Judgment Day"

Many people probably don't think any longer of a heaven of golden streets and pearly gates up above the sky, or a hell of fire and brimstone down below the earth. For one thing, now that we know our earth is a planet spinning around on its axis, there is no longer any "up" or "down." Furthermore, such a heaven is designed to please bodies, and such a hell is made to punish bodies. But if in the future life we don't have bodies, or at least bodies like the ones we now live in, there would be little satisfaction in golden streets and little pain in endless fire. You can't very well burn a spirit. There is something to be said for picturing the life beyond in spiritual terms, rather than in bodily terms.

This not to say that there will be no judgment, and no rewards or punishments awaiting us. Indeed, we are being judged all the while, and the rewards and punishments can be seen even now. Every day is Judgment Day.

—NEVIN C. HARNER

Reaching Heaven

MIAMI BEACH, FLA. (AP)

Heaven, to Bill Graham, is real and reachable.

"I don't know here it is, or how large it

is, but I believe it is a literal place," the evangelist told an audience of 13,000 at Miami Beach Convention Hall last night.

Graham described heaven as devoid of sin, sorrow, disasters, darkness and armies. He said the only way to be sure of reaching heaven it "to repent, accept Christ by faith as Savior, and obey him as Lord."

—*The Kansas City Times*

Meaning of salvation

To the Jew salvation means redeeming the world from evil. And that can come only through the constant disciplining and refining of the individual, so that he can discern right from wrong and not only discern it but learn to enjoy the good and reject the evil. This is the definition of ancient Hebrew wisdom. To this ultimate end has Jewish learning been directed. This is the message of Israel to mankind.

—DR. JOHN J. TEPFER,
Professor of Jewish History and Talmud,
Hebrew Union College–Jewish
Institute of Religion

The coming world

The Baal Shem Tov was once so depressed that it seemed to him that he would have no place in the coming world. Then he said to himself, 'If I love God and enter into relationship with God here, in this world, what need have I of a coming world?"

SELECTED READINGS

FACKENHEIM, EMIL L., *Paths to Jewish Belief,* Chapter 9

GITTELSOHN, ROLAND B., *But Little Lower Than The Angels,* Chapter 17, "What Happens To Us When We Die?"

HARNER, NEVIN C., *I Believe—A Christian Faith For Youth*

SILVERMAN, WILLIAM B., *The Still Small Voice Today,* Chapter 8, pp. 222–226

15

Religion and Social Justice

The soapmaker and the rabbi

A soapmaker and a rabbi once took a walk. The soapmaker said: "What good is Judaism? Look at the condition of the world: hatred, war, hunger, sickness, misery, man hating his fellow man. All this after 4,000 years of Judaism!

"What good is Christianity? After almost 2,000 years of Christian teachings we still find nation fighting nation, people through the world are starving, and man persecutes his fellow man, and there is the ever-present threat of someone pushing a button and destroying humanity with atomic death.

"What good is Judaism? What good is Christianity? What good is religion?"

The rabbi was silent as they continued their walk. Soon they came upon a dirty child playing in the gutter. The rabbi said: "Look at this filthy child. What good is soap? With millions of bars of soap coming off the assembly line, just look at the condition of this child. What good is soap?"

The soap manufacturer became angry. He protested, "Soap isn't any good unless it is applied and used!"

The rabbi said, "So it is with Judaism and Christianity, my friend. Religion isn't of much value unless it is applied and used."

THE RIGHTEOUS SHALL LIVE BY HIS FAITH

We hear so much about the teachings of religion, but too often we forget that religion must be applied to life, to our homes, our work, the community, the nation and the world in which we live.

This is what the prophet Habakkuk meant when he said, "The righteous shall *live* by his faith" (Hab. 2:4).

When the children of Israel received the Torah they said, *"Na-aseh v'nishma.* We will *do,* and we will obey." Time after time the Torah urges the children of Israel to learn the teachings of God *to do them, to live by them.*

The prophets of Israel insisted that God's teachings must be applied to every aspect of life. Amos spoke in the name of God saying:

I hate, I despise your feasts,
And I will take no delight in your solemn
  assemblies.
Yea, though ye offer me burnt-offerings
  and your meal offerings
I will not accept them.
Neither will I regard the peace-offerings
  of your fat beasts.
Take thou away from Me the noise of thy
  songs;

And let Me not hear the melody of thy
psalteries.
But let justice well up as waters,
And righteousness as a mighty stream.
—AMOS 5:21–24

Because he spoke out so bluntly against sacrifices without justice, and because he criticized the people for not living by their faith, Amos was stoned and driven out of Beth El.

Isaiah demanded that the children of Israel do more than offer sacrifices and prayers. He lashed out at those who made a mockery of religion by offering sacrifices and forgetting justice. Speaking in the name of God he said:

I cannot endure iniquity along with the
solemn assembly.

Your new moons and your appointed
seasons
My soul hateth;
They are a burden unto Me;
I am weary to bear them.
And when ye spread forth your hands,
I will hide Mine eyes from you;
Yea, when ye make many prayers,
I will not hear;
Your hands are full of blood.
Wash you, make you clean,
Put away the evil of your doings
From before Mine eyes,
Cease to do evil;
Learn to do well;
Seek justice, relieve the oppressed,
Help the fatherless, plead for the widow.
—ISAIAH 1:13–17

"Justice, justice, shall ye pursue," proclaim the placards.
They were carried by members of the Commission on
Social Action of Reform (UAHC) Judaism, who took part in
the August 1963 March on Washington, when Dr. King
made his "I have a dream" speech.

GOD IS EXALTED THROUGH JUSTICE

How do we praise and glorify God, asked Isaiah? Through words, prayers or ritual, or Holy Days or festivals? No! Listen to him as he speaks:

*The Lord of hosts is exalted through
   justice
And God the Holy One is sanctified
   through righteousness.*

Isaiah was hated by many of his own people because he insisted that God demands justice and righteousness from those who worship Him. The people did not like to listen to this constant criticism, but Isaiah persisted, always speaking in the name of God, saying to those who forgot the real meaning of the day of Atonement:

*Is not this the fast that I have chosen?
To loose the fetters of wickedness,
To undo the bands of the yoke,
And to let the oppressed go free,
And that ye break every yoke?
Is it not to deal thy bread to the hungry,
And that thou bring the poor that are cast
   out to thy house?
When thou seest the naked, that thou
   cover him.
Then shalt thou call, and the Lord will
   answer;
Thou shalt cry, and He will say:
"Here I am."*
                              —ISAIAH 58:6–9

THUS SAITH THE LORD

You may be asking yourself: "Does this mean that the prophets were against prayers, ritual, Holy Days and festivals because they lash out at the people who observed them?"

No, the prophets were not against prayer, ritual, Holy Days and festivals. They were against making sacrifices and ceremonials *substitutes* for social justice and for ethical action. They believed that the sacrifices, the prayers and the ritual should inspire the people to deeds of kindness and justice. They believed that the Holy Days and the festivals should make the people more mindful of their obigation to help their fellow man, and to be holy as God had commanded them.

The prophets used their religion and applied their faith to the problems of society. This got them into trouble and made lots of people angry.

Jeremiah condemned even kings for injustice to the people. He criticized the mightiest authorities of the land when they oppressed the people. He predicted destruction and doom for Judah because the people had strayed from the paths of the living

*Thus saith the Lord:
Woe unto him that buildeth his house by
   unrighteousness,
And his chambers by injustice;
That useth his neighbour's service without
   wages,
And giveth him not his hire.*
                              —JEREMIAH 22:13

Many people mocked Jeremiah, and even threatened him, but he persisted. And because he demanded social justice for the rich and the poor, for the weak and the strong— because he had the courage to condemn the rulers for their sins, they hated him and lowered him into a dungeon where he would have died if an Ethiopian had not rescued him.

MODERN PROPHETS

This same thing is happening today with some ministers, rabbis and priests. We read about clergymen being arrested and put into jail because they are trying to help the Negro people, or because they picket, or join in protests for peace, or work for some unpopular cause. They are being mocked and jeered at, just as the prophets were.

Ministers, rabbis and priests are insisting that religion must be used, must be applied to the problems of life. They say that the church and the synagogue must no longer remain silent when there are injustices, but must speak out in the words of the prophets: "Thus saith the Lord."

But more than words are needed. These modern prophets are demanding that the church and synagogue must move forward to an ever greater participation in social action. They maintain that religion must be concerned with race relations, with international amity, with slum clearance, with the elimination of poverty, prejudice, of crime and disease, with the furtherance of mental health, education, nuclear testing, and above all with the effort to bring peace to the world.

Something new and wonderful is happening in our generation. Ministers, priests and rabbis are meeting together and working together, and sometimes walking arm in arm as they fight for justice. Members of churches, cathedrals, synagogues and temples are joining together to discuss problems and take action against the wrongs of society. Judaism and Christianity are becoming partners, partners in faith, partners in the building of a better world.

SIMILARITIES AS WELL AS DIFFERENCES

Of course, there are differences between Judaism and Christianity, and very important differences, or there wouldn't be two distinct religions, but there are many great ideals that Judaism and Christianity share.

Today it is the custom for Christian groups to visit synagogues. When this happens the rabbi tells about the Eternal Light, the *Menorahs,* the *Aron ha-Kodesh* and the *Torahs.*

He also explains the meaning of Jewish ceremonials and Jewish beliefs. The following is what happened at one synagogue when a group from the Methodist church visited. Maybe it happened at your synagogue, too.

Rabbi: Judaism believes in the Fatherhood of God and the Brotherhood of man.

Boy (from Methodist group): But, Rabbi, that is Christian. We believe that, too.

Rabbi: That is so. Judaism and Christianity both believe in the Fatherhood of God and the Brotherhood of man.

We also believe that God wants us to "Love thy neighbor as thyself."

Boy: But that's Christian, too.

Rabbi: That is right, and there is the Jewish belief that man is created in the image of God, and the Jewish belief in justice, mercy and peace.

Boy: We believe that is Christian.

Rabbi: And so it is. What do you say about the Jewish belief in the building of God's Kingdom on earth, the good society of tomorrow?

Boy: We would say that is Christian.

Rabbi: Son, you are right. There are Christians and Jews here today, and although we may differ on many points, there are many great ideals that both Judaism and Christianity share together.

THE JUDEO-CHRISTIAN ETHICAL HERITAGE

When it comes to religious practices, Judaism and Christianity may differ. We may differ in our beliefs about God, Jesus, original sin, salvation and the next world, but when it comes to ethics, we share the same great tradition that is called the Judeo-Christian ethical heritage.

Ethics means the way we act. It has to do with our behavior, our conduct, the difference between right and wrong. It means choosing the right way, the good way, the way God wants us to act.

Christian ethics and Jewish ethics are basically the same. When Christianity began, the early Christian leaders carried over into their new religion many of the ethical beliefs of Judaism. That is why these ideals of justice and mercy and kindness have been given the name, the Judeo-Christian ethical heritage or tradition.

This should help us to understand how it is possible for Judaism and Christianity to work together as partners for the building of a better world.

What do you think a Christian and a Jew should say about these letters which were written in jail?

We have known humiliation, we have known abusive language, we have been plunged into the abyss of oppression, and we decided to rise up only with the weapon of protest. It is one of the greatest glories of America that we have the right to protest.

If we are arrested every day, if we are exploited every day, if we are trampled over every day, don't ever let anyone pull you so low as to hate them. We must use the weapon of love. We must have compassion and understanding for those who hate us. We must realize so many people are taught to hate us that they are not totally responsible for their hate. But we stand in life at midnight; we are always on the threshold of a new dawn.

—Excerpts from a letter written by the leader of the Negro resistance movement, the late Reverend Martin Luther King, Jr., after his arrest in Alabama.

WHAT DO YOU THINK?

1. How would you compare the Reverend Martin Luther King, Jr., with the prophets

of Israel? How does he differ from the prophets?

2. How would you compare the plight of the Negroes in the South with that of the children of Israel who were slaves to Pharaoh in Egypt? What are the similarities? What are the differences?

3. What did Reverend Dr. King mean by "the weapon of protest" and "the weapon of love"?

4. Do you think the Negroes are right in using sit-ins, pray-ins, demonstrations and marches to gain the right to vote, and the other rights of American citizenship? Do you think they are hurting or helping their cause by being arrested and going to jail?

What of the Negroes who say passive resistance is no longer sufficient, and force and hatred are the only possible weapons? Have they a valid point? Are they doing the Negro a disservice?

5. Ministers, priests and rabbis have protested, marched and worked for Negro freedom and have been arrested in Montgomery, Selma and Birmingham, Alabama; in Americus, Georgia; in St. Augustine, Florida; in communities in Minnesota, Pennsylvania and Mississippi and other states. Why do you think they feel they must do this to be true to the teachings of Judaism and Christianity?

JUSTICE, JUSTICE SHALL YE PURSUE

It is against the teachings of both Judaism and Christianity to be prejudiced against Negroes. Discrimination against Negroes is not only against our American way of life, it is against everything that Judaism teaches.

God is the creator and universal Father of all people, and therefore if God is the Father, then all men must be united in the bond of universal brotherhood.

When we affirm through the *Shema* that God is One, we are also declaring our belief that mankind is one. According to Judaism,

Three nuns from the Queen of the World Hospital, Kansas City, Mo., joined
in singing freedom songs with other civil rights demonstrators in Selma, Alabama.
Day-and-night demonstrations followed the death of a Unitarian minister
who had been beaten by white segregationists.

God created man in His divine image. There-fore, every man and every woman is sacred and holy because every man and every woman has a part of God within. When we help our fellow human beings, we help God and glor-ify God. When we hurt our fellow human beings, we hurt God and profane the name of God.

Through the Torah, God commands us to follow His moral laws and seek justice. Social justice is the will of God, and that is why Judaism must always think in terms of justice for all of God's children.

Judaism must never tolerate hatred, cruelty or injustice to any of God's children. To hate or to be prejudiced against a person because of the color of his skin, or his religious faith, or his nationality, is to hate God. All people,

whether rich or poor, wise or ignorant, are children of God, and therefore they must be given equal opportunities and rights because they are created in the image of God.

The Torah teaches: "Justice, Justice shall ye pursue" (Deut. 16:20). Notice that jus-tice is repeated twice. The sages taught that there is a reason for this. Justice is repeated twice to teach us that there must be justice for those of our faith, and justice for those who are not of our faith.

The decision of the Supreme Court

On May 17, 1954, the United States Su-preme Court declared that segregation by race in the public schools is illegal. This de-cision caused a great deal of controversy, especially in the South, because many Southern people object to what is called "the mixing of races" in the public schools.

The Union of American Hebrew Congregations and most Jewish religious organizations approved of and supported the decision of the Supreme Court. In February 1955, the Union of American Hebrew Congregations voted the following resolution:

As proponents of Judaism which first enunciated the concept of the fatherhood of God and the brotherhood of man, we pledge ourselves to do all within our power to make the decision of the highest court in the land meaningful in our respective communities.

We therefore urge our congregants and congregations in all sections of the country to join with forward-looking racial, religious and civic groups in the community in using their influence to secure acceptance and implementation of the desegregation decisions in every community in our land.

Some people didn't like the decision of the Supreme Court and in some communities, particularly in the South, there were riots, schools were bombed, and there were other ugly efforts to prevent Negro children from going to school with white children.

Despite the ugliness and the resistance, amazing progress has been made. In many communities integration of the schools took place quietly and peacefully. Not only the National Association for the Advancement of Colored People, but other, newer, organizations worked to strengthen the decision of the Supreme Court and to give Negroes their rights as Americans. The churches and the synagogues, together with local Human Relations groups, were most active in educating the people to accept the decision of the Supreme Court.

We still have much work to do. Congress passed the Civil Rights Act in July 1964, but unfortunately in both the North and the South there is still considerable prejudice against the Negro. That is why many Catholics, Protestants and Jews have dedicated themselves to securing equal rights for the Negro, to allow the Negro to register and vote, to help the Negro get jobs and suitable employment, and to see to it that Negroes are permitted to rent or buy homes in all neighborhoods.

What do you care?

A rabbi whose congregation was in the South tells what happened before he moved to another congregation in the Middle West:

Just before I moved to the mid-West with my family I went into a drugstore in the Southern community in which I lived, and sat at the lunch counter to have a cup of coffee.

A man sat down next to me. He was dirty, unkempt and had been drinking. The waitress looked at him with distaste as she took his order. It was then that a clean-cut Negro youth wearing the uniform of the United States Army approached the lunch counter and started to sit down. The waitress rushed over to him and said, "I'm sorry, but Negroes aren't permitted to sit at this lunch counter."

"But I'm hungry and I would like some breakfast,'" said the young man.

"I'll serve you breakfast," said the waitress. "But you'll have to eat it standing up, or go outside and sit on the curb. What will you have?"

The soldier said, "O.K. I'll have some coffee and two fried eggs up."

While he stood and waited, the waitress fried two eggs, put them on a paper plate, and then put another paper plate on top, and handed it to the soldier up-side-down.

When the soldier held the paper plates, the egg yolk dripped all over his uniform. The young man looked down at his soiled uniform. Then he looked at those of us who were sitting silently at the lunch counter and he said, "What do you care?"

Without another word he put the paper plates dripping with egg yolk on the counter, picked up several napkins, and walked away.

The dirty, intoxicated man, who was sitting next to me, shouted after him, "If you know what's good for you, you won't try to sit and eat with decent white folks." He put a large piece of pancake in his mouth, and the syrup dripped down his chin.

I don't think I'll ever get out of my mind the image of that fine, clean-cut looking Negro soldier standing there with egg yolk dripping on the uniform of the United States Army. Those words, "What do you care?" burned themselves into my brain.

That is the question that all of us must answer if we are to be true to our faith, whether it is Judaism or Christianity: "What do you care?" We must care and be concerned as Americans and as Christians and Jews — and our concern must inspire us, motivate us, challenge us to see to it that such things do not happen in our beloved America, whether in the North or in the South.

It isn't enough for us to become angry about discrimination and prejudice against the Negro. We have to do something about it, through education, through law and legislation, through our churches and synagogues.

Today the Catholic and Protestant churches and the synagogues and temples are taking a more active role in the Nego struggle to attain to the rights of American citizens. Councils on Religion and Race are making a great contribution by studying the best ways

Desegregation is most opposed in regions that generally have used Negroes as low-paid manual labor.

of giving the Negro equal rights and encouraging proper and dedicated action.

Not only the clergymen, but men and women who are business and professional people have formed Social Justice Committees in their churches and synagogues and have been of tremendous help in promoting good race relations and educating the people to understand how important it is to bring justice and equal rights to the Negro.

Many of our temple and synagogue youth groups are very active now in helping the Negro cause by working with civil rights groups, answering the telephones in offices, passing out literature and by doing something even more important. That is the wonderful and exciting projects of the youth groups—projects where Negro boys and girls are invited to youth group meetings, to Jewish worship services, Jewish homes, as colored and white, Christians and Jews get to know each other, and show each other that as Christians and Jews they really care, care about justice, care about brotherhood and care about working for the rights of man.

QUESTIONS FOR DISCUSSION

1. What is your opinion of the wisdom of the Supreme Court Decision about the desegregation of our public schools? Do you favor or oppose the decision? Give your reasons.

2. Why does Judaism oppose race prejudice?

3. Those who oppose desegregation argue that the mixing of Negroes and whites in the public schools will contribute to interracial marriages. What do you think?

4. If Amos and Isaiah were alive today, what do you think they would say about segregation and prejudice against the Negro? What do you think Paul and Jesus would say, if they were alive today?

5. What do you think about the wisdom

of ministers, priests and rabbis taking an active part in protests, marches and demonstrations in behalf of Negro rights?

6. Rabbi Fackenheim wrote:

Perhaps the most frequent misunderstanding is that Judaism is only a religion of justice, while Christianity is a religion of love. This mistaken view is often supported by quoting a saying of Jesus to his followers. Jesus said to love your neighbors and to love God. But Jesus is actually quoting the Hebrew Bible (Lev. 19:18 and Deut. 6:5). Judaism does emphasize love. The Deuteronomy passage is part of the Sh'ma, the principal declaration of belief of every Jew.

Christianity differs from Judaism by pushing the idea of love to a radical extreme. In the famous Sermon on the Mount, Jesus asks his followers to love their enemies. If your enemy hits your right cheek, says Jesus, then turn your left cheek to him. But even for this argument we can quote Isaiah who said, "Say, 'Ye are our brethren,' to those who hate you." And similar ideas were expressed among the rabbis of Jesus' time, such as Hillel. But very few Christians know anything about Hillel.

Do you think of Judaism as a religion of love or justice or both?

Give your reasons.

THINGS TO DO

1. Make a list of the ways that the synagogue can contribute to social justice in your community. What projects would you suggest to temple and synagogue youth groups? What can your class do?

2. Interview a Catholic priest, a minister and a rabbi about their views on social justice,

The cause of social justice—and of happiness on earth—may be served in quiet but profoundly important ways. This young couple has just adopted a baby to whom they will give all the advantages of a secure and loving home. Baby and adoptive parents were selected for each other and brought together by the Louise Wise Services, one of many helpful agencies affiliated with the Federation of Jewish Philanthropies of New York.

and what the church and synagogue can do to practice social justice in your community.

3. Make a list of some of the Negro organizations working for Negro rights. Make a list of some of the non-Negro organizations working in behalf of justice for the Negro.

4. Write an essay on the work of the National Association for the Advancement of Colored People.

5. Write to the CORE office (Committee on Racial Equality) address and ask the office to send you some pamphlets on the work and purpose of this organization. Discuss the work of CORE in class. Has it changed its philosophy through the years?

6. If you do not have a Committee on Social Action in your congregation, what can you do to stimuate the organization of such a committee? What would be its purpose? What are some of the things it should do?

7. Ask a Negro who has been active in the civil rights program to speak to your class. Be prepared to ask questions about Negro problems, and how the synagogues and temples may be of help.

8. Write to the Commission on Social Action of Reform Judaism, 838 Fifth Avenue, New York, New York 10021, and the Social Action Committee of the United Synagogue of America, 3080 Broadway, New York, New

Some two hundred and seventy Protestant ministers and laymen marched from the Lutheran Church of the Reformation to Capitol Hill, in Washington, in 1964, urging the immediate passage of a strong civil rights bill.

York 10027, and ask for information about the work of these committees.

9. Write the United Synagogue Commission on Jewish Education for filmstrips:

    a. When the Prophets Spoke
    b. Thus Saith the Lord

SELECTED QUOTATIONS

Peculiar sensitivity

Out of the centuries of tribulation and suffering and wandering, by virtue of a peculiar sensitivity to revelation, out of a hunger for social solidarity, and a passion for righteousness, there came to the prophets of Israel and Judah a new conception of God that has ever since spurred men to higher action and has kept before them the haunting realization that apart from His service there is no true hope or happiness for mankind.

—DR. NATHAN PUSEY,
President of Harvard University

The Synagogue speaks against segregation

We cannot deny that we live in a day when mankind looks to America for leadership in the struggle for freedom. The denial of justice to any of our citizens dims our moral standing and prestige among the nations. When this denial of Justice is predicated on the color of a man's skin, we make suspect the whole concept of democracy in the eyes of the billion colored people whose friendship we want and need.

—Commission on Justice and Peace of the Central Conference of American Rabbis

The Protestant Church speaks against segregation

We urge Christian Statesmen and leaders in our churches to use their leadership in positive thought and planning to the end that crisis in our national history shall not be made the occasion for new and bitter prejudices, but a movement toward a united national embodying and proclaiming a democracy that will commend freedom to all peoples.

—Southern Baptist Christian Life Commission

Catholics speak against segregation

We sincerely hope that the day will come when the ideal of Christian brotherhood will displace from our Southern scene all traces of the blight of racism. Let us Catholics, true to our convictions, set the pattern.

—The Catholic Committee of the South

SELECTED READINGS

FREEHOF, LILLIAN S., *The Right Way*

GOODMAN, HANNAH GRAD, *The Story of Prophecy*

KING, MARTIN LUTHER, *Stride Toward Freedom*

REINFELD, FRED, *The Great Dissenters*

SILVERMAN, WILLIAM B., *The Still Small Voice Today*, pp. 252–256

TARSHISH, ALLAN, *Not by Power*

UNIVERSAL JEWISH ENCYCLOPEDIA, Volume 8, Prophets, pp. 658–664

VORSPAN, A., and LIPMAN, E., *Justice and Judaism*

16

Religion in Action

KEEP RELIGION OUT OF POLITICS

Some people say they would like to help the Negroes, but insist that the church and the synagogue should stay out of politics, and that ministers, priests and rabbis shouldn't get involved in the Negro's struggle for freedom or in any other controversial subject. They believe that ministers, priests and rabbis should stick to religion and stick to the Bible.

In Biblical times there were people, too, who said that the prophets had no right to become involved in politics. They didn't like it when the prophets spoke out against injustice and evil. They said that the prophets shouldn't be concerned with the problems of the poor, with housing, with righteous business practices, or even with war and peace. But the prophets insisted that God is a God of justice, and that God demands the practice of justice by those who worship Him. That is why these "spokesmen of God" refused to be quiet, or refused to stop their efforts to bring about justice. God had commanded them to speak, and they thundered against evil and injustice—even though it meant that some people hated them and even tried to destroy them.

Perhaps we should stop here and study a little about what the Bible says about getting involved with the wrongs and injustices of society. A long time before the age of the prophets, the laws of Moses commanded the people to apply Judaism to the world in which they live.

THE HOLINESS CODE

Some people speak about religion as if it had nothing to do with the way we live and act. They think that religion is limited to a synagogue, or cathedral, mosque or church, or that religion is to be observed on the Sabbath, festival and Holy Days alone.

This just isn't true. Religion must be concerned with every part of life, and all the experiences of day-to-day living. According to our faith, Judaism is a way of life and holiness is not retreating from the world, or fasting, or praying for hours. Holiness is the way God wants us to treat our fellow human beings. Holiness is concerned with social justice and the rights of man.

If you really want to know the Jewish requirements for holiness, then open your Bibles to the Book of Leviticus, the 19th Chapter. This chapter is called "the holiness code" of Judaism. Just run your eye down the page and you will read:

"Ye shall be holy: For I the Lord your God am holy."

Following this you will see the requirements for holiness: respect for parents; to keep the sabbath, to take care of the stranger and the poor.

Ye shall not steal; neither shall ye deal falsely, nor lie one to another . . . Thou shalt not oppress thy neighbour, nor rob him; the wages of a hired servant shall not abide with thee all night until the morning . . . Ye shall do no unrighteousness in judgment; thou shalt not favor the poor or the rich in law cases . . . Thou shalt not go up and down as a talebearer . . . neither shalt thou stand idly by the blood of thy neighbor . . . Thou shalt not hate thy brother in thy heart . . . Thou shalt not take vengeance, nor bear any grudge against the children of thy people, but thou shalt love thy neighbor as thyself.

THE WELFARE OF MAN

Judaism is a religion that concerns itself with the practical affairs of life, and with the welfare of man. In the Talmud, we are taught

Nuns and priests man relief and resettlement stations in South Vietnam. CARE, the Red Cross, FOA, UNICEF, and the National Catholic Welfare Conference combine in meeting urgent refugee needs for food, soap, clothing, mosquito netting.

that synagogues must have windows, and it wasn't because of fresh air.

We understand this to mean that synagogues should have windows so that when we pray, we may look out and see people— the parade of humanity passing by — those who are hungry, poor and needy—those who are sick—those who have problems that weigh on their hearts. We must never separate our prayers from the needs of our fellow man, the sages taught. We must always keep in sight the needs of humanity. That is why a synagogue should have windows.

In the Midrash the rabbis tell us that when Adam was created, he was made as large as the world.

Most of us will say: "Impossible! There is no man who could be the size of the world."

That's what other rabbis said, too, until the wise men explained that they didn't actually mean that Adam would be the size of the world in physical stature.

What they meant is that God gave Adam a human heart, a heart of compassion and pity, and that the human heart can reach out from one end of the world to the other in compassion for the poor, the suffering and the needy.

As beautiful as this Midrash is, we must remember that Judaism teaches that compassion and mercy aren't enough. We are commanded to *do* something, to take action to feed the hungry, to clothe the naked, to release those who have been imprisoned unfairly, and to help those who are in trouble, by our deeds.

A medieval rabbinic tradition reads: "If a man says, 'What have I to do with the concerns of the community, with their problems, why must I listen to their talk? Peace to thee, O my soul!'—such a man destroys the world, and is a disgrace to his religion and his people."

Sometimes we forget that we not only show our love of God with prayers and words, but that we also show our love of God by our deeds. Every time we do an act of kindness and helpfulness to others, that, too, is a prayer that is most pleasing to God. This is worship without words. This is *avodah*, which not only means "prayer" but "service"—service to God and our fellow men. That is why those who believe in God must always take action to help His children.

The rabbi makes an announcement

Once, in the eighteenth century, in a little village in Poland, called Berdichev, the Jewish people forgot this. They were surprised when one day the town crier came around and said that their Rabbi, Levi Yitzchok, had an announcement to make, and wanted the people to assemble at the town square at noon that very day.

The housewife grumbled as she left her domestic chores. The shopkeeper complained as he left his little shop, but their rabbi had commanded them to gather together and hear his announcement.

When the people assembled the rabbi said: "I have an announcement to make. I wish to announce that there is a God in this world!"

That's all he said, but the people went away humbled and chastened. They understood what the rabbi was telling them.

He was telling them that while they said they believed in God and loved God and offered praises to God, they forgot what God had commanded them. They forgot to help the poor, and heal the sick, and take care of the widows, the orphans and the strangers. They forgot to live their Judaism every day through acts of loving-kindness and *ma-asim tovim,* good deeds. That is why the rabbi reminded them that there is a God in this world, a God who is a God of mercy and wants His children to be merciful; a God who is God of justice, and wants His children to do deeds of justice.

The good samaritan

Christians, also, believe that we should help our fellow man and that God wants us to do deeds of loving-kindness and show mercy to our fellow human beings. Christians also believe in helping the oppressed and the persecuted.

There is a parable in the New Testament that you should know. Jesus taught, according to the gospel of Luke (Chap. 10).

"A man was going down from Jerusalem to Jericho and he fell among robbers who stripped him and beat him and departed leaving him half-dead. Now by chance a priest was going down the road, and when he saw him passed by on the other side. So likewise a Levite, when he came to the place and saw him, passed by on the other side. But a Samaritan, as he journeyed, came to where he was, and when he saw him he had compassion. And he went to him and bound up his wounds, pouring on oil and wine; then he set him on his own beast and brought him to an inn and took care of him.

"The next day he took out two coins and gave them to the innkeeper saying, 'Take care of him, and whatever more you spend, I will repay you when I come back.'

"Which of these three," [asked Jesus] "do you think proved neighbor to the man who fell among the robbers?"

And he [the man who was conversing with Jesus] said: "The man who showed mercy on him."

And Jesus said to him, "Go and do likewise."

To understand the story you have to remember that the Jews did not like the Samaritans, and the Samaritans did not like the Jews. But the good Samaritan helped the stricken Jew in need, even though he was his enemy, because he, too, believed that God is the Father of all, and that each man must show his love of God by helping God's children.

This parable or story is in harmony with the spirit of the Jewish tradition. Remember that Jonah was sent to ask the people of Nineveh to repent even though they were the enemies of the Jewish people. God's love reaches out to all His children.

Many of the stories and parables of the New Testament were taken from Jewish sources. According to Jewish law, the priest and the Levite were wrong in walking past the man who was in need of help. They were not worthy of being priests or Levites in the service of the Lord, when they refused to serve their fellow man.

In the Gospel story, Jesus follows the teachings of Judaism as he makes it clear that to hate your fellow man is to hate God. To love your fellow man is to love God. Jesus said: "He who says he loves the Father and hates his brother, is a liar!" (I John 4:20)

This is strong language, but Jewish teachers were taught that to love God is to help and serve your fellow man. God is a God of justice and demands the practice of justice to all people.

THE PRACTICE OF JUSTICE TODAY

In a book called *Justice and Judaism,* by Albert Vorspan and Eugene Lipman, we learn why modern Jews must also be concerned with justice and problems dealing with race relations, housing, unemployment, education, marriage and the family, crime, civil rights, immigration and international peace.

The authors not only believe that Jews must be concerned with social justice, but they also urge each synagogue to have a committee on social action to study and practice the principles of democracy, justice and peace.

Christian groups also have such social action programs. The Roman Catholic Church and virtually every Protestant denomination have social action programs functioning nationally and in many local churches.

Let us consider some important aspects of social justice, and see why Judaism and Christianity must become involved in meeting the great challenges of our times.

Civil liberties

The Preamble to the Declaration of Independence states that every citizen is entitled to "life, liberty and the pursuit of happiness." In addition to the Declaration of Independence, The Bill of Rights, the first Ten Amendments to the Constitution, part of the Constitution of the United States, guarantees civil rights and liberties to the American people. It assures the freedom of the individual right to speak and live in a land of liberty.

This is our Bill of Rights:

Amendment I. Freedom of Religion, Speech and the Press; Right of Assembly and Petition

Amendment II. Right to Keep and Bear Arms

Amendment III. Freedom from Quartering of Soldiers without Consent

Amendment IV. Regulation of Right of Search and Seizure

Amendment V. Protection of Persons and Their Property

Amendment VI. Rights of Persons Accused of Crime

Amendment VII. Right of Trial by Jury in Suits at Common Law

Amendment VIII. Protection Against Excessive Bail and Punishments

Amendment IX. Constitution Does Not List All Individual Rights

Amendment X. Powers Reserved to the States and the People

Try to imagine what our democracy would be like without these rights. Think of what it might be like to live in a country where the citizen can't worship God or follow his religion according to his convictions, where there is no free speech and spies report on everything you say. Imagine a country where the press is not free, and the newspapers must publish what the government commands them to publish; a country where you cannot meet with others without official permission. There are, alas, many countries today where there are none of these guarantees of fundamental liberties that we take for granted.

Imagine how you would feel if there would be a sign in front of your synagogue:

BY ORDER OF THE GOVERNMENT

Jews are prohibited from worshiping their God.

Jewish prayers are prohibited.

Jews may no longer observe their Sabbath, their festivals or their Holy Days.

Any Jew who observes his religion will be put to death.

Imagine what it would be like!

In Communist countries, all religions are quite often treated as enemies of the state. Somehow, in most Communist lands, though the churches have few rights and little freedom, Jews and the synagogue have even worse treatment. Zionists are often punished with long jail terms at hard labor.

We should realize what a blessing it is to live in America, and how fortunate we are to have laws that protect our rights, instead of laws that take away our rights.

Be vigilant to protect the rights of American citizens

Sometimes people forget what freedom really means and because of selfish interests, fear, ignorance or prejudice, they ignore the Bill of Rights, and try to take away rights and liberties from other Americans.

The church and synagogue must always be vigilant and take action to protect these rights of the American people. It's hard to believe, but there are some who say that the church and synagogue should stick to religion, or stick to the Bible and not interfere in these controversial matters. No matter how controversial a problem might be, Judaism and Christianity must be involved and concerned.

Inscribed on the Liberty Bell is: "Proclaim liberty throughout the land, to all the inhabitants thereof." This is from the 25th Chapter of the Book of Leviticus. How fitting were these words on the bell that pealed out the news that the people of the new United States of America had founded their country on the basis of freedom for every citizen of the land.

If liberty is to be proclaimed throughout the land and throughout the world, then people must be really free; they must have freedom from hunger, freedom from disease, freedom from ignorance, freedom from crime, and freedom to work and live in peace.

Young civil rights enthusiasts spent a day demonstrating outside Independence Hall in Philadelphia, in support of Negro rights. At night they were permitted to sleep in the room that houses the Liberty Bell.

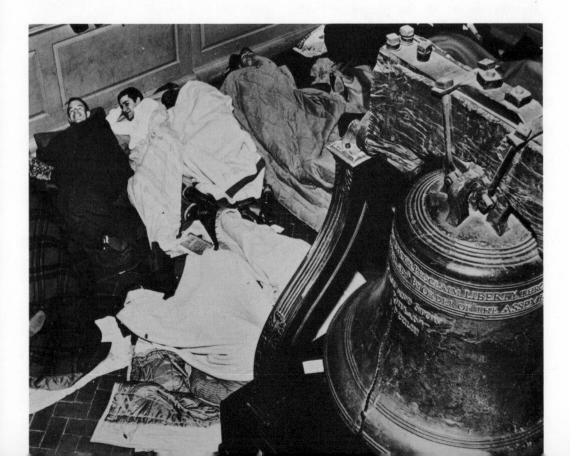

Freedom from hunger

During the great depression of 1929, when 15 million men and women were unemployed, it was estimated that a full third of the people in America were living without enough food, without proper housing and without money for medical care.

The churches and synagogues, together with social and government agencies took action to bring about legislation to provide unemployment insurance, minimum wage laws, Federal child labor laws, old-age insurance, pensions, and state and Federal construction projects. All of these helped millions to get food, shelter and medical aid.

It is shocking for us to hear that in our own time, nearly one quarter of Americans still live in poverty, denied sufficient food, clothing and housing and unable to take advantage of educational opportunities. Through the world, the picture is much worse. Almost half the human family is hungry. Millions upon millions of children live out their few years of pain without ever having enough to satisfy their gnawing hunger.

Even as you read this, in India carts are being hauled along filth-ridden alleys picking up the bodies of children who died of starvation during the night.

In China and in other countries, millions of children go to bed at night without enough to eat, hungry, yearning for a crust of bread, waiting to dig into garbage cans and rubbish heaps, hoping to find something that will keep them alive.

We are so well-fed that it is difficult for us to believe that there are people who are starving. How can they think of God and religious values when their stomachs are empty and the prospects for the future are dismal?

Religion must join in the war against poverty. What good are all our churches and synagogues if they ignore the misery of human beings created in the image of God?

Today ministers, priests and rabbis are becoming more and more active in fighting this war against poverty.

The Commission on Justice and Peace of the Central Conference of American Rabbis reported:

> Poverty remains one of the world's major evils. Two-thirds of the earth's population do not have adequate food, clothing, and shelter. In an age when goods and food can be mass produced, we cannot accept such widespread poverty as inevitable. . . . We call for a sustained attack upon all the social and economic conditions which make for poverty. We affirm that it is the obligation of the United States and other advantaged nations to co-operate in a program of development for those areas of the world where hunger and suffering are today so prevalent.

Freedom to live in decent homes

In many communities in the United States people live in slums that are filthy and unsanitary. The church and the synagogue have important work to do so that people may live in decent and clean homes.

Sometimes people cannot buy or rent in certain neighborhoods. There are efforts made to keep out those of the Jewish faith, though these have diminished in recent years. Negroes find it very difficult to find decent housing, even though they can afford it. In some places Puerto Ricans, Mexicans, Japanese and Chinese-Americans are discriminated against, and are not allowed to rent or buy homes.

Fair housing commissions and other groups are working desperately to convince real estate agents and homeowners that it is wrong to keep people out of decent housing because of their color, their religion or their nationality.

Adequate clothing and shelter are not the possession of some people, even in America. Recent reports show that some 10,400,000 housing units are rated substandard. In rural communities 23% of the housing fails to measure up to satisfactory living standards.

—Report of the Council on Christian Relations

Our heart is filled with a deep sadness in contemplating the immeasurably sorrowful spectacle of vast numbers of workers in many lands and entire continents who are paid wages which condemn them and their families to live in homes that suggest subhuman conditions of life.

—Encyclical letter, "Mater et Magistra" Pope John XXIII

The throne of judgment

Modern rabbis are concerned with the everyday problems of life — civil rights, health, poverty, housing and peace.

That is part of our Jewish tradition, to be worried about human welfare. But it isn't enough to worry, or to brood or think about the injustices of our world. A Jew is commanded to do something about them.

Rabbinic tradition tells us that when a man appears before the throne of Divine Judgment, God doesn't ask: "Have you performed ritual?" God doesn't ask, "Have you said your prayers?" The question God asks is, "Have you dealt justly with your fellow man?"

Freedom from disease

Sickness and poor health not only cost the nation great sums but also deprive the individual of happiness and life itself. The church and the synagogue cannot afford to sit back and ignore the problems of disease.

Government and private research groups are spending billions of dollars to rid the nation of terrible diseases. Vaccines, serums, wonder-drugs, and other discoveries of science are bringing renewed health to millions of people.

We still have many problems to solve and many diseases to conquer. We need more clinics for the poor, better equipped hospitals and more and more research.

One of the greatest threats to health is the increase of mental illness. There is an immediate need for the prevention and treatment of mental illness, more hospitals for the mentally ill and funds for the estabishment of mental health and child guidance clinics.

With the great progress made in medical science people are living longer. There is a need for more work in the field of geriatrics, the care and health of old people. Too many old people feel unwanted and hate being a burden. A great deal of work has to be done in caring and providing for the senior citizens of our nation.

There are many problems, but we must never stop in our effort to solve them. Religion must be concerned with all the problems that beset our society. Judaism has a special responsibility, because we say that religion is a way of life, and because we have a commitment to God to fight injustice, destroy evil, and bring health, justice, freedom, brotherhood and peace to all mankind.

Freedom from crime

The church and the synagogue are deeply concerned about the problem of crime and juvenile delinquency. Slums are the breeding place of crime and juvenile delinquency. But crime and juvenile delinquency are not limited to the slum dwellers. Those coming from middle and high income groups are also involved.

Special congressional committees are study-

*Ḥasidic Jews in Brooklyn, N.Y., have formed a group to patrol the
streets, unarmed, in radio cars and report any impending trouble to police.
By a strict policy of non-violence, they help control crime and have
attracted volunteers of other faiths to help in this work.*

ing the effects of comic and crime books,
television and motion pictures upon juvenile
delinquency. Special juvenile judges and family courts are trying to combat the alarming
spread of juvenile delinquency and organized
crime.

Confidence men, swindlers and rackets
take millions from the public each year. Innocent people are preyed upon and made to
pay "protection" to operate their businesses.
The selling of dope and drugs to adults and
minors wrecks many lives. Gambling syndi-
cates feed on the hunger of people to make
money the easy way. With gambling there are
usually associated crime and other vices.

The church and the synagogue must take
an active role in bringing about changes in
laws for human betterment, and in the social
conditions that breed crime.

WHAT DO YOU THINK?

1. What is your opinion of this statement
by the Central Conference of American Rabbis: "The time is overdue for the abolition
of the death penalty wherever it is still util-
ized."? Are you in favor of or against capital
punishment? Give your reasons.

2. The Central Conference of American
Rabbis has called for prison reforms.

We need a complete overhauling of our criminal codes and probation systems. We need greatly improved prison administration and much improved programs for training prison personnel. Many of our prisons are archaic, ill equipped and provide inferior food. These conditions only foster criminality and produce hardened criminals.

What is your reaction to this statement? Do you think the purpose of prison should be to punish or to cure? Do you think that criminals should be put in hospitals instead of prisons? Are they sick people? How should they be treated? What makes a person a criminal?

Freedom to learn

Most Jewish congregations have a very active program of adult Jewish education. Part of this program is to study about the need for religion to fight poverty and how Judaism and Christianity must get involved with problems of housing and medical care and crime.

Religious education is important, but general education is essential if we are to build a better world. How sad is it that some people have no opportunity, or very limited opportunity, to obtain a good education. In America and throughout the world, we have many problems to solve in the field of education.

There is the need for more adequate schools and equipment, competent teachers and special instruction for handicapped and exceptional children and adults who are blind, deaf, crippled, mentally retarded or unusually talented and bright.

The Council on Christian Relations recently issued the following report on urgent needs in our public school system:

It is in the Protestant tradition to support the public school system for a free public education is the handmaiden of democracy. Ignorance and prejudice are the weapons of tyranny. Yet we find our school system in jeopardy. There is a shortage of qualified teachers, buildings are inadequate or obsolete, indecision reigns.

The Central Conference of American Rabbis in its report stated:

We are in danger today of . . . permitting our school system to deteriorate for lack of funds. Physical facilities are in adequate and unequal. Schools are undermanned and teachers unpaid. . . . If we can afford to spend billions on armaments, luxuries, and vacations, we can afford the new classrooms we need as well as salary schedules for teachers which will attract the best qualified individuals to the profession. . . . It is our duty as teachers of spiritual values to help arouse public spirit in the citizens of our respective communities to vote the tax funds to meet the legitimate needs of the schools.

Freedom to work

We should remember how it is when there is unemployment, when people can't get jobs to feed their families, pay their rent and have the funds to buy medicine and get medical attention for their families. When a person is out of work and hungry, it is difficult to think about religious values and making this a better world.

Sometimes even those who do have jobs don't make enough money to enable them and their families to live in suitable homes and pay their bills. Then too, there was a time when the laboring man was exploited and treated miserably. Today labor unions protect the laboring man, but with labor unions there have arisen tensions between employers and employees, strikes and labor disputes. The government has been of great assistance in arbitrating many of these disputes, but the conflict between labor and management is still a problem.

While our sympathies go out to the laboring men, we must never forget the rights of management. Our system of free enterprise and competition is business has made America prosperous and great. Justice is due not only to the laboring man, but to management as well.

Freedom to live

War is a terrible thing, and atomic war is too horrible even to think about. When we read about the atom bombing of the Japanese cities of Hiroshima and Nagasaki, with people running into the night as human, blazing torches, screaming in their burning agony, we solemnly resolve that never again shall a rain of nuclear death be showered upon human beings.

Nuclear bomb testing also brings its dangers to human life. Fallout, with the possibility of strontium 90 destroying bone marrow and deforming future generations, is a very serious and dangerous problem that confronts the church and the synagogue and calls for action.

This isn't a very pleasant subject to discuss, but we cannot ignore it—not when so many scientists tell us that there can be no possible victory in an atomic war—not when they tell us that with the development of the megaton bombs, at the push of a button, almost all of the civilized world could be destroyed.

The great hope for the world in renouncing war as a method of solving disputes between nations is the United Nations — but an even greater hope is that those who believe in One God and the moral teachings of

God will put their faith to work and make religion a vital force for world peace.

Freedom from war

With the threat of the atom bomb, guided missiles and other terrible instruments of war, the United Nations organization is all the more necessary.

There is opposition to the United Nations, and true, it isn't perfect or without weaknesses. But what other organization do we have that will enable the nations of the world to meet together and attempt to find a solution for the discord and conflicts among nations that make for war?

The Charter of the United Nations written in 1945 in San Francisco begins:

> WE THE PEOPLES OF THE UNITED NATIONS, DETERMINED to save succeeding generations from the scourge of war . . . and to reaffirm faith in fundamental human rights, in the dignity and worth of the human person, in the equal rights of men and women and of nations large and small, and to establish conditions under which justice and respect for the obligations arising from treaties and other sources of international law can be maintained, and to promote social progress and better standards of life in larger freedom, AND FOR THESE ENDS to practice tolerance and live together in peace with one another as good neighbors and to unite our strength to maintain international peace and security, and to ensure . . . that armed force shall not be used, save in the common interest, and to employ international machinery for the promotion of the economic and social advancement of all peoples, HAVE RESOLVED TO COMBINE OUR EFFORTS TO ACCOMPLISH THESE AIMS.

This is really a Bill of Rights for all nations. It is difficult to estimate how much good has been accomplished through the United Nations. It has prevented armed conflicts and provided education, economic aid and medical care for millions of underprivileged people.

It is true that the United Nations has failed to stop all wars, but that is not the fault of the United Nations. It is the fault of those who have failed to permit the United Nations to make vital decisions. It is the fault of those nations who did not turn over problems to the United Nations, but used their own armies and military power.

The fact is we don't have any other international organization that is as effective in harmonizing the efforts of nations to bring nearer the time when there shall be understanding, brotherhood, justice and peace.

We need peace so desperately in our world. Peace. Shalom. That was the dream of Isaiah: when nations would break their swords into plowshares and their spears into pruning hooks, and men would learn war no more. Shalom. That means more than peace. It means completeness — wholeness — the hope, the ideal of the prophets and of the teachers of our faith—the time when nations will live together as one great brotherhood, complete, united, whole!" That is why we need social action to make that dream come true. That is why Judaism and Christianity must show the way by becoming partners for the building of a moral future for all mankind.

QUESTIONS FOR DISCUSSION

1. Would you object if a Negro family wanted to move next door to you? Why or why not? What do you think would happen if Negro families moved into your neighborhood? What is the attitude of Judaism toward the effort to permit Negroes to rent and buy in what are now restricted neighborhoods?

2. In what way does the Bill of Rights apply to the problems of youth?

3. Why do you think that the rate of juvenile delinquency and crime have been so low among Jews?

4. Do you think an unemployed person who steals to feed his family should be punished by law—even if his children were hungry?

5. Do you think that labor unions have a right to call a strike during a war or a national emergency?

6. Do you think that the state should spend large sums of money on the mentally ill, the mentally retarded, the aged and the incurably sick? Would it be better to use that money to help those who might be able to contribute to the welfare of society or the future of our civilization?

7. Do you think that the censorship of books, magazines and newspapers is justified? What are the advantages and the dangers of censorship?

8. Do you think that our immigration laws should be relaxed? Do you think the government should keep former Nazis and suspected Communists out of our country?

9. If your rabbi became involved in a controversy over social justice, do you think he should be asked to drop the matter for the sake of peace in the congregation? What are your reasons?

10. What do you think Professor Abraham Heschel meant by this statement?

God will return us when we shall be willing to let Him in—into our banks and factories, into our Congress and clubs, into our courts and investigating committees, into our homes and theaters. For God is everywhere or nowhere, the Father of all men or no man, concerned about everything or nothing. Only in His presence

Four Nike guided missiles speak of modern man's reach for power.
Until cooperation replaces rivalry, international power races
will grow ever more ominous.

shall we learn that the glory of man is not in his will to power, but in his power of compassion. Man reflects the image of His presence or that of a beast.

11. What do you think Pope Paul VI meant by this statement?

The Church must enter into a dialogue with the world in which it lives. It has something to say, a message to give, a communication to make.

THINGS TO DO

1. Diagram a comparison between the Bill of Rights and quotations from Exodus, Leviticus and Deuteronomy, showing that the Bible offers man a sacred bill of rights.

2. Write to the American Civil Liberties

Union, 170 Fifth Avenue, New York, New York, 10010 for a statement of its principles.

3. Write an essay setting forth the reasons why the members of your congregation should join the American Association for the United Nations.

4. Write to the following organizations for information on their purpose and program, and then discuss in class:

National Religion and Labor Foundation
349½ N. High Street,
Columbus, Ohio 43215

National Probation and Parole Association
1790 Broadway,
New York, N.Y. 10019

National Committee on Immigration and Citizenship
40 East 40th Street,
New York, N.Y. 10016

National Committee Against Discrimination in Housing
35 West 32nd Street,
New York, N.Y. 10001

Through the United Nations Development Program nations can use their knowledge to help one another. Here an engineer and UNESCO expert from Argentina talks with a mechanics student at the National Polytechnic Institute, Barquisimeto, Venezuela.

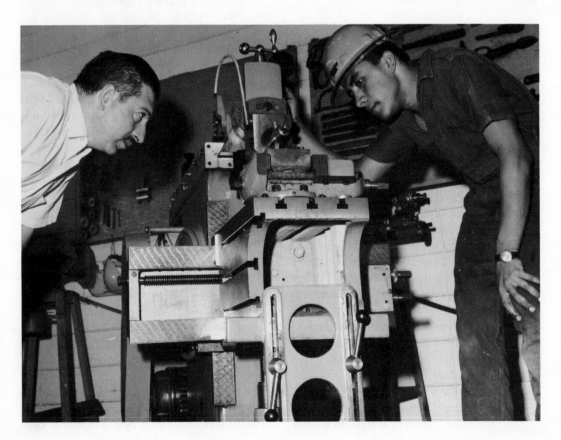

The Community Relations Service
386 Fourth Avenue,
New York, N.Y. 10016

5. In the Jefferson Memorial, we read this quotation: "I have sworn upon the altar of God, eternal hostility against any form of tyranny over the mind of man." Write an essay setting forth what Thomas Jefferson might say about modern controversial problems if he were alive today.

6. Find out about the need for slum clearance in your community, and the problems that are created by slums. Discuss in class.

7. Write an essay on the Biblical and rabbinic attitude toward capital punishment.

8. Obtain a copy of the play by Rabbi Louis I. Newman, called *Go North, Young Man,* and enact it in class.

SELECTED QUOTATIONS

Jewish, Catholic and Protestant leaders and religious bodies are calling for social action to meet the crying needs of our time.

Action must follow

Religious teachings are meaningless if they remain within the confines of the synagogue, or of the church, or are limited to words in prayer books. Action must follow. The love of God and the love of man must be felt so fervently that it will lead us out of the wilderness of bigotry and reveal the vistas of the future when men's hearts will not only beat with the rhythms of social justice and liberty or pulsate with sympathy for a brother's cause; when their lips will not only proclaim a resounding affirmation to the question: "Am I my brother's keeper?" but when they will move to translate their beliefs into the relationships of the daily world.

—Race Relations Message, Central
Conference of American Rabbis

Youth gives prophetic witness

Catholic, Protestant and Jewish youth have an unparalleled historic opportunity to give vivid Prophetic witness to their faith by taking part in this demonstration of the moral commitment of Americans to equal opportunity for all citizens.

—RABBI MARC H. TANNENBAUM

Human life is sacred

Human life is sacred. From its very beginnings it calls for the creative action of God. By the violation of His laws, the Divine Majesty is offended, individuals themselves and humanity become degraded and likewise the community of which they are members is gravely enfeebled.

We reaffirm strongly that Christian social doctrine is an integral part of the Christian conception of life. . . . It is not enough merely to publicize a social doctrine; it has to be translated into action. This is particularly true of Christian social doctrine, whose light is truth, whose objective is justice and whose driving force is love.

—POPE JOHN XXIII

Presbyterians support freedom of speech

The Christian Church advocates the right of free speech even if the idea expressed be wrong. Freedom of speech involves the right of dissent; yet of late America has been compelled to struggle for this right both within and without her own borders. The fear of Communism has bred suspicion and distrust which is injurious not only in arresting creative thinking but in bringing our nation into disrepute among the free nations. . . . A congressman is not re-elected, a school teacher faces investigation, a health officer is dismissed, a journalist is forced to leave the community, a man suddenly loses his credit, and a minister loses his congregation — all because they exercised their right to speak freely.

—Presbyterian Church of the United States

SELECTED READINGS

COHON, BERYL, *God's Angry Men*.

CRONBACH, ABRAHAM, *Judaism for Today*

DOUGLASS, WILLIAM O., *A Living Bill of Rights* (pamphlet)

GOODMAN, HANNAH GRAD, *The Story of Prophecy,* Edited by Eugene B. Borowitz, Part II, Chapters 12 and 13.

MANWELL, REGINALD D., and FAHS, SOPHIA L., *The Church Across the Street*

SILVERMAN, ALTHEA, *Behold My Messengers*

UNIVERSAL JEWISH ENCYCLOPEDIA, Volume XVI, Justice, pp. 268–270

VORSPAN, A., and LIPMAN, E., *Justice and Judaism*

WAGNER, RUTH H., *Put Democracy to Work*

17

Partners in Faith

A STRANGE STATEMENT

"Nathan, sure
You are a Christian, by Heaven you are,
None better ever breathed."
And Nathan answered: "That which
makes me a Christian in your eyes,
Makes you a Jew in mine."

This is a famous statement taken from a play written in 1779. The play was called *Nathan der Weise,* which means Nathan the Wise. It was written by a famous German writer, Gotthold Lessing.

In the play, a Christian bishop meets this wise and good Jew, Nathan, and the bishop calls him a Christian. Nathan then sincerely returns the compliment by calling the bishop a Jew.

What is significant is the fact that while each man followed a different religion, both followed the same principles, and both acted in kindness, both were known for their truthfulness, their mercy, their devotion to justice, and their love of their fellow man.

Therefore, the wise and good Nathan was considered by the bishop to be like a Christian. Nathan could say to the wise and good bishop that he was considered to be like a Jew.

This is just like the Christian students who come to visit synagogues and when they hear about the Jewish belief in the Fatherhood of God and the brotherhood of man, and the holiness of man and the ideals of justice, brotherhood, mercy, kindness and peace, say, "That's Christian, and that's what we Christians believe, too."

While it is true that Christians and Jews aren't and shouldn't be so far apart, and while there are many similarities and many ideals that we share together, we always have to be honest and remember that there are basic differences between Judaism and Christianity.

The fact that there are differences doesn't mean that we can't be brothers and work together for great and exalted objectives. Remember that brothers are different, too. They may have different opinions, different ideas and different convictions, but more important than the differences is the fact that they are brothers and should love each other.

TWO SACRED BELIEFS

There are two sacred ideals that should bring Judaism and Christianity very close together, despite differences. One is the belief in God, the creator and Father of all mankind.

The other is that Judaism and Christianity agree on what is called the Judeo-Christian ethical heritage. This means that Judaism and Christianity agree on moral values and ethical principles and ideals.

We shall now consider the Jewish-Christian teaching about the Fatherhood of God and the brotherhood of man.

God, the Father of all

Our Jewish tradition teaches that when God created man, he caused the winds to blow and dust gathered together from the four corners of the earth, and from the accumulated dust God created man. This is only a legend, but it has an important lesson to teach us. The sages reasoned that if God created the first man from the dust of Palestine, then the Jews would say, "We are superior and better than others." If God created the first man from the dust of Egypt, then the Egyptians would have said, "We are superior." But God created man from the dust from the four corners of the earth to teach that no people is superior to the other, and that we all have the same beginning, and the same creator.

Once Rabbi Akiba and Ben Azzai had a discussion. Rabbi Akiba said that the greatest verse in the Bible is "Love thy neighbor

At a Convention of the National Conference of Christians and Jews the late President John F. Kennedy lauded the NCCJ for doing more than "perhaps any other factor in our national life to provide for harmonious living among different religious groups."

as thyself." Ben Azzai disagreed and said the greatest verse is:

"This is the book of the generations of *man*"—meaning mankind, all mankind created in the image of God.

This is why Judaism does not consider itself the only true religion, nor does it teach that God loves the people of Israel alone. According to Jewish tradition, God gave 613 laws to Israel, but through Noah, God gave seven laws to all mankind.

These laws require that man shall refrain from (1) idolatry; (2) adultery and incest; (3) bloodshed; (4) blasphemy; (5) robbery; (6) social injustice; (7) eating flesh cut from a living animal.

We believe that a Gentile who observes these basic seven laws of morality is as beloved of God as a Jew who observes all 613.

Our sages taught that God loves even a pagan or an unbeliever who keeps the laws of morality as much or more than a high priest of Israel. Again and again we read the sentiment: "Heaven and earth I call to be witness, be it non-Jew or Jew, man or woman, man-servant or maid-servant, according to the acts of every human being does the holy spirit rest upon him."

That is why it is important for us to remember that God looks upon our deeds, not the color of our skin, or the label of our religious faith. That is why it is important for us to always keep in mind the Jewish belief that God is the Creator, and that all people are His children.

Because man is a child of God we are obligated to help men, whoever they are and wherever they may live. By helping and serving our fellow man, we most beautifully and truly show our love of God.

Go forth and serve my children

That is why the rabbis told of the subjects of a king who came before their sovereign and said: "Oh, King, how can we show our love for thee. What words shall we say before thee? What gifts may we give to thee?"

The king said, "My subjects, I appreciate your goodness in coming before me to express your love. As for your words, do I not understand the sentiments of your hearts? As for your gifts, remember that I am the King and own the entire kingdom. What can you give to me? But I have children. When any of my children suffer hunger, feed them. When they are naked, clothe them. When they are oppressed, free them. When they cry out of the depths for help, respond to them and help them. If you would truly show your love for me, the father, go forth and serve my children."

In the same way, the sages imagined that when we go before God, the King of all kings we say: "How may we express our love for Thee? What words may we give thee? What gifts may we offer thee?" And they imagined the King of all kings saying: "My dear ones, I appreciate your coming before me to express your love. As for your words, do I not know your thoughts, expressed and hidden? Do I not probe into the deepest recesses of your souls? As for your gifts, what can you give me? I am King and own the heaven and the earth. But if you would show your love for me, remember that I have children, and they are scattered all over the world. Some of my children are Jews and some are Christians. Some are Moslems and some are of many other faiths—some are white, and some are black, some are yellow and red. When my children are hungry, feed them. When they are naked, clothe them. When they are enslaved, free them. When they cry out of the depths, answer them, respond to them and help them. If you would show your love for me, the Father, then go forth and serve my children."

This means that we have to serve God's children everywhere, but it tells us something more. It tells us about the great and sacred purpose of Judaism.

This is what is meant by the mission, the purpose, the destiny of the people of Israel, to build God's Kingdom on earth. But we need help for this great and lofty goal. We can't do it alone. We need allies and partners, those who will join with us to help make this dream of Judaism a sublime reality.

That is why we call Christianity our partner, our partner in faith. Christianity and Judaism are partners in the building of a moral future which means that they are partners in the building of God's Kingdom on earth. But before we become partners with Christianity, we must first understand that we have another partner, and that Jews must see themselves as copartners with God.

COPARTNERS WITH GOD

Many religions teach that man needs God. Judaism is one of the few religions that teaches that God needs man, too. We may wonder for what purpose the eternal, almighty God of the universe would use mortal man.

The answer of Judaism is that God needs man for the fulfillment of His divine plan, the building of His Kingdom on earth. God needs man to help perfect the world, and to help create a just and moral society for the future.

For this great and sacred purpose, our sages have taught that each Jew must enter into a partnership with God. Each Jew must regard himself as a partner of God in bringing about a new society where people will live by the teachings of God and follow God's ways, a society where poverty, disease, hatred, ignorance, injustice and war will be eradicated—a society in which every individual will have the opportunity of finding *shalom*—of becoming complete, of fulfilling himself as a child of God, and living his life

with no one to make him afraid. Throughout his history the Jew longed for this day and called it the Messianic Age. Sometimes he called it God's Kingdom on earth. But regardless of the name this has ever been the dream of the Jew: a magnificent dream of a world of universal justice, brotherhood and peace for all mankind.

This is the hope and dream of the future expressed in the prayer that is said just before the *kaddish* prayer. This prayer is called the *Alenu* and affirms the Jewish hope for the future. Read the prayer carefully and you may understand a little better why the Jew believed and believes to this day that he must enter into copartnership with God:

May the time not be distant, O God, when Thy name shall be worshiped in all the earth, when unbelief shall disappear and error be no more. Fervently we pray that the day may come when all men shall invoke Thy name, when corruption and evil shall give way to purity and goodness, when superstition shall no longer enslave the mind, nor idolatry blind the eye, when all who dwell on earth shall know that to Thee alone every knee must bend and every tongue give homage. O may all, created in Thine image, recognize that they are brethren, so that, one in spirit and one in fellowship, they may be forever united before Thee. Then, shall Thy kingdom be established on earth and the word of Thine ancient seer be fulfilled: The Lord will reign forever and ever. On that day the Lord shall be One and His name shall be One.

JUDAISM AND CHRISTIANITY: RIVALS OR PARTNERS?

Some Jews and some Christians think of Judaism and Christianity as rival or competing religions. This is against the spirit of both Judaism and Christianity and is grossly unfair to both religions. Actually, they are not in competition one with the other, but are allies and partners in the sacred task of bringing light to the world and building God's Kingdom on earth.

Our hope is to bring to reality God's Kingdom on *earth*. It is not a kingdom for the next life or the next world. It is not a kingdom for a distant place called Heaven. It is God's Kingdom in *this* world, on *this* earth. It is a Kingdom with God ruling as the King of all kings, as people of all religions live together in harmony and brotherhood as God's children.

Judaism and Christianity both share this hope and this dream. Despite all the differences in beliefs and ritual, differences in Holy Days and festivals, both religions are united in their determination to join forces to make the dream a sublime reality.

Although Judaism and Christianity may part on many beliefs, here is where they meet. Here is where they agree and work together because they are united in the determination to fashion the future in accord with the Judeo-Christian ethical heritage.

What Christian could reject this?

Leviticus: "And thou shalt love thy neighbor as thyself."

Micah: "It hath been told thee, O man, what is good and what the Lord doth require of thee, but to do justly, to love mercy and walk humbly with thy God."

Deuteronomy: "And thou shalt love the Lord thy God with all thy heart, with all thy soul and with all thy might."

Psalms: "The Lord is my shepherd, I shall not want. He maketh me to lie down in green pastures; He leadeth me beside the still waters. He restoreth my soul; He guideth me in straight paths for His name's sake."

Amos: "Let justice flow as the waters and righteousness as a mighty stream."

Exodus: The Ten Commandments

Malachi: "Have we not all one Father? Hath not one God created us? Why then do we deal treacherously every man against his brother?"

Isaiah: "And they shall beat their swords into plowshares, and their spears into pruning-hooks; nation shall not lift up sword against nation, neither shall they learn war anymore."

Hillel: "Do not unto others, what you would not have others do unto you."

Psalms: "How good and how pleasant it is for brethren to dwell together in unity."

We could go on and on considering quotations from the Bible and from Jewish teachings, other ideals that are equally precious and sacred to Christianity. Now let's consider some other quotations.

What Jew could reject this?

Jesus: "Do unto others what you would have them do unto you."

St. Francis of Assisi: "Lord make me a channel of Thy peace that where there is hatred I may bring love, that where there is wrong I may bring the spirit of forgiveness, that where there is discord I may bring harmony, that where there is doubt I may bring faith, that where there is despair I may bring hope."

There are many quotations from Catholic and Protestant writings that would be acceptable to Judaism because there are so many ideals, values and hopes that Judaism and Christianity share.

If we changed the names of the authors of the quotations and jumbled them all up, it wouldn't make a bit of difference as to the meaning and spirit of the ethical teachings.

We would accept them for what they have to teach us, and not because of who wrote them. We could say that the quotations from Christian sources are Jewish, and the Christians could say that the quotations from Jewish sources are Christian, and both would be right.

THE ENEMIES OF THE JUDEO-CHRISTIAN DREAM

There are some people in this world who do not accept the ethical teachings of Judaism and Christianity. They don't believe in God or in God's teachings of mercy, justice and love. They don't believe in trying to make this world a Kingdom of God on earth. They want the earth to be their kingdom. They scoff at mercy and regard it as weakness. They sneer at justice, and say that this is an old-fashioned and outmoded ideal. They don't believe in letting others differ. They want everyone to believe their way. They laugh at such ideals as kindness and brotherhood and say the world is a jungle, and that men are really beasts ready to tear each other apart.

There are some people who are not evil, and who do not hate the Judeo-Christian dream. They just believe that the dream is an impossible one, and that the hope of Judaism and Christianity for God's Kingdom on earth is unrealistic, impractical and impossible.

These are the pessimists, the doubters, the prophets of doom, who despair of the future and have given up all hope that man might build a good society for the future. They say that man will use the atomic bomb to destroy himself and his civilization.

There are others who say that religion has failed, and only science will be able to train man to be like a machine and react properly so that he may survive and not destroy himself.

According to legend, Saint Francis preached love even to the birds. This thirteenth-century miniature shows them listening attentively.

There are still others who are not against the Judeo-Christian dream, or who may even possibly be in favor of it, but who don't care enough or believe enough to be willing to work to make that dream come true. These are the indifferent, the passive, the ones who are so busy making money or enjoying themselves that they aren't one bit concerned about building God's Kingdom on earth or working for a moral future for all mankind.

I WILL LIFT UP MINE EYES UNTO THE MOUNTAINS

Some may ask: With all this opposition, do you think we have a chance to win out and make the dream of the future come true?

Throughout our Jewish history there have been those who laughed and mocked at the dream and who tried to destroy the dreamers, but we have survived and persisted because of our covenant with God, because of our sacred mission and because of our faith in the glorious possibilities of the future.

The Communists don't believe in the Judeo-Christian dream, nor do the Fascists and the dictators who hate those who are different, and use their power to persecute the weak and the helpless.

Communism and Fascism are vicious enemies of the dream, but there are many other enemies, such as war, the threat of nuclear destruction, poverty, disease, man's indifference to the welfare of his fellow man, and those who make money, power and pleasure their god.

Those of the Jewish faith have ever turned to God for hope and direction. In every age our people repeated the words of the 121st Psalm: "I will lift up mine eyes unto the mountains. From whence shall come my help? My help cometh from the Lord who made heaven and earth."

Today, many people who need help say: "I will lift up mine eyes unto my material resources, to my stocks, bonds and possessions." Others say: "I will lift up mine eyes unto the bookshelves," thinking that education alone will help them. Still others turn to science and say: "I will lift up mine eyes unto the test tubes, unto the atoms, unto guided missiles." They appeal to the scientists for help, but many of the scientists are frightened at the horrible and terrible power of the nuclear bombs they have made. The scientists now say: "We can't help you. You

must help us!" They are appealing to the ministers, priests and rabbis, to the educators and people of good will to take action, to apply the teachings of Judaism and Christianity to the world in which we live to save the world and bring peace, understanding, brotherhood and international justice to our civilization.

Do we think we can do it? Do we think we can win and make the Judeo-Christian dream come true? We believe with all our hearts that we can do it, and that we will win, and make our dream come true. But more than anything else we have to work to apply religion to life. We have to be strong, courageous and never give up hope. This is why it is so urgent for Judaism and Christianity to become partners and join together, work together, serve together to build God's Kingdom on earth and conquer the enemies of the dream in order, with God's help, to advance to the moral future of tomorrow.

NEW FRONTIERS OF FAITH

Judaism and Christianity are being challenged today to become pioneers of the future and to advance to new frontiers of faith. Like the pioneers of America, who made their way through forests, climbed mountains, and cleared the way as they went forward to explore new territory and establish settlements, we must be pioneers, advancing to new frontiers of religious cooperation.

There are pioneers in science. For instance, the scientists who worked to invent new things such as electric generators, and the telephone, the automobile, and the airplane —and now how to use atomic power to help people—and scientists who work in laboratories to find new drugs, to fight disease and conquer cancer, heart trouble and other sicknesses that destroy people.

Scientists are pioneering, exploring and trying to find ways of eradicating disease.

They are pioneering into new frontiers of science and knowledge all the time, and never give up no matter how discouraged others may get.

The same determination is shown by those who are going forward to new frontiers of space, the pioneers who will someday make it possible for man to travel to the moon and to Mars. Even here on earth there will be new inventions and new discoveries, like moving highways and control of the weather, food from oceans and little gadgets that will enable us to fly through the air so that we won't need automobiles anymore, and television wristwatches.

There will be many new and marvelous scientific inventions in the future. There will be great advances in education through teaching machines and educational television. Through automation, man will have more leisure time for recreation and study. There are endless possibilities for the future, but we must not forget that if man is to survive to enjoy these wonderful new discoveries, it will

The factory system raises living standards—and reduces man to tending machines. Religion is now challenged to offset the nonhuman use of human beings, to keep alive "the spirit of man."

be necessary to advance to other frontiers, frontiers of faith so that people will be able to live together in peace.

It is important to have pioneers in science and in education, but it is equally important to have pioneers of faith, men and women who will help us advance to new frontiers of brotherhood, understanding, justice and peace.

If our civilization is to survive so that we can enjoy the new discoveries of the future, then it will be necessary to find ways of ending war, the threat of atomic destruction, and the danger of nuclear fallout.

If our civilization is to survive, then we need pioneers of faith to help find ways of bringing different religions, peoples and races together so that they will understand each other and learn to live with each other in harmony and peace.

That is why Judaism and Christianity must become partners and pioneers of God to create a new society—a new way of life where the teachings of religion will be applied and used. That is why we must learn to conquer poverty, disease, prejudice, cruelty, ignorance and strife. That is why we must work to bring about the brotherhood of all peoples and all the races in the world.

Is there an adventure more exciting than this? Is there a challenge more difficult than this? Is there a pioneering effort more important than this? Is there a hope and a dream more sacred than this? You are the pioneers of the future. Some of you will be scientists, doctors, teachers, architects, technicians, astronauts, business men and women, and whatever your work may be—at the same time, you must be pioneers of God, advancing to new frontiers of faith. That is why we have to put our faith to work. That is why we have to live by our faith, and that is why you will have to join with your Christian friends and neighbors in a great and sacred partnership.

Before we conclude our study of Judaism and Christianity compared, there is a true story that has something important to teach us.

JOINING HANDS AND HEARTS

It happened in Minnesota, where a wheat farmer's four-year-old son was playing in the kitchen. His mother didn't notice him as he opened the door and wandered out to the field where the wheat was stacked up in sheaves. It was dangerous for a little child to be in the wheat fields that extended acre after acre because of the possibility of smothering.

In a little while, the mother noticed the child was missing. She ran through the house calling to him, but there was no answer. Becoming more and more frantic, she rushed outside and looked everywhere, but her child was nowhere in sight.

She screamed for someone to get her husband. Soon he came running and when he found out that his child was lost, terror struck his heart because he knew the terrible possibility that a child could smother in the dense wheat field.

Without another word, he ran out to the field and started to beat down the sheaves of wheat, calling to his child. There was no answer. Soon he was joined by some of the hired hands who breathlessly turned this way and that way, shouting the child's name. The news of the lost child reached the village near by, and before long many of the townspeople joined in the frantic search for the little boy. They were rushing, pushing, walking, in all directions, beating down the sheaves in desperate haste. Finally, someone said: "This is wrong. We are going off in all directions and we'll never find the child this way. Let's join hands and form a gigantic circle and work our way in toward the center of the field and perhaps we'll find the boy."

And so they joined hands, the farmer with the custodian of the school, the preacher with

Pope John XXIII brought hope to millions that Christians and
Jews may yet work together for God's kingdom, without old
condemnations. The late Pope is here shown receiving the
$160,000 Balzan Peace Prize, in 1963.

the grocer, the banker with the street-cleaner, the plumber with the lawyer, the postman with the butcher. There they were with joined hands: those of every religious faith, those who were white and Negro, the rich and the poor, the learned and the ignorant, those from every station of life.

It wasn't long before someone reached down and picked up the child and handed him to his father. The father held the lifeless body of his child in his arms and knew with terrible certainty that the child was dead. In his anguish, he cried out: "God! God! Why didn't we join hands before it was too late?"

This isn't a very happy story but it is a true one. We hope that the time will never come when after a terrible atomic-nuclear catastrophe the few people who survive will look at the rubble of their towns and the burning destruction and cry out: "God! God! Why didn't we join hands before it was too late?"

This must never happen to us and we will not permit it to happen if we act now. It is essential for the survival of our civilization that Judaism and Christianity join hands and hearts together for a great and sacred purpose. It is a vital necessity for Jews and

Christians to recognize and understand the differences that separate them, but it is even more vital and more crucial for Jews and Christians to concentrate on the great ideals and the sacred objectives that unite them.

QUEST FOR THE STARS

Some of you may be thinking: "What can I do? How can I possibly help to pioneer into the future and contribute to the building of God's Kingdom on earth?" It's hard to know how and where to begin.

That is why the Ḥasidic sages told of the time when the disciples of a great rabbi went to their teacher and said: "There's so much darkness and evil in the world, and we are so discouraged. Do you think anything can be done, or must we throw up our hands in despair and say that it's impossible to do anything about it? Show us, our teacher, how we can help to drive the evil and the darkness from the world."

The rabbi said: "My students, my disciples, go down into that dark cellar and beat at the darkness."

The disciples found large sticks and they descended into the dark cellar and beat at the darkness, striking out against it time after time. But to no avail. The darkness was still there.

They went back to their teacher who said: "My disciples, take brooms and descend into the dark cellar and sweep out the darkness!" So the students found brooms, went down into the cellar and swept vigorously, but to no avail. The darkness was still there.

They went back to their teacher who said: "My subjects, my disciples, go into that dark cellar and protest against the darkness. Curse the darkness!" They descended again into the cellar, protesting against it and cursed the darkness. But to no avail.

This time when they went back to their teacher he said: "And now my subjects, my disciples, go down into the dark cellar, and let each of you light one candle." They descended into the cellar and each one kindled a candle. They looked, and behold, the darkness was no more.

That story should have meaning to every one of us. When we feel that there is so much darkness in our world, and we want to do something to drive out the evil and the darkness, it isn't enough for us to beat at it, or try to sweep it away, or even to protest against it and curse it. Wherever we find darkness, each of us must kindle a light, and the darkness will be no more.

If every Jew and every Christian would resolve not just to kindle a light, but to *be* a light, to identify himself with the light of truth, the light of justice, the light of brotherhood and the light of peace, how much of the evil and darkness would be driven out of our world!

Each of us has to begin with himself, and resolve to be a light, remembering that God called upon the children of Israel to be a covenant of the peoples and a light unto the nations. We, as Jews, have to show the way, so that other religions may join with us in our efforts.

Isn't it strange. With all the differences that exist between Judaism and Christianity, there are so many more things to unite us? Isn't it strange, too, that just as the Bishop in Lessing's play considered Nathan to be like a good Christian, and Nathan considered the Bishop to be like a good Jew, both the Bishop and Nathan were thinking of the same qualities of character and goodness? The Bishop called those qualities "Christian." Nathan called those qualities "Jewish"—and both meant the same thing.

So it is that Judaism and Christianity, different though they are, share the same great ethical ideals for the future. Faithful adherents of both religions would agree with the poet who wrote:

The devastating power of the atom bomb—now superseded by the hydrogen bomb—has alerted man to the need for a better way than the paths of force and rivalry. Faith in God and wise obedience to Law must show the way.

We are the heartbeat of a world that wills
To find its noblest self and to fulfill
The law of justice which it seeks to know.
We are God's people, for, we will it so.
The stars our quest, and truth
  our watchword still.

We are God's people. Jew will say "that refers to us." Christians will say "that refers to us," and both will be right. Listen to these magnificent and lofty words: "The stars our quest, and truth our watchword still." Christians could say "that is Christian." Jews could say "that is Jewish"—and both would be right.

Think of it! Judaism and Christianity inspiring Jews and Christians to regard themselves as the heartbeat of the world, as "God's people, God's children";—Jews and Christians questing for the stars together.

This is our cause. This is our hope. This is our sacred covenant with God. This is our sacred destiny, and this is our dream: Judaism and Christianity, not rivals, but partners, partners in faith for the greatest and most sublime building project ever revealed to man —the building of God's Kingdom on earth.

QUESTIONS FOR DISCUSSION

1. What are the practical possibilities of a universal religion, acceptable to both Christians and Jews? Would you be willing to give up the Jewish faith for such a uinversal religion? Do you think Christians would give up their faith for a universal religion?

2. Would you favor a type of church-synagogue, in which Christians and Jews would worship together? What are the arguments for and against such a church-synagogue?

3. How can Judaism and Christianity join forces to achieve the great ideals that both share? What are the factors that now prevent Judaism and Christianity from joining forces and becoming real partners in faith? What do you think could and should be done to eliminate those factors?

4. What is your opinion of the following statement by an American Rabbi, Ferdinand M. Isserman?

What matter it to God whether men seek Him before the ark of the synagogue, before the crucifix of the church, under the dome of the mosque, before the image of the Buddhist? What matter it to God whether men pray to Him in the classic accents of Hebrew, in the musical cadence of Latin, in the rhythmic poetry of the Upanishads, in German, in French, in English? What matter it to God whether men call him Yahveh or Christ, Buddha or Confucius, Jupiter or Osiris? What matter it to God what the form of worship, what the style of ritual, what the theological definition as long as men seek Him with their whole hearts? Then He will answer them. Even therefore in this seemingly divided field of religion there is unity, the unity of eternal human aspiration, the unity of worship before the Creator of the universe.

5. What is your opinion of this statement by Rabbi Fackenheim?

We as Jews can assign a very special place to Christianity, as a religion which directs its followers into righteous paths. In the end what Jew and Christian share is far more than what they disagree on. They share, not only the basic laws of morality and the belief in the One God, but also the belief that God is concerned with man, and that man ought to be concerned with God. They share the belief that the world stands in need of being redeemed, and that it ultimately will be redeemed. They share, perhaps above all, the belief that redemption if and when it is finally achieved, must be the union of men, through love, with God as well as with each other.

Thus, ultimately, Jew and Christian may each disagree with the way the other understands his own position in history. But there is no reason why each should not admit that the other is a part of the fulfillment of God's purpose for the world and man.

6. Rabbi Balfour Brickner writes of man as a partner of God. Read his statement and then explain what you think he means.

Judaism is not now, and never has been structured around any idea of redemption or salvation, whose reason for being is a depraved, helpless, irredeemable humanity. Judaism does not see man as rotten; neither worthy nor capable of redemption. To the contrary, everything in Jewish thought speaks of man as a valuable partner with God, jointly involved in the making of a cosmos out of a chaos. . . . Judaism gives no acceptance to those views of man which describe him as originally sinful.

7. Jewish tradition teaches:

When the Shofar is sounded the Jew lifts his voice to God and prays: "O hasten the blessed time when all dwellers on earth shall hearken unto the sound of the shofar and shall worship as one brotherhood at Thy holy mountain."

On the Day of Atonement the Jew cries out: "Father of mercies, we do not pray for ourselves alone but for all Thy children." The prayer continues: "Unite us in a brotherhood of service to Thee and to our fellow men."

How should we apply these teachings to help us achieve brotherhood in a jet and space age?

8. The rabbis of Yavneh liked this saying:

I am a creature of God and my neighbor is also His creature, my work is in the city and his is in the field; I rise early to work, and he rises early to his. As he cannot excel in my work, so I cannot excel in his work. But perhaps you say, I do great things, and he does small things. We have learnt that [it matters not whether] a man does much or little, if only he directs his heart to heaven.

—BERAKHOT 17a (Talmud)

How is it possible for someone your age to direct his heart to God?

THINGS TO DO

1. Interview an Orthodox, Conservative and Reform Rabbi and ask for a statement of "Judaism and Christianity: Rivals or Partners—Which?

2. Interview a Catholic priest and a Protestant minister and ask for opinions on the best way that Judaism and Christianity may unite as partners without giving up convictions and sacred beliefs.

3. Write to the National Conference of Christians and Jews, 43 West 57th Street, New York, N.Y. 10019 and request material for class study.

4. Discuss in class the theme: "How good is the good-will movement in the United States? In our community?" What are the practical results of Brotherhood Week in your community?

5. Write an essay on "The Four Chaplains" (Washington, Goode, Poling and Fox), who gave their lives in World War II.

6. Write an essay on "How can I make my contribution to the building of God's Kingdom on earth."

7. To illustrate the truth that no man sins against himself alone, Rabbi Simeon ben Yohai said:

Several men were sailing together when one of them began to bore a hole in the bottom of the boat. The others protested. "What are you doing there?" He replied, "What concern is it of yours? I am only boring a hole beneath my own seat." They replied: "Of course it is our concern, for the water will fill the entire boat and drown us all."

Discuss in class how we are all in the same boat today.

8. Christian scholar, Travers Herford, wrote:

Christianity and Judaism can never blend without the surrender by the one or the other of its fundamental principle. But they could learn to understand and respect each other, and recognize that each religion has God's work to do, and cannot do it without the help and presence, yes, even the sympathy of the other.

Write an essay telling how Jews and Christians together may do God's work.

SELECTED QUOTATIONS

Rivals or partners?

Cathedral and temple, church and synagogue, share convictions in a God above, a soul within and a life beyond. They accept as fundamental the belief in the Fatherhood of God and the brotherhood of man. They seek to promote individual righteousness and social justice. They desire to see God's Kingdom established on earth.

They should, therefore, be not rivals nor competitors but partners. They can, with mutual respect and in a spirit of cooperation, wholeheartedly work together towards many common objectives. They can be natural allies in the fight against the forces of evil in the life of the community and the world at large. They can unite in furthering all good causes for man's uplift and the higher life of society. They have a kindred stake in salvaging the ethical and spiritual values of civilization.

—RABBI HARVEY W. ETTELSON

One world is not a fairy tale

In our day Jews and Christians must unite in the building of the one world—a world of freedom for all under God. There will be one world or no world. There will be co-existence or no existence. This is a great age for humanity. Millions have cast aside chains and gained nationhood and self-determination. At no time have the conditions of the common man been more improved than today in every direction of life. This is the hour where Jew and Christian must battle on all fronts against illiteracy, poverty and racial inequality, and, too, we must do all we can toward the abolition of war. The dream of the one world as visioned by the great prophets of Israel is not a fairy tale. It will come sure as this is day. We however must patiently toil in the building of the one humanity.

—RABBI HARRY JOSHUA STERN

Jew and Christian share

We as Jews can assign a very special place to Christianity, as a religion which directs its followers into righteous paths. In the end what Jew and Christian share is far more than what they disagree on. They share, not only the basic laws of morality and belief in the One God, but also the belief that God is concerned with man, and that man ought to be concerned with God. They share the belief that the world stands in need of being redeemed, and that it ultimately will be redeemed. They share, perhaps above all, the belief that redemption, if and when it is finally achieved, must be the union of men, through love, with God as well as with each other.

Thus, ultimately, Jew and Christian may each disagree with the way the other understands his own position in history. But there is no reason why each should not admit that the other is a part of the fulfillment of God's purpose for the world and man.

—RABBI EMIL L. FACKENHEIM

The candle and the star

Christmas and Chanukah are largely festivals of the home and have a particular appeal to children. Both teach the eternal lessons of freedom, of justice, of love, of peace! Both are symbolized by light—the one by a candle and the other by a star.

Consider how equally precious to Christian and Jew are the mottos of these festivals! "God grant that there may be peace on earth and good-will toward men," prays the earnest Christian! And every Jew echoes this prayer with all his heart and all his soul.

Not by physical power nor by material strength, but by My Spirit shalt thou prevail, sayeth the Lord of Hosts" — the famed verse from the prophet Zechariah —is the watchword of the Chanukah observance. Where is the Christian, worthy of the name, who is not aware of the need for strengthening and undergirding spiritual and religious values in our time?

Some follow the candle! Others the star! Shall we who live in an age which stands in such desperate need of light declare that one is superior to the other? Shall we say that one should be eliminated and the other prevail? Both are needed, urgently, desperately, in a world still darkened by hatred, conflict and lack of brotherliness. I say, therefore, let more and more Christian homes be illuminated by the Star of Bethlehem and more and more Jewish homes be made bright by the candles of the Maccabees. . . . It is not a question of the star *or* the candle, but rather of *the need of both* to illuminate the world and make glad the hearts of men.

—RABBI JULIUS MARK

God's kingdom on earth

In a day of deep despair and even more threatening terror of world devastation, from the pillar of fire by night and the mushroom cloud of death by day, when all of us helplessly cry out, "When shall come our help," let us, with forebears of old, assert, "My help cometh from God— who will not forsake me nor leave me in my need. My help cometh from God who has commanded me to build His Kingdom

on earth; yea verily, His kingdom of decency and equity among all the children of men. His kingdom of brotherhood for all."

—RABBI MAURICE N. EISENDRATH

Chain reaction of love

For centuries now we've tried everything else; the powers of wealth, of mighty armies and navies, and combinations of nations, machinations of diplomats. All have failed. Before it's too late, and time is running out, let us turn from trust in the chain reactions of exploding atoms to faith in the chain reaction of God's love. Love — love of God and fellowmen, that is God's formula for peace. Peace on earth to men of good will.

—ARCHBISHOP RICHARD R. CUSHING

From the jungle to the stars

Christianity has been the instrument for bringing the ethical treasures of Judaism to mankind. Jesus, who was a child of Israel and the father of Christianity, is thus a perpetual reminder that the two great faiths have a common basis and a common goal. There is no need for either to conquer or absorb the other. In spite of their genuine differences, they have much more in common. Today, the challenge is directed not against Jewish ritual or Christian theology, but against the great body of common religious and ethical ideals that constitute the Judeo-Christian tradition . . . Judaism and Christianity must cease to eye each other like jealous rivals and recognize that they are allies in the long and desperate struggle to raise man from the jungle to the stars.

—RABBI ROBERT GORDIS

SELECTED READINGS

ELLIOT, JOHN, *Building Bridges,* National Conference of Christians and Jews

FACKENHEIM, EMIL L., *Paths to Jewish Belief,*

PLAUT, W. GUNTHER, *Judaism and the Scientific Spirit*

SILVERMAN, WILLIAM B., *The Jewish Concept of Man,* B'nai B'rith Series

UNIVERSAL JEWISH ENCYCLOPEDIA, Volume II, Brotherhood of Man, pp. 558–561

WHITNEY, PHYLLIS A., *The Highest Dream*

Film

The Toy Maker, ADL

Today the Shofar still sounds its stirring call—awakening man to the word of God and to respect and love for his fellow man.